# Contributions to Management Science



For further volumes:
http://www.springer.com/series/1505

Julia Koralun-Bereźnicka

# Corporate Performance

## A Ratio-Based Approach to Country and Industry Analyses

Springer

Julia Koralun-Bereźnicka
University of Gdańsk
Faculty of Management
Sopot
Poland

ISSN 1431-1941
ISBN 978-3-319-03295-5 ISBN 978-3-319-00345-0 (eBook)
DOI 10.1007/978-3-319-00345-0
Springer Cham Heidelberg New York Dordrecht London



Printed on acid-free paper

Springer is part of Springer Science+Business Media (www.springer.com)

# Introduction

How to search for the factors determining corporate performance is a question asked by many researchers in the area of finance. The factors could be both external, e.g. macroeconomic, industrial, political or social conditions affecting an enterprise, as well as internal, i.e. controlled by an entity, such as the size or managerial competence of an enterprise. This study focuses on external aspects of corporate performance, specifically on the country and the industry in which a company operates. Both factors are believed to have a significant impact on corporate activity and therefore economic results, which are reflected in financial ratios.

The following research is involved in an important stream of contemporary economy and finance, which can be defined as the analysis of reasons and consequences of the diversity of objects. The objects can be treated here either as countries (country effect) or industries (industry effect). Most of the hitherto analyses focus on corporate performance reflected mainly in stock returns. There are few of those considering fundamental ratios, however, which can be an equally important criterion for investment decisions, especially long-term ones. Therefore, updating and broadening the study of the country and industry effects within the European Union area seems a useful addition of knowledge to this area.

Analysis of the country and industry effects is of particular importance for the theory and practice of modern finance. Projects undertaken by financial investors, especially institutional ones, are not limited to the local or national markets, but are often implemented at the sub-regional level and therefore have a global dimension. Identifying the factors responsible for the risk diversity for the selected groups of objects, measuring these differences as well as evaluating their significance are therefore important research tasks. The results of this type of research are used in the process of making investment decisions aiming at risk diversification both internationally and across industries.

On the one hand, the issue of corporate performance diversity depending on the industry, namely the industry effect in financial ratios, is of crucial importance for cross-industry diversification of investments. On the other hand, the country effect, understood as a variation of corporate performance due to the country of operation, is important mainly in the context of the integration processes taking place in Europe. Studies of ratios diversity across countries are therefore justified in terms of international investments diversification.

The main purpose of this book is the comparative evaluation of international and industrial factors affecting the financial condition of enterprises in the selected European Union countries. In order to implement the above formulated concept, some theoretical and empirical studies were performed concerning the occurrence of the country and industry effects in the financial health of companies located in the analysed area. In the theoretical part, the results of previous research on this issue were reviewed. The aim of the empirical study was to determine which factors – national or industrial ones – have a greater impact on the performance of economic entities. The cross-country and cross-industry comparative analysis of corporate economic and financial results was performed in order to solve the main research problem of this book, which can otherwise be described as an assessment of the relative importance of the country effect and the industry effect in the financial condition of companies.

To characterise the financial condition of entities, a set of appropriately selected ratios was used, which enabled a comprehensive assessment of the examined objects. The adopted financial ratios reflect two basic criteria used for assessing corporate performance, i.e. the broadly understood effectiveness and solvency. These criteria represent some of the most important factors taken into account when making investment decisions. For the purpose of this study, the analysed ratios were grouped into three categories: profitability and turnover ratios, liquidity ratios and long-term solvency ratios.

The analysis of empirical data derived from the aggregated and harmonised financial statements enabled the verification of the research hypotheses concerning the existence of the country and industry effects, which involve the differentiation of corporate performance depending on the country and industry, respectively. The research also allowed indicating which of these two effects prevails in affecting the financial health of companies.

Thus, the hypothesis to be verified in this study can be formulated as follows: the national factors have greater impact on the corporate performance of enterprises than the industrial factors. Rejecting the tested hypothesis would be a statistical proof of the truthfulness of the alternative hypothesis, i.e., that industrial factors affect financial conditions of enterprises more than national ones.

If there is no reason for rejecting the hypothesis, it could be concluded that companies from different industries of the same country have more mutual similarity than companies in the same industry but from different countries. Rejecting the hypothesis would mean that companies in a given industry but from different countries should be less diverse than companies from different industries of the same country. It might also occur that cross-country and cross-industry diversity of corporate performance is fairly uniform and that none of the examined factors can be identified as the dominant one. Simplifying, the main research problem can be reduced to the question whether, e.g., the performance of the construction industry enterprises in France is more similar to the performance of French transport companies or rather corresponds to the situation of enterprises in the construction industry, e.g., in Italy.

In addition, several more specific research tasks were formulated. One of them was to find out whether corporate financial parameters differ significantly across industries as well as internationally. Another problem to be solved was the question of the scope of the observed differences, i.e. whether they relate to all industries, countries and financial ratios or just to some of them. Financial analysis of companies in individual industries and countries was applied to establish whether and to what extent the corporate performance differs in these two sections and in which countries and industries the disparities are most apparent. In addition, the study was meant to specify which ratios or groups of ratios best reflect these differences. Consequently, one of the ancillary purposes was to identify financial ratios with the best discriminating properties, i.e. the most different in the analysed sections.

The study includes a total of thirteen industries (in line with the European Classification of Activities) in ten European Union countries. The territorial scope of the research was deliberately restricted mainly to the countries which have long been integrated in the European structures. In addition, most of the countries are also members of the euro zone – the highly integrated area. This helps to avoid artificial exaggeration of the country effect which might happen if the study included countries with significantly different levels of development. The only exception to this relatively homogeneous population is Poland. The inclusion of Poland, for which the accession to the common currency area is probably a close prospect, allowed to compare it with other peer EU countries and thus to show the likely gap between them.

The subject of the study is the economic and financial standing of enterprises, characterised by a set of financial ratios for each industry, each country and each year in the period 1999–2005. The calculation of ratios is based on the harmonised and aggregated annual accounts from the BACH database.

The methodology of this study involves mainly multivariate statistical analysis, the choice of which is justified by the nature of the data – its range and numerousness. Some methods of data classification were also applied, such as cluster analysis, factor analysis, or multidimensional scaling.

Due to the relatively wide range of data characterising many objects, the natural procedure of the research was to organize the elements of the analysed population, i.e. to classify them according to certain criteria. Therefore, grouping the objects into categories characterised by a greater within-group similarity was one of the purposes of the analysis. The classification was applied to the objects treated either as industries or countries. The binomial objects – industries in countries – were also systematised. Some kind of categorisation was also employed for the diagnostic variables, i.e. the financial ratios used in the study.

The classification of industries and countries based on the economic and financial condition of enterprises was meant to distinguish such categories of objects (countries, industries, or industries in countries), which differ in terms of performance. The identification of such groups of objects – described by many features – was possible with the use of taxonomic methods.

Apart from this introduction, the study consists of five chapters and the ending which contains the summary and conclusions of the research.

The first chapter is a prolegomenon to the issues of cross-country and cross-industry diversification of business activity results. It discusses the various interpretations of the concept of corporate performance and also formulates its definition which is the most appropriate from the point of view of the empirical research performed in the later part of the study. It also outlines the theoretical foundations of the industrial economics which is the starting point for discussing the cross-industry diversity of enterprises. A classification of the factors influencing corporate performance was also attempted here. The author also discusses the nature, genesis and practical application of the financial ratios as measures of the corporate financial condition. Finally, various classification systems of ratios were presented and their limitations were signalled.

The second chapter is a methodical one. First of all, it reviews the previous research on the diversity of economic and financial performance of companies. The author also synthetically presents conclusions from earlier studies on the prevalence of the industry and country effects. This review was treated as the basis for the formulation of the essential methodical assumptions used in the following empirical research. Therefore, the chapter specifies the scope and methodology of the study of corporate performance diversity depending on the country and the industry.

The following part of the discourse contains a discussion of the findings of empirical research. The third chapter includes a preliminary analysis of corporate performance diversity. It mainly considers the basic statistics of financial ratios and, later, the diversification of corporate performance in various sections with the use of the analysis of variance.

The next – fourth – chapter aims to present the results of the classification of objects. It discusses the results of agglomerative cluster analysis of countries and industries as well as industries in countries. An important stage in the study was to assess the similarity of the clustering results between countries and industries. This part of the study also focused on the characteristics of the identified clusters.

The purpose of the last stage of analysis, presented in Chap. 5, was to identify the factors influencing corporate performance in different countries and industries. The factors isolated with the use of factor analysis were then compared across countries and industries. In order to simplify the data structure, a two-dimensional map of objects was constructed with the use of the multidimensional scaling method. Reduction of the number of dimensions was meant to increase the clarity of the detected patterns.

Deciding which of the two categories of factors considered in this research influences corporate performance more is an important theme of many studies on the coexistence of the country and industry effects. The evaluation of the relative importance of national and industrial factors may be significant in the context of investment diversification. If these are mainly industry factors which are responsible for the performance of enterprises, investment portfolios management strategies should be based mainly on cross-industry sections. However, the traditional strategy of portfolio diversification by countries would be more justified in the case of the country effect domination.

Multiple attempts to solve the problem of the mutual relation between the country effect and the industry effect have led to formulating some suggestions about the methods of portfolio diversification as well as ways about conducting research in the area of finance. However, the apparent lack of consensus among researchers on the relative importance of the country and industry effects gives rise to further verification of this problem. Some contradictions between the results obtained by different researchers, depending on the method used, the period of study or the research sample, prove that it is purposeful and advisable to use alternative methods of resolving the issue and continue exploring the research problem, which particularly concerns the area of integrated Europe.

# Contents

# List of Tables

# List of Figures

# List of Appendices

# Chapter 1
# Corporate Performance Interpretation and Measuring Problems

## 1.1 Interpretation of Corporate Performance on the Grounds of the Industrial Organisation Theory

Corporate performance, though a term commonly used both in business practice and by academics, provides a field for wider discussion due to its ambiguity and information capacity. One of the starting points for considering the meaning of corporate performance could be the theory of industrial organisation. Along with the progress of knowledge, as well as the economic and social development, many specific disciplines, also known as the applied sciences, have appeared and are still growing in the economic sciences. One of them is the industrial organisation or industrial economics, which aims at researching production system and strategies of entities operating within this system. The discipline comprises a number of research streams concentrating on corporate strategies, performance results, production structures and government intervention (Rainelli, 1996, p. 7). The traditional paradigm of industrial organisation deals with exploring the relations between industrial structure, conduct (strategy) and corporate performance, particularly focusing on the factors and effects of the market force of firms (Scherer & Ross, 1990).

The main function of the industrial economics is the exploration of the occurrences taking place in an industry in order to determine regularities and make generalisations, which are then used to formulate certain recommendations concerning the industry and its enterprises (Blajer-Gołębiewska & Zielenkiewicz, 2005, p. 85; Cabral, 2000). The basic range of the industrial organisation issues involves the market and industry structure, production concentration, localisation, innovations, the firm theory, the development theory, diversification, firm jointing, investment decisions and public interventionism in the private and public sector (Pierścionek, 1992). The analysis is performed in two areas; the subject of the research is mainly the competitive environment of an enterprise and the mutual interaction of the participants on the imperfect competition market, particularly the oligopoly. The contemporary research applies e.g. the game theory, which is one of

J. Koralun-Bereźnicka, *Corporate Performance*, Contributions to Management Science, 
DOI 10.1007/978-3-319-00345-0_1, 

the main instruments of the industrial economics (Fudenberg & Tirole, 1987, 2001, p. 176; Tirole, 1988). The other research area is the enterprise itself, whose development is affected, among others, by the technology, investment processes and knowledge or marketing policy. Viewing the corporate performance through the theory of industrial economics has important implications for the complex enterprise analysis (Blajer-Gołębiewska & Zielenkiewicz, 2005, p. 85).

Due to the distinct development of the industrial economics in different countries, the two basic models can be distinguished: the Anglo-American (Jacquemin, 1985; Schmalensee & Williga, 1989) and the French one (Arena, Benzoli, Bandt, & Romani, 1991; Morgan, 1990). The main concept of the first stream is the sequence: structure – conduct – performance (Bain, 1968; Łyszkiewicz, 2003). The aim of the analyses according to the Structure Conduct Performance Paradigm (SCPP) is to explain the corporate performance through the characteristics of the market on which the enterprise operates (i.e. structures), and also through the way in which they operate on the market (conduct). However, the interpretation of the relations between these three elements is not unquestionable, as on the one hand they can be treated as a cause-result approach, where the structures determine the conduct and the performance, but on the other hand they can be attributed an independent character (Demsetz, 1973; Peltzman, 1977; Rainelli, 1996, p. 12).

The SCP model, which constitutes an important research instrument in the industrial economics, is also susceptible to different interpretations, depending on whether it is treated as a cause-result relation (the structure as a variable which explains the performance) or as the coexisting parallel occurrences (structures, conduct and performance). Moreover, the introduction of the strategic behaviours of enterprises considerably changes the concept of the relations between these three categories (Rainelli, 1996, p. 23). In a traditional SCP model the analysis is based on empirical research, which aims at explaining the differences in effectiveness of industrial enterprises. It is assumed that they result from the market structure, which directly influences corporate performance. This kind of analysis is strongly supported by the concept of the cross-section comparisons, where enterprises belonging to different industries are examined. The starting point in the above mentioned cause-result sequence is the market structure, which determines the conduct, which in turn influences the performance.

Summing up the above reflections in the context of their relationship with the interpretation of *corporate performance*, it should be stated that it constitutes one of the main research themes in the industrial economics, especially in terms of the reasons for its diversity. However, the literature does not provide a precise definition of the term corporate performance. In the theory of the industrial economics, corporate performance is attributed such features as: profitability, development, product quality, technological progress and productive and allocative efficiency.

In the analyses based on the SCP concept, the profitability is considered as the most adequate measure of corporate effectiveness. At the same time, it is also the most commonly applied measure. However, measuring profitability can be performed with the use of different methods, based for example either on book values or on market values. In practice, the most frequently used ratios include the following (Lipczynski, Wilson, & Goddard, 2005, pp. 318–328):

- Tobin's q ratio, which is the relation of the market value of an enterprise to its recreation value,
- Profit margin, which is the relation of the generated profit to the turnover,
- Book value profitability rates, which are the relation of the net or gross earnings to the selected book values, such as assets, equity or sales.

Despite the utility of the profitability ratios as the effectiveness measures for firms oriented at profit maximisation, they seem less adequate for enterprises aiming at other goals, such as sales, growth or managerial competence increase. In such cases, the alternative effectiveness measures are suggested, such as the growth rate of sales, assets or employment. The use of such rates also enables comparisons of corporate performance between different size firms. From the point of view of a customer or a group of customers, the quality of products or services should also be considered as an important effectiveness measure.

Another ratio characterising financial condition of an economic entity is the technology progress, which is a derivative of investments in the research and development. In the long term, technological progress is probably also one of the most important factors affecting the market structure by influencing the demand (the consumers' preferences and likings evolve as the new products emerge) and supply (technology and cost structure change as the new and more effective production processes are developed).

The last, but not least symptom of corporate financial condition recognised in the theory of industrial economics is the productive and allocative efficiency. The productive efficiency is associated with the extent to which an enterprise reaches its maximal, technologically feasible level of production from the employed combination of production factors. The productive efficiency may also refer to whether an enterprise uses the optimal combination of factors in terms of costs in order to attain a given production level. Therefore it can be brought to the rational rule, according to which a firm operates rationally if it maximises the effects at a given level of expenditure or minimises the expenditure in order to reach a given effect. The allocative efficiency refers to maximising the social welfare in the state of economic equilibrium (Lipczynski, Wilson, & Goddard, 2005, p. 10).

However, when referring to the practice of the industrial organisations, the corporate performance is almost exclusively identified as profitability. Despite this fairly narrow interpretation of the term, still there is no conformity concerning the universal measure of this economic feature. The ambiguity of the term 'profitability' is revealed in a number of studies on the diversity of this profitability under the influence of various factors, such as industry, corporate strategy or branch. The profitability ratio which is definitely the most commonly used in empirical research is the return on assets (ROA), i.e. the relation of the earnings to the total of assets (Adner & Helfat, 2003; Claver, Molina, & Tari, 2002; Hawawini, Subramanian, & Verdin, 2003, 2004; Mauri & Michaels, 1998; McGahan, 1999a, 1999b; McGahan & Porter, 1997, 2002, 2003; Powell, 1996; Roquebert, Phillips, & Westfall, 1996;

Ruefli & Wiggins, 2003; Rumelt, 1991; Schmalensee, 1985; Spanos, Zaralis, & Lioukas, 2004). Sometimes, however, some alternative profitability ratios are utilised, such as the return on sales (ROS), i.e. the relation on the earnings to the turnover (Kessides, 1990), the very amount of operational profit (Furman, 2000) or even the level of earnings measured on an ordinal scale, indicated by the managers in comparison with the competition (Caloghirou, Protogerou, Spanos, & Papagiannakis, 2004).

The corporate performance is sometimes also interpreted as the firm value measured with the use of e.g. Tobin's q (Wernerfelt & Montgomery, 1988), economic value added (EVA), i.e. the difference between the operational earnings after tax and the cost of total capital invested or the total market value (Hawawini et al., 2003, 2004). There are also some studies, where the corporate performance is measured by the firm's market share (Chang & Singh, 2000).

## 1.2 Corporate Performance Versus Corporate Finance Theory

A considerably different interpretation of the term 'corporate performance' is provided by the theory of corporate finance. According to the most general definition, it is considered as an economic financial condition of an entity in a given time, which is also known as financial effectiveness (Bień, 2002). In order to comprehensively recognise the financial condition of a firm, i.e. to diagnose it, various analytical methods are utilised. The classification of those methods is shown in Fig. 1.1.

The environment analysis is used to determine those factors influencing corporate performance which are mainly independent from an enterprise. It aims at identifying the opportunities and risk involved with the environment and therefore also at determining the strengths and weaknesses of a firm. The market analysis in the above classification involves such aspects as e.g. demand analysis, product distribution, price forecasting, market segmentation, as well as demographic and geographic characteristics of the market, etc. The competition analysis, which is performed e.g. by sales volume and sales dynamics analysis, is meant to identify the main competitors (Sierpińska & Jachna, 2004, pp. 14–15).

The fundamental part of corporate activity analysis is the economic analysis, involving technical and economic analysis, as well as financial analysis. The first one focuses on evaluating individual sections of corporate economic activity, such as production (quantity, product range, production methods), employment, pays, labour productivity, technical equipment, inventory management and technical progress (Bednarski & Kurtys, 2001). In a market economy, it is the financial analysis which plays the crucial role and therefore constitutes the main field of economic analysis. Traditionally, it consists of the initial firm evaluation based on the structure and dynamics analysis of financial reports (balance sheet, profit and

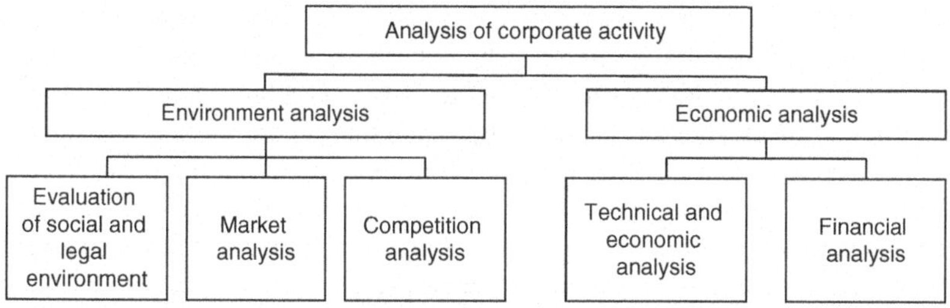


**Fig. 1.1** Classification of corporate performance analysis (Source: Author's own compilation based on: Gabrusewicz, 2002, p. 15; Sierpińska & Jachna 2004, p. 14)

loss account and cash flow) and also of the deepened ratio analysis of the corporate condition in the area of liquidity, solvency, profitability, efficiency and market value (Jerzemowska, 2004; Sierpińska & Jachna, 2004, p. 16).

In the practice of corporate finance, the firm evaluation is often limited only to the financial analysis, which might be due to the easiness of its application. The data necessary for performing the financial analysis is usually freely accessible, as the traditional financial analysis is based on accounting reports. Sometimes it is limited exclusively to the ratio analysis in the basic areas under examination. In such case, the corporate performance is usually characterised with the ratios of profitability, liquidity, efficiency, solvency and capital market (Bień, 2000, pp. 97–128, 2002, pp. 64–102; Gabrusewicz, 2002, pp. 207–251; Jog & Suszyński, 2000; Libby, Libby, & Short, 2009, pp. 716–732; Sierpińska & Jachna, 2004, pp. 144–221).

Despite the fact that there are many different ways in which the analytical areas contributing to the whole of corporate performance are classified, the very analytical tools formed by financial ratios are usually similar. Therefore, the corporate performance can be affected by profitability, assets utilisation, long-term financial situation and liquidity (Bednarski et al., 2001, pp. 57–139).

Considering the variety of aspects influencing the overall financial condition of an enterprise, as well as taking into account the nature of the empirical study, one can formulate a definition of the corporate performance best corresponding to the needs of this study. The term can be interpreted as an economic and financial state of an entity in a given time, described by its effectiveness and solvency. Due to the fact that the examined enterprises are not public companies, the important aspect of the market value of the company has to be omitted.

The issue of efficiency is of interest to many fields of science, although it is a very complex question and the very concept of efficiency is sometimes interpreted differently, both in the economic literature, as well as in business practice (Fedorowicz, 1990; Felbur & Ważniewski, 1994; Fiszel, 1973; Kornai, 1986; Kotarbiński, 1973; Leibenstein, 1978; Łubieński, Makowski, & Rybak, 1988; Melich, 1980, 1985). Considering the fact that the essence of the economic efficiency evaluation of an enterprise – as a complex economic category – should cover its multiplicity, i.e. the combined assessment of the many diverse elements that determine it (Czechowski, 1997, p. 130), the efficiency can be interpreted as a relation of the broadly defined results obtained from economic activities to any expenses incurred for that purpose, where both the inputs and the effects are quantifiable values (Biliński, 1987; Nahotko, 1992; Żółkiewski, 1993). Using the terminology of financial analysis, it can be stated that efficiency is characterised by ratios of profitability and effectiveness. The other aspect of financial condition, i.e. solvency, can be defined as the ability to repay debt. In the financial analysis this ability is decomposed to the long-term and short-term solvency, known as liquidity.

Thus, the above interpretation of corporate performance is much wider than the concept used in the theory of industrial economics, where practically the term was reduced to a selected profitability ratio, but narrower than the traditional approach used in financial analysis. The presented interpretation of the corporate performance is probably the closest to the definition proposed by Kowalak (2003, p. 11), who defines it as the financial condition at a given time, expressed by the ability of a company to maintain the solvency, generate profits and expand the assets and equity.

The two basic areas included in this definition – efficiency and solvency – cover a large and important part of the problems associated with the analysis of corporate performance, although certainly do not cover all the related issues. Some important aspects of financial condition were consciously abandoned in the definition constructed for the purpose of this study. On the one hand, the adopted limitations arise from the range of data available in the database. On the other hand, they are the result of a compromise between the desire for a comprehensive business characteristics and the risk of excessive number of diagnostic variables, which increases the likelihood of difficulties in detecting regularities. Including too many ratios may lead to a situation, where one wants to describe everything, but in fact does not discover anything.

On the one hand, using data exclusively from financial statements raises awareness of the limitations resulting from imperfections of book values, e.g. due to manipulations performed on financial items, especially on the profit. The problem is particularly noticeable in the case of some profitability ratios, such as earnings per share or return on equity, which are often subject to management in a pejorative sense, for example, in order to meet the desirable threshold values. The Chinese listed companies may serve as an example here. The probability of profit manipulation in these companies appears to be greater than in other countries due to the statutory requirements concerning the possibility of raising capital on the stock exchange (Yu, Du, & Sun, 2006). Studies on this kind of phenomena, referred to as the earnings management, are more and more frequent and often concern the distribution of rates of return around some threshold values, such as zero or the value of the ratio from the previous reporting period. The expected result of profit manipulation is the asymmetric distribution, where the values from above the threshold occur much more frequently than the values from below it (Burgstahler & Dichev, 1997; Charoenwong & Pornsit, 2009; Dechow, Sloan, & Sweeney, 1995; Moreira & Pope, 2007). The activities of this type are also observed in other countries, and – although companies surveyed in this study are not public companies – the presence of such phenomenon is also not unlikely. On the other hand, referring to the accounting data – although less frequently used in the empirical research – will create an opportunity to compare the impact of national and industrial factors between market and book values.

## 1.3 Classification of Corporate Performance Determinants

The progress of the European economic integration intensifies internationalisation process of companies and the resulting growth of market competition. Consequently, the role of financial analysts who compare business performance with their competitors, both nationally and internationally, is increasing. The main tool employed by financial analysts are the ratios, used for regional comparisons, as well as to assess the progress of companies in time, that is to compare the performance between the subsequent reporting periods (McLeay & Stevenson, 2006).

The reasons for diversification of the corporate financial results are various and numerous. The most general classification of these reasons, distinguishes two categories: external and internal factors. This categorisation, along with some examples of specific factors, is shown in Fig. 1.2. Factors in the first group depend on the business environment, which means that they are affected by such aspects as geographical location, development of the region, distribution of natural resources, the country's economy, etc. The other group of factors, also known as microeconomic factors, is controlled by an enterprise. They are therefore largely dependent on business management.

Apart from the categorisation of corporate performance determinants according to the criterion of their impact on an enterprise, i.e. into the external and internal factors, there can be a number of other classifications of these factors, for example according to the value for the owners, which they affect (e.g. sales, assets or working capital) or according to the strategic success factors (e.g. factors related to customers, internal processes and development) (Wędzki, 2006, p. 21). However, as the above-mentioned classification criteria and the types of factors have no direct connection with the country and industry effect which constitute the main focus of this study, they will not be further characterised here. The external factors, however, deserve more elaborated classification. These factors can be broadly divided into factors of macro- and micro- environment (Mączyńska & Zawadzki, 1997).

Factors in the first group (macro-environment) apply to all businesses, and can include: government policy, economic cycle, national financial system (including the organisation and regulation of capital markets, interest rates, exchange rate policy), tax system (particularly the income tax, tax on goods and services, concessions and preferences), accounting procedures, inflation, and legal regulations, especially concerning business. These factors, therefore, correspond in general to the domestic factors, as they vary across countries, but are usually homogenous within one economy.

Micro-environmental factors are associated with the industry in which the enterprise operates, and therefore can be identified with the industrial factors.

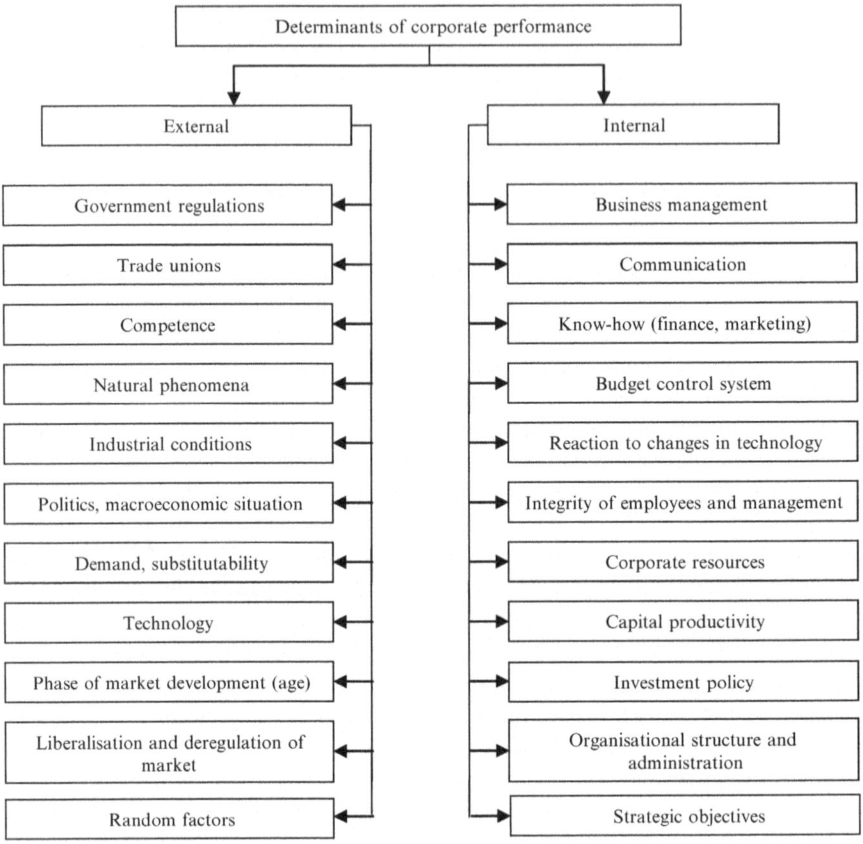


**Fig. 1.2** Corporate performance determinants (Source: Author's own compilation based on: Kowalak, 2003, pp. 33–47)

They include: industry cycle, the bargaining power of suppliers (i.e. the degree of business dependence on resources, deliveries, price, timing, seasonality) and buyers (related to the demand for company products, the degree of substitutability, competition), the risk of entry of large competitors, the emergence of new products and technologies, changes of customers' needs, competitiveness in the industry (intensity of the entry of new competitors, pricing and marketing fight) (Siemińska, 2002). One of the first comprehensive summaries of industrial factors affecting the level of profitability in the industry is presented by Porter's model (Porter, 1992), in which he lists five main groups:

– Competition in the industry – competition among the existing firms, the industry growth rate, operating leverage, product differentiation, concentration of production, capacity utilisation;
– Threat of new entry – economies of scale, capital requirements, concerns about the brand, access to distribution channels;

- Bargaining power of suppliers – the concentration of suppliers, the cost of changing supplier, the threat of integration on the part of manufacturers or suppliers in order to obtain a monopoly-like conditions;
- Bargaining power of buyers – the concentration of buyers, the cost of changing buyer, price elasticity of product;
- Threat of substitutes – technical progress in the field of substitute products.

Empirical verification of the influence of industrial factors on the profitability carried out under the research program called PIMS[1] confirms a strong positive impact on profitability mainly of such factors as market share and product quality, while the negative impact of the following factors: capital intensity, mass purchase of products and expenditures in marketing and in research and development (Buzzel & Gale, 1987).

In practice, there are mutual relationships between internal and external factors which strengthen or weaken their impact on the financial condition of companies. This interaction can also vary depending on the time horizon (Mączyńska & Zawadzki, 1997).

Financial efficiency of enterprises is one of the main research themes in industrial economics. According to the SCP paradigm the distribution of the number and size of enterprises in an industry (market structure) determines the manner in which these actors interact with each other (strategies), which in turn affects the profitability of enterprises (the conduct). According to this concept, the market structure depends mainly on technological factors, such as economies of scale, while the presence of high profits is the evidence of monopolistic power. Studies in the tradition of SCP, which mainly attempt to assess the empirical regularities, were often based on cross-sectional data for the market, understood as different industrial sectors (Bain, 1951). A common measure was the regression of the average profitability rates in relation with different market variables, such as horizontal concentration index, measures of economies of scale, barriers to entry or intensity of research and development and advertising. Summarising the results of many studies, it can be concluded that the relationship between market structure and profitability of the company was generally positive, but not necessarily significant (Weiss, 1974).

Much of the research in this area aims to clarify the causes of unequal financial strength of companies, which is most commonly measured with profitability ratios. These studies are based on the assumption that the formation of the corporate efficiency is affected by various industrial factors, as well as those concerning the company itself (Lipczynski et al., 2005, pp. 318–328). To identify these determinants, a decomposition of variance is often used. The tool is employed to decompose the total variability into components, explained by industry effects, corporate effects and business unit effects. A portion of the total variability may remain unexplained by these effects (Schmalensee, 1985).

[1] *The Profit Impact of Market Strategy.*

Industry effects are common to all companies operating within the given industry. Each industry has certain characteristics, resulting e.g. from the concentration of companies, barriers to entry and exit or from product differentiation.

Corporate effects apply to all industries where an enterprise operates. Therefore, every company has some distinct features, reflecting the impact of strategic decisions concerning the size and scale of an enterprise, vertical and horizontal integration or long-term investment.

Business unit effects (also called line of business effects) are factors specific for each organisational unit, which functions within a company. These include the impact of operational decisions on the effectiveness of each department of an enterprise in such areas as: production level, allocation of resources in various departments, research and development and marketing.

If the data can be seen not only in the horizontal cross-section, but also in time series, it is also likely that the impact of macroeconomic factors called year effect will be detected. It includes economic fluctuations, changes in government policy or taxation, which equally influence the condition of all industries and all enterprises (Lipczynski et al., 2005, pp. 329–330).

Studies of the extent to which various factors affect the economic corporate performance have a broad tradition, especially in the United States, but are becoming increasingly popular also in Europe. The review of studies involving mostly the U.S. companies and the impact of the effects of industrial and corporate-level effects (Lipczynski et al., 2005, pp. 333–334) shows that industrial factors are usually not the most important determinants of corporate profitability compared to other effects which are subject to analysis. However, these studies do not provide conclusions about the relative importance of the industry and country effects.

According to the SCP concept, a company's financial condition (conduct) depends on the company's strategy, which in turn is influenced by factors related to the market structure. The diagram of the SCP paradigm is shown in Fig. 1.3, where the main relationships are marked with a continuous line (from the structure to results through the strategy). However the opposite interactions have also been proven possible, i.e. for example that the strategy may depend on the results, the market structure on the strategies and the financial condition (Clarke, 1985; Phillips, 1976). These links correspond to the dashed lines.

The common assumption for virtually all branches of the economics is the concept that companies seek to maximise their profits. However, although some companies are much more profitable than others, most of them only reach profit levels characteristic for a competitive market. In view of these circumstances in the various disciplines of economics, models were developed in order to forecast which companies will achieve higher rates of return and how these levels can be maintained in a situation where profits attract new market players. Slade (2004) describes four such models: two derived from the industrial economics, one – from financial economics, and one – from the economics of non-renewable resources. Each of them exposes another factor as the main determinant of profitability. The first one stresses the importance of the market structure in which the enterprise

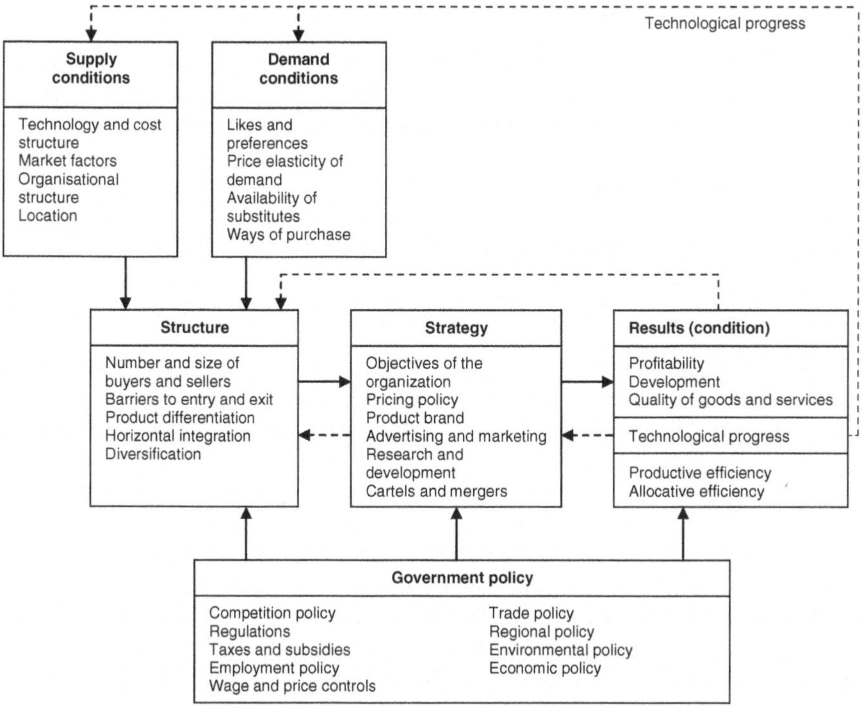


**Fig. 1.3** The SCP paradigm (Source: Lipczynski et al., 2005, p. 7)

operates, the second focuses on the company's market share, the third – on the company's risk class, and the last highlights the scarcity of resources.

When discussing the characteristics of an industry, which is one of the sources of corporate performance differentiation, it is purposeful to define the term of the industrial sector, especially that there is no overall consensus on the substance of the term in the literature (Bieliński, 2006; Foster, 1986). Sometimes, an industry is examined in terms of similarity of the raw materials used, whereas sometimes in terms of the resemblance of the production process, final product or the final recipient (Faulkner & Bowman, 1996, p. 50; Gierszewska & Romanowska, 1994, p. 57; Porter, 1992, p. 23, 1998, p. 33; Stonehouse, Hamill, Campbell, & Purdie, 2001, p. 57). In practice, however, some or all of these attributes often overlap with each other, which makes it more difficult to isolate industries. In addition, assigning precisely particular enterprises to the relevant industry can be further complicated by the fact that some companies may operate in different industries simultaneously. For the purpose of this study, an industry will be interpreted as one of several basic types of economic and social activity in line with the European Classification of Activities (NACE), distinguished as a result of applying the one-digit division of these activities into sections.

Each industry is characterised by certain distinctive features. The specificity of the industry, in turn, affects the functioning of enterprises, including their financial standing. Industry-specific factors can be grouped as follows (Bieliński, 2006, pp. 62–64):

- Demand factors – depending on market and product characteristics (such as product homogeneity or differentiation, market fragmentation or segmentation),
- Supply factors – resulting from the necessary resources and the production process (e.g. location, type of materials used, knowledge and technology needed to produce the product, the type of machinery, the production cycle length, the organisation of production, distribution and supply channels),
- Factors common for both groups – characteristics associated mainly with the objective of increasing competitiveness and defining relationships between enterprises in the industry.

Another industry-specific feature affecting corporate financial parameters is the amount of the necessary investment expenditures. Operating in some industries requires substantial expenditure on fixed assets, such as land, buildings, machinery and equipment, whereas in other industries these charges are much smaller. The industry-specific raw materials and semi-finished products, including their availability and cost, are also an important determinant of corporate performance. They affect both the competitiveness of the industry and the rate of corporate profitability. Another feature differentiating the industries is the method of product pricing, which either allows for achieving high profits from the sales or forces the realisation of low margins. However, in most industries with relatively low ratio of earnings to sales, companies face a relatively high turnover.

Another factor is the credit terms, or – more broadly – the cost and availability of capital, which might be convenient in certain industries, while in others – limited for example due to cash sale only. In a similar manner, the performance of enterprises in an industry is affected by the labour factors, including its availability, cost and level of employees' qualifications. The corporate efficiency is also under the influence of the state through subsidising certain activities or goods produced or due to financial support for research and development.[2]

The cost structure, where the ratio of fixed to variable costs of production varies depending on the type of activity, could also be taken as a feature differentiating between industries (Kotler, 1994, p. 208). Some other indicators suggested for differentiating between industries include a relationship of expenditure on research and development to sales, advertising expenditure to sales and the ratio of expenditure on intermediate goods to sales (Rainelli, 1996, p. 37).

Users of financial ratios, both practitioners and academics, search for some common characteristics of ratios across industries, as it is expected that ratios are more uniform within an industry and more diverse in industrial cross-section (Gupta & Huefner, 1972), which indicates that when assessing business performance, it is

[2] *Analysis of the International Competitiveness of U.S. Commercial Shipbuilding and Repair Industries*, United States International Trade Commission, Washington, April 1985, p. 47 (United States International Trade Commission, 1985).

necessary to take into account the industrial specificities. It can be achieved for example by comparing ratios of an enterprise with the industrial mean of the ratio. Another method of more accurate comparability is the reference to another company in the same industry (Ketz et al., 1990). Similar rules should be followed when constructing bankruptcy prediction models on the basis of financial data from two groups of companies: the bankrupts, and the healthy companies, where each pair of firms is from the same industrial sector. Some other methods of eliminating the influence of industry on comparability of financial ratios are also proposed, such as dividing all the ratios by the industrial mean (Lang & Lundholm, 1993) or the analysis of time series residuals only, i.e. after removal of the industrial mean (Lev, 1974).

Almost equally important as the industry effect is the effect of company size. It has been shown in the literature that small firms differ from the large ones in a number of ways. Studies on the size effect and the way it impacts financial ratios have a long history (Hall, 1987), as expanded upon later in this chapter.

Another factor affecting financial ratios is the corporate management policy. The various policies include e.g. minimising production capacities, adapting them for only short-term sales targets, or maintaining unused production capacity, considering the prospects for the future.

An obvious factor differentiating the business performance is also the very quality of management, which has its source in the managerial competence. Then in the same external conditions of the industry and with the same strategic policy two companies can achieve completely different financial results only because of the way of management.

Another determinant of financial ratios, especially those referring to capital structure is the policy of asset financing – with equity or debt. According to the traditional approach to capital structure issues, the financial structure of companies differs not only by countries (Delbreil et al., 1997), but also within the same country, where corporate leverages vary depending on the requirements for funding, particularly regarding the different needs in terms of financial flexibility, which in turn depends on the characteristics of the company's products. Despite the dilemmas concerning the measures of capital structure (Leary & Graham, 2011; Welch, 2011), the diversity of financial structures should also be considered as a derivative of the local customs adopted in the area of financing, which determine the financial relations between a company and the capital providers. They include customs concerning business cooperation with customers, legislation in the field of bankruptcy proceedings or providing guarantees. These habits provide framework for analysis of financial structure, which is a result of complex interactions between the nature of the company, its products and market environment.[3] This means that the decisions of individual companies in the field of financing are conditioned by the quality of relations with financial partners, as well as specific institutional factors.

---

[3] *Corporate Finance in Europe from 1986 to 1996*, European Committee of Central Balance Sheet Offices, Own Funds Working Group, www.ssrn.com, p. 4.

Knowledge of the characteristics of financial systems in different countries, as well as industrial specificity is therefore a condition for explaining the differences in financial structures of companies (Fan et al., 2012). However, it is not always a sufficient condition. According to the survey of the capability of the Stock Exchange Industrial Classification (SEIC) to create uniform groups of companies, the fact that an enterprise belongs to a given industry does not determine its economic or financial features. The analysis shows that although there are significant differences between industries, some of them demonstrate considerable internal non-homogeneity in terms of basic economic and structural characteristics. In the absence of this uniformity within sectors, the classification system does not always meet its goal, which is to distinguish companies from different industries (Sudarsanam & Taffler, 1985).

Identifying the factors influencing corporate profitability was also attempted by financiers. In their models, however, the returns in relation to the assets of businesses vary widely, depending on the characteristics of the company. One of the more prominent features is the systematic risk, i.e. the non-diversifiable risk. Thus, the assets with higher levels of systematic risk should generate higher returns. The simplest model describing this concept is the capital asset pricing model (CAPM), which in contrast to the models of industrial economics is derived from the theory of optimisation of the decision by the market (Lintner, 1965; Sharpe, 1964). In this model, the only risk that matters is the systematic risk, while the idiosyncratic risk is irrelevant because investors can avoid it through diversifying their portfolios. A number of empirical studies aiming at evaluating the predictions obtained with the use of the CAPM reject this model in its simplest form, but justify its modified versions, which take into account additional explaining variables (Brennan, 1987; Huberman, 1987). Most of these variables are, however, market factors, not related to a specific industry or company.

Differentiation of the corporate performance caused either by the industry, the country's economic policy, the quality of management or managerial competence is reflected in the financial statements of companies and can be displayed with the use of financial ratios (Haskins, 2001).

## 1.4 The Nature and Genesis of Financial Ratios as Characteristics of Corporate Performance

On the one hand, the profusion of information conveyed by corporate financial reports is a rich source of knowledge about enterprises. On the other hand, however, it may also procure certain problems with selecting the most important or relevant occurrences and make their comparison more difficult. Solving this kind of problems to some extent can be facilitated by the application of financial ratios, which – when referring to corporate evaluation – are supposed to be defined as the results of comparing at least two quantitative economic features. The result is expressed in one figure (Westwick, 1988, p. 2). The connection – usually in the form of a quotient – of two essentially interdependent financial values, i.e. the parameters mutually connected on the cause-result basis, makes it possible to directly compare different enterprises, as well as makes it easier to comparatively evaluate one firm across different periods.

The beginnings of the use of financial ratios for analytical purposes should be sought at the beginning of the last century, when they were means of assessing the financial situation of enterprises, mainly for banks and other financial institutions (see also: Zarzecki, 1997). This assessment focused primarily on the ability of the timely repayment of debt. Hence the important role was played by the short-term liquidity ratio (called current ratio), being a relationship of current assets to short-term liabilities. Later, to evaluate the financial health of companies, more ratios were successively introduced, but even a broad set of ratios did not guarantee the accuracy of the analysis, which suggests that both the selection of ratios, as well as their interpretation should be treated with an appropriate caution.

By contrast, in the middle of the last century, the concept of using financial ratios was spread into tools for eliminating or reducing the size effect in the comparative analyses of financial statements. Since then, the financial ratios have been used in many analyses. However, as studies show, they are not completely unbiased by the size of an entity, and therefore can lead to distortion of cross-sectional comparisons (Hopwood & McKeown, 1998). Analyses show that both the mean and standard deviations of ratios do depend on the size of a company, which confirms the existence of the size effect.

Currently, the use of financial ratios has become common practice in evaluating the performance of companies. A financial ratio, i.e. the relationship of two or more amounts, allows comparing a company to the industry or competition. Financial ratios are also used as tools in forecasting stock prices, profits from securities, financial risk and the likelihood of the acquisition of an entity, its financial difficulties or bankruptcy (Ketz et al., 1990, p. 1).

Industrial comparisons may have different degrees of reference, depending on how detailed the classification of industries is. However, comparisons between companies with similar characteristics should take into account such parameters as size of the assets, market capitalisation or equity (Muresan & Wolitzer, 2004).

The source of information to calculate ratios is the corporate accountant reporting included in financial reports, mainly in the form of the balance sheet and the profit and loss account, but also the information contained in the statement of cash flows, statement of changes in equity and in some cases resulting from the notes. In order to properly use a ratio, i.e. to calculate and interpret it, the thorough knowledge of accounting principles is necessary. The utility of the ratio analysis is beyond doubt, if only because of the interest it creates in a broad spectrum of individuals and institutions, both internal and external.

The group of internal users of analysis, who are inside the company itself and have a direct impact on its performance, includes mainly managers. The category of external users, from outside the enterprise and without any direct influence on the effects of a company's activities, is much wider. It certainly includes the owners

**Table 1.1** Users of financial information

| User category | Expected financial information |
|---|---|
| Company management | Current and projected financial situation of enterprise, information facilitating the effective management, control and planning decisions |
| Shareholders (owners) | Information to assess the effectiveness of management, mainly the company's profitability |
| Contractors | |
| Suppliers | Firm's ability to repay debts |
| Consumers | Security of the company as a source of supply |
| Providers of capital | Firm's ability to service debt (debt plus interests) |
| Tax authorities | Amount of taxable income generated |
| Employees | Sustainability of the company as an employer, the amount of wages depending on the financial situation |
| Analysts and financial advisors | |
| Brokers | Necessary information for investors in shares and the value of shares |
| Rating agencies | Information needed by suppliers, contractors |
| Journalists | Information for the public, the readers |
| Public | Information about the company's activities for members of the public as taxpayers, consumers, workers |

Source: Own compilation based on: *Accountancy,* 1991, pp. 2–3; Subramanyam & Wild, 2009, p. 10.

(shareholders), contractors (both suppliers and consumers), providers of capital (e.g. banks), tax authorities, analysts and financial advisors, rating agencies, employees, journalists and public opinion. However, each of these bodies reveals the need for a different type of reporting information. A detailed range of the information expected by individual groups of financial statement users is presented in Table 1.1.

The common use of financial ratios is associated firstly with the fact that they are intuitively easy to calculate and simply defined as a set of book values – in the numerator divided by certain book values – in the denominator. Secondly, their interpretation is usually quite clear due to the fact that they are based directly on accounting values. However, these user-friendly tools are not free from some shortcomings, of which the most important will be discussed further in this chapter.

Despite the likelihood of an easy abuse of financial ratios, resulting from their simplicity and widespread availability of source data, they facilitate the creation of certain patterns, supporting the management process considerably. The ratios also provide a starting point to investigate the diversification of companies and their positioning in the environment.

## 1.5 Selected Classification Systems of Financial Ratios

The systematics of financial ratios, also called taxonomy, is defined as a specific classification of ratios into groups, whose elements show a great similarity (Ketz et al., 1990, p. 2). It can therefore be expected that e.g. various cash ratios, such as the ratio of cash resources to current liabilities, sales or assets are combined into one category. Their membership in the same group stems from the fact that they measure the same characteristics of a company, which is the monetary situation in relation to other aspects of the entity.

By contrast, elements of the different categories should reflect different aspects of business, which means that the ratios derived from various categories should be more differentiated among themselves rather than similar. It is therefore reasonable to assume that e.g. current ratio will be in another category than the rate of return on sales or assets, as these ratios examine different aspects of business, i.e. short-term solvency and profitability, respectively. In fact, one may be faced with a company which is profitable and at the same time solvent, but also profitable but insolvent or unprofitable but solvent. Therefore, the taxonomy of ratios is based on combining similar elements, and separating elements directly unrelated.

The most general classification of financial ratios involves only two categories: ratios of financial situation, i.e. the solvency ratios indicating the ability of the timely repayment of debts, and the ratios indicating the achieved outcomes of the business, i.e. the efficiency ratios (Fess & Warren, 1984, pp. 570–580). More often, however, a more detailed categorisation of the ratios is encountered, where they are divided into four groups: ratios of debt or capital structure (also called gearing or leverage ratios), liquidity ratios, activity ratios (also called productivity or management performance ratios) and profitability ratios (Smith & Skousen, 1984, pp. 1162–1179; Wędzki, 2006). Sometimes also the capital market ratios or ratios of market value are distinguished as a separate category (Dębski, 2005, pp. 99–102). Most other classifications, however, are dominated by the division of ratios into just four categories: liquidity, long-term debt, activity and profitability (White, Sondhi, & Fried, 1994, pp. 198–199; Rees, 1995, p. 120).

Another method of organising ratios is based on the system of data in the financial statements. In such case, the following analytical areas are distinguished: analysis of assets situation (ratios mainly based on the combination of assets or their components with other interdependent values), analysis of the financial situation (ratios comprising elements of liabilities), analysis of the economic situation (ratios based mainly on the amounts from profit and loss account) and analysis of the monetary situation (ratios based primarily on the information from the cash flow statement) (Żurek, 2007, p. 300).

An interesting alternative to the traditional classification of ratios is a mnemonic method, which is based on using fingers as tools to help identify and remember the five most frequently used categories of financial ratios characterising the overall condition of a company (Muresan & Wolitzer, 2004, p. 15). The first letters of the names of groups of ratios (Profitability, Asset utilisation, Long-Term Solvency,

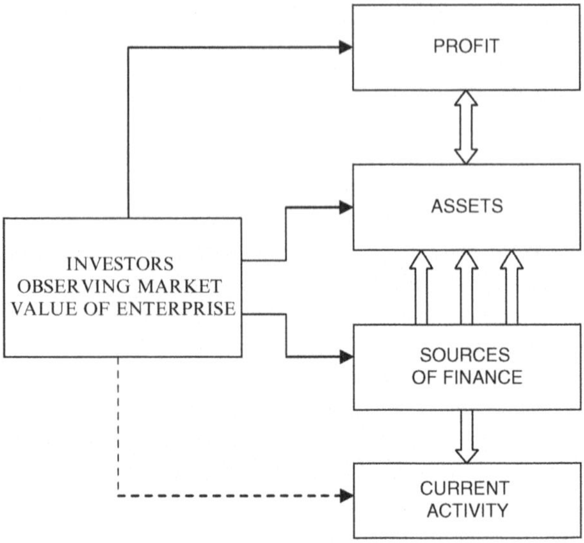


**Fig. 1.4** The basic process of business analysis (Source: Muresan & Wolitzer, 2004, p. 15)

Market value, Short-Term Solvency) form the word PALMS and thus may help to organise the process of analysing companies in the five key areas.

The process of analysis based on the method of PALMS is also convergent with the course of financial transactions held by a company during the financial year, as well as the approach to the analysis from the perspective of an investor, who, in order to diagnose a firm, intuitively starts the analysis from the final effects of its activity, that is profits. This approach is illustrated in Fig. 1.4.

Profits are generated through properly managed assets. To come into possession of the assets that generate profits, the sources of their funding must be known and found. A well thought-out way of shaping the capital structure is also important for the survival of a firm. If an entity is overly indebted, in an effort to exploit the effect of financial leverage, the necessity of the debt and interest repayment might decrease the profit generated from operations. This in turn will not be satisfactory for the owners (shareholders), whose perception of the company plays a key role in the expectations concerning its future.

However, when taking decisions regarding the capital structure, one must take into account the usually lower cost of raising external capital compared with the equity, as well as its greater availability. The last, but not less important stage of the analysis is to evaluate the company's ability to manage operations in the short term, i.e. the management of current assets and liabilities (Muresan & Wolitzer, 2004, pp. 5–6).

Regardless of the classification method of ratios, their construction is such that they aim at evaluating one of the two aspects of a company: either the broadly defined solvency (regardless of the time horizon), i.e. the financial risk, or efficiency – on a gross basis (based on turnover) or on a net basis (profitability). At the same time, these two groups of ratios reflect the two fundamental criteria for evaluating the economic activities of companies, i.e. efficiency and safety, which are both important qualifiers taken into account when making investment decisions (Koralun-Bereźnicka, 2008a, 2009a, 2010).

## 1.6 Limitations of Financial Ratios

Irrespective of the classification method of financial ratios, they are tools that are characterised by significant limitations in the application, which is an imperfection one should be aware of when using them. First of all, having the very values of financial ratios, without any wider context enabling their comparison, largely limits their utility as a source of information and hinders the process of interpreting them. Consequently it limits the inference process based on the values of ratios. Obviously, it is difficult to formulate an objective opinion on the effectiveness of a company without the knowledge of the industry in which it operates, or without the information about the behaviour of the ratio in the past. However, even the exact knowledge of the nature and history of the analysed enterprise can sometimes be insufficient for a reliable ratio analysis due to the limited comparability of financial ratios.

One of the basic accounting rules is the principle of consistency, assuming a constant use of the once adopted rules and practices from one period to another to ensure comparability of the financial data. Since the financial ratios are usually the relation of two quantities taken from the financial statements, it is important to maintain consistency in the calculation of these ratios. Neglecting the principle of continuity means, that the calculated ratios lose their real meaning and comparability, both between periods of the same entity and between other firms. Comparability is also disturbed if the numerator or denominator of a ratio is calculated incorrectly, for example, as a result of erroneous recognition of long-term receivables as short-term ones. The inclusion of receivables with a repayment period of more than 12 months to the receivables turnover ratio expressed in days would cause overestimation of the proportion. Similarly, improper classification of the loan with a repayment period of 9 months as a long-term commitment would cause underestimation of short-term liabilities and therefore falsely improve liquidity ratios. Similar classification errors may occur in relation to the components of any ratios, which in turn distorts the obtained results and reduces their usefulness (Muresan & Wolitzer, 2004, p. 9).

Disruption of comparability may also result from a variety of changes, which the analysed objects experience, such as methodological, financial, objective and organisational. Methodological limitations of comparability result from a change in the information content of ratios, which represent a different range of phenomena, or are the result of changes in accounting rules. Disruptions of a financial nature are associated with the changes including product prices, exchange rates, depreciation rates or tax rates. As a result of technological progress and continuous improvement of the production process, the differences of quality in the manufactured products occur, which in turn are the cause of objective interference. Lastly, comparability difficulties of an organisational nature have their origins in changes in the organisational structure of enterprises, e.g. as a result of their merger or division (Zarzecki, 2007, p. 569).

Another important factor significantly influencing the process of analytical inference is the use of various benchmark values, such as industry-average values of a ratio, the historical values, or the supposedly universal normative values. This latter type of the reference value, though easy to use, is the major reason for concern. This is evident even on the basis of the discrepancies in the commonly used short-term liquidity ratio, whose lower critical values vary depending on the source from 1.2 to 1.6, while the upper ones from 1.9 to 2.5 (Bednarski, 1999, p. 79; Benninga & Sarig, 1993, p. 354; Dudycz & Wrzosek, 2000, p. 54; Ostaszewski, 1991, pp. 54–55; Tarczyński, 2002, p. 103; Tyran, 1992, pp. 162–163; Waśniewski, 1997, p. 313; Waśniewski & Skoczylas, 2002, p. 173; Westwick, 1988, p. 178).

In fact, the application of uniform standards for different companies may lead to erroneous decisions made under the influence of the analysis, while ignoring the impact of such important factors as the industry, company size and finally individual circumstances, such as relationships with contractors. It can therefore be suggested that these normative reference values should be treated as indicative rather than categorical, and absolutely obligatory ones. Striving to achieve them at all costs could cause the effect opposite to the intended one.

The proper selection of ratios and the corresponding reference values facilitates the management process aimed at optimising the corporate results. However, the possibility of manipulation by the managers should be detected by the appropriately performed analysis. Off-balance sheet transactions, simulating the results, related party transactions or premature revenue recognition are just some examples of a false modifying of financial ratios. The use of such embellishing practices leads to a situation in which the evaluation of a corporate financial position does not reflect the reality.

Another trap lying in wait for an inexperienced user of financial ratios is the excessive confidence in the calculated numerical values deprived of any critical overview of the primary parameters influencing a given ratio. An example of frequent misinterpretation can be supplied by one of the most commonly used profitability ratios ROE, the return on equity, which is the relation of net income and equity. Companies which have relatively low book values of equity can often be characterised by high rates of ROE, although at the same time they may show over-indebtedness, which elevates the insolvency risk. The ROE increases with the decrease of the denominator of the ratio, so it can signify high rates of return, while the condition of the company deteriorates. In addition, the book value of equity can be negative (when the value of liabilities exceeds the value of business assets), resulting in the value of the ratio of a completely different meaning in the analytical sense. Finally, if both the numerator and denominator of the ratio (net profit and equity, respectively) take negative values, the company could demonstrate a falsely positive ROE, which would be the most explicit example of an error generated by the inappropriate use of ratios for analytical purposes. The superficial treatment of the final value of the ratio would in fact lead to recognising an enterprise as a thriving business, when in fact it could be a bankrupt (Trimbath, 2001, pp. 2–6).

The above mentioned possibilities of ratios misinterpretation do not only refer to the discussed situations. Similar reasoning errors may be committed also when using other ratios, especially those containing in their construction the equity value, and when the denominator of the ratio may take the zero value. Thus, the skilful use of analytical tools in the form of ratios should not be limited to purely arithmetical calculation of their value, but, to ensure fairness and reasonableness of the performed analysis, it should be complemented by a thorough look at the meaning of primary structural elements used in synthetic ratios.

Another major disadvantage of ratios is their reliance on book values, which are not always fully reliable and accurate. For example, significant differences were detected in the area of liquidity, solvency, indebtedness and profitability of companies depending on the accounting methods adopted (Lanez & Callao, 2001). Results of other empirical studies, in turn, confirm the limited ability of financial ratios to detect and (or) predict fraudulent financial statements (Kaminski, Wetzel, & Guan, 2004). Imperfections of the ratios also result from their properties consisting of a limited proportionality as applied to the evaluation of enterprises of different sizes, i.e. the presence of the earlier mentioned size effect (McLeay & Trigueiros, 2002).

A multitude of different ratios may also cause difficulties in choosing the most appropriate measures to assess the analysed entity. The similarity of ratios structure sometimes contributes to duplicating information, instead of bringing new, valuable analytical content. So far, there has not yet been developed a set of ratios which would be a universal method allowing to perform a systematic and fully complete analysis of a business.

A financial analyst, therefore, to support the conclusions from the study of the condition of a firm, cites a number of subjectively selected ratios representing each category of activity, which are supposed to answer questions about the five key areas: profitability, asset management, ability to survive through the efficient management of funding sources, maintenance of the market value and efficiency in the current activity management (Muresan & Wolitzer, 2004, p. 15).

Some difficulty in international comparisons of ratios, especially in the context of the following empirical study, may also result form the differences in the use of accounting methods by individual countries. This issue was considered, for example, with reference to the impact of accounting differences on financial ratios and valuation of companies based on the corporate data from France, Germany and the UK (Frost, 1994). The aim was to assess the effectiveness of the efforts taken by the European Union to reduce this diversity, i.e. to increase harmonisation, treated as the comparability and transparency of information in accordance with the EU directives, emphasising the concept of "true and fair view of the company" (Walton, 1993, 1997). The harmonisation is achieved in various areas, which include rules, regulations and practices. However, achieving harmonisation in one of them, such as e.g. the regulations, does not automatically mean the overall consistency at another level, especially in accounting practice (Tay & Parker, 1990).

The occurrence of so many weaknesses of financial ratios, in principle, should disqualify them as tools for measuring the financial health of a company. It should be noted, however, that the ability of ratios to relativise financial phenomena, as well as the attractiveness and ease of their application, outweigh their shortcomings and determine their widespread use, both in theory and practice of corporate finance.

# Chapter 2
# Country and Industry Factors as Determinants of Corporate Performance: Research Methodology

## 2.1 Review of Previous Research on Corporate Performance Diversity

Corporate performance diversity has long been the subject of a number of studies performed with various research methods in such areas as finance, accounting or industrial economics. Researchers focus on different aspects of this diversity, for example, depending on geographical region, industry, company size or strategy.

In industrial economics there have been at least three different methodological approaches employed for analysing markets. The primary – and still the most common methodology – is a case study of an industry. The case studies, however, do not lend themselves to easy generalisations. This weakness has led the industrial economists of the 50s of the previous century to the cross-sectional econometric analyses. Econometric methods based on panel data were also used. This kind of methodology was established at the beginning of the last decade of the previous century. This allowed the observation of market dynamics based on time series. Another methodological approach in this area was the study of cases observed in a long time, covering almost the entire history of the market. The attractiveness of this method in comparison with the panel data was based on the use of long time series (according to the age of the industry), which enabled the formulation of reliable conclusions about the dynamics of the market and eliminated the possibility that the panel could reflect the characteristics found only in a few years, when the panel was created (Geroski & Mata, 2001).

An important tool widely used in contemporary research of corporate performance is the discrimination analysis, which is gaining more and more supporters in the area of business diagnostics. The discrimination analysis enables constructing a formula that identifies the belonging of objects to the distinguished classes. The simplest practice in this methodology is the division into two groups. The construction of the membership rule is based on multi-dimensional information about each object and its assignment to a given category (Lipiec-Zajchowska, 2003; Rószkiewicz, 2002).

J. Koralun-Bereźnicka, *Corporate Performance*, Contributions to Management Science, DOI 10.1007/978-3-319-00345-0_2, © Springer International Publishing Switzerland 2013 

One of the discrimination methods most commonly used in practice and the most popular is a linear discriminant function, i.e. the hyper-plane which separates two or more groups. Bankruptcy prediction models, also called early warning systems, are designed to reveal deteriorating economic and financial situation of an enterprise (Zaleska, 2002, p. 12). Identification of problems should occur well in advance, thus enabling the introduction of appropriate measures to prevent the failure.

The increasing popularity of discrimination methods, mainly due to their easy application, sometimes leads to an alternative use of traditional financial analysis and discriminant analysis. When referring to enterprises, the discriminating functions are designed to classify them, i.e. to categorise them into groups according to some specific criteria. A typical example of such categorisation with the use of discriminating function is to assign companies to one of two groups: the solvent ones and the ones threatened with bankruptcy. This is meant to identify the risk of a failure early enough – before it becomes a fact (Koralun-Bereźnicka, 2006).

The issue of predicting corporate bankruptcy with the use of financial ratios is also one of the most frequent themes of research in the area of corporate finance. Studies in this area often focus on the predictive abilities of ratios when identifying the bankruptcy risk. These studies have their origins in the first half of last century – initiated by Fitzpatrick (1932), and then continued by Smith and Winakor (1935), and Horrigan (1965). In the early studies a one-dimensional methodology prevailed, which was meant to identify the ratios with the best abilities to separate unthreatened business from the bankrupts. A milestone in this area is the study by Beaver (1966), which in turn was a starting point for another important study on the theory of financial ratios as predictors of bankruptcy (Wilcox, 1970). The research shows, among others, that some ratios are characterised by stronger predictive abilities, which makes that they perform their function of predicting bankruptcy better than other ratios. This is particularly true about the ratios which include cash flows.

The discrimination models owe their popularity largely to E. Altman (1968, 1993, 2001; Altman, Haldeman, & Narayanan, 1977), whose contribution to the development of these functions, including multivariate ones, resulted in the significant spread of knowledge in this area. Over the past several decades, a number of models were constructed, which aimed at an early detection of potential bankruptcy. The variables used in them were both financial ratios, as well as information about cash flows which are crucial to the survival of a company. In fact it is argued that more companies go bankrupt as a result of the cash problems than due to unprofitability. As a result of a series of modifications of the primary discriminating functions, meant to predict the solvency of companies, the set of workable models for discriminant analysis has now become quite numerous. It is suggested however, that in order to improve the predictive accuracy of the bankruptcy forecasting models, they should be constructed separately for each industry (McGurr & DeVaney, 1998). Therefore, it could be concluded that the industrial specificity is strong enough to affect the quality of the results obtained with the use of the models. A comparative analysis of bankruptcies across industries, carried out among others in Canada, is empirical evidence that the industrial membership can be a factor influencing the probability of bankruptcy (Fisher & Martel, 2000).

Apart form the evaluation of the bankruptcy probability of individual companies, there have also been attempts to assess the risk in a wider context – by industries (Falk & Heintz, 1975). The aim of the study by Falk and Heintz was to classify industries according to the risk level measured with financial ratios. The relationship between business risk and financial ratios was also the subject of many other studies, most of which, however, focused on the factors relating to companies. It turned out, for example, that financial ratios are characterised with good predictive properties with respect to the quality of securities issued by companies, as well as financial difficulties (Beaver, McNichols, & Rhie, 2004).

Financial ratios were also the basis for classification of companies into categories with a similar level of risk with the use of cluster analysis (Melnyk & Mathur, 1972). The grouping results resembled to some extent the industrial categorisation of companies. Similar conclusions result from a study by Gupta (1969), who detected that certain patterns in the industrial financial ratios show a systematic resemblance to the characteristics of industries. The occurrence of the industry effect was also identified in a study of the profitability ratios of enterprises from different industrial sectors (Ball & Brown, 1968). Another notable conclusion was that companies seek to coordinate the values of some ratios with the industry mean (Lev, 1969).

Methods which employ artificial intelligence, such as neural networks, prove an appropriate and increasingly popular tool for classification of businesses (Brabazon & Keenan, 2004). Neural networks were applied for example in order to search for isolated groups within the same industry, namely banking sector, which distinguishes this study from those seeking for differences between industries (Serrano-Cinca, 1998). A preceding research in the area of finance is a study, which uses cluster analysis to verify the ability of financial statements to reveal the hidden industrial characteristics (Gupta & Huefner, 1972). It was meant to verify if the companies from different industries were characterised with some similar values specific to each industry. This type of study has later become a broad stream of research.

A common research theme in terms of financial ratios is their distribution properties, particularly the question of normality of this distribution. An example might be an attempt to determine the characteristics of distributions of the selected financial ratios of the listed companies in Malaysia from the period 1980 to 1996, some of which were bankrupt (Sori, Hamid, Ali, Annuar, & Shamsher, 2006). Observations from the three industries were subjected to normality tests, which showed that in all examples only one variable (current to total assets) was normally distributed. The improvement in terms of normality was noted after eliminating unusual observations and data transformation and only when individual industries were analysed separately. However, in many studies of ratios, the assumption of normal distribution was treated as a necessary condition for multivariate analyses. Verification of this assumption in the early stage of the analysis is also recommended by other researchers (Afifi & Clark, 1990; Karels & Prakash,

1987), who suggest that multivariate discriminant analysis procedure will be optimal if the condition of normality is met; otherwise some of the conclusions might be erroneous. Other authors, however, point to the difficulties in meeting the normality assumption, arguing that the deviation from the normal distribution, at least in the area of economics and finance, appears to be the rule rather than an exception (Eisenbeis, 1977). Some aspects of the ratios' distribution are also discussed in the study by Deakin (1976). Rejection of the normality assumption is also confirmed by some British publications (Bougen & Drury, 1980). Similar conclusions can be drawn from other studies focusing on the selected aspects of financial ratios' distribution, which were undertaken in European countries, for example, in relation to larger industrial enterprises from the stock exchange in Ireland (Lucey, 2003). The research shows that many of the fundamental assumptions underlying the traditional financial analysis, including the normality of distribution are no longer met.

One of the key elements of assessing the corporate attractiveness is the financial statements analysis, which however entails certain difficulties. The purpose of the traditional ratio analysis, based on the financial statements is to enable comparability between companies and at different points in time by eliminating the size effect. The removal of the size effect is based on the proportionality of the numerator and denominator in a financial ratio. The problem of proportionality of ratios caused a major debate in the literature (Fieldsend, Longford, & McLeay, 1987; McLeay & Fieldsend, 1987; Whittington, 1980). The research on this controversial issue (Lev & Sunder, 1979; McDonald & Morris, 1984, 1985) show that the assumption of proportionality is not satisfied in all the industries analysed. Lack of proportionality in ratios is also confirmed by the results of other studies based on the data from Finland (Perttunen & Martikainen, 1989), Spain (Cinca, Molinero, & Larraz, 2005) or France (McLeay & Fieldsend, 1987). However, the degree of failure of this theoretical assumption depends on the industry and company size. The issue of proportionality in ratios was also examined in terms of its dynamics in time, which also confirmed the existence of the industry effect (Feildstein, Longford, & McLeay, 1987).

An important research topic of financial ratios is also the question of their cross-industry comparability. A study by Ketz et al. (1990, p. 2) of the similarities and differences between different taxonomies of ratios in several industries provides evidence for this comparability. In a review of several industries in the United States, they look for certain patterns of ratios as well as try to determine the degree of similarity between the identified structures. The authors challenge the traditional ways of ratios classification, which do not necessarily reflect the actual relations between them. Statistical approach provides, according to the authors, an empirical verification of these relationships and classifications based on real data. The study involved a set of 32 ratios in seven industries (automotive and aerospace, chemicals, electronics, food, textile, retail and steel industry) in over 10 years' period from 1978 to 1987. The selection of ratios was guided by their common use in other studies and practice, which ultimately led to the inclusion of the following ratios:

1. Cash/current liabilities,
2. Cash/sales,
3. Cash/total assets,
4. Cash/total liabilities,
5. Operational cash flow/sales,
6. Operational cash flow/total assets,
7. Operational cash flow/total liabilities,
8. Cost of goods sold/inventory,
9. Cost of goods sold/sales,
10. Current assets/current liabilities,
11. Current assets/sales,
12. Current assets/total assets,
13. Current liabilities/total liabilities,
14. Inventory/current assets
15. Inventory/sales
16. Inventory/working capital,
17. Long-term liabilities/total assets,
18. Operating profit/sales,
19. Operating profit/total assets,
20. Operating profit/total liabilities,
21. [Operating profit + depreciation]/sales,
22. [Operating profit + depreciation]/total assets,
23. [Operating profit + depreciation]/total liabilities,
24. Liquid current assets/current liabilities,
25. Accounts receivable/inventory,
26. Accounts receivable/sales,
27. Sales/accounts receivable,
28. Sales/total assets,
29. Total liabilities/total assets,
30. Working capital/sales,
31. Working capital/total assets,
32. Working capital/total liabilities.

When analysing the above list of ratios, one must notice the duplication of variables, such as ratios 26 and 27. The inclusion of a ratio which is nothing but a reciprocal of another ratio does not provide any new information. Not including the ratios of return on equity or return on assets, which are so common elsewhere, is also puzzling.

The main methodological tool used in the study was the factor analysis as a method to ensure the effective representation of the variables in the form of ratios by a smaller number of variables called factors. Similar variables are therefore combined to form one common factor. An example of similar variables can be a pair of ratios 10 and 24, both of which have a similar structure: the same denominators and similar nominators, including cash, short-term investments and receivables. They describe the same analytical area, i.e. corporate liquidity, and therefore it can be expected that they are influenced by the same factor. However, the ratios 3 and 18 may serve as an example of dissimilar variables as they measure different business areas: monetary situation and profitability. Furthermore, these variables do not have to show a similar way of variability; the increase of ratio 3 may be accompanied by the decline of the ratio 18, which would be unlikely in the previous couple of ratios. Although the factor analysis used in this study, does not fully resolve all the problems of ratios classification, it offers a more reliable basis for the creation of taxonomies. In addition, the established ratio classification schemes for the analysed industries allow for further exploration of the similarities between these taxonomies, and as a result for studying the stability of the ratio structures both across industries and in time.

Another important research issue is the international diversification of corporate financial condition and its variation depending on the size of the company, which means the occurrence of the country effect and the size effect in financial ratios (Cinca et al., 2005). In a study based on the BACH database, the authors calculated a set of 16 financial ratios, which were then subjected to multivariate statistical analysis meant to identify the effect of country and size. The data refers to three size groups of enterprises in 19 industries of 11 countries in 14 years. In total, including the missing data, there were 6,428 observations. The examined ratios include the following:

1. Gross operating profit/net turnover,
2. Net profit/net turnover,
3. Net profit/equity,
4. Consumption of goods and services/net turnover,
5. Value added/net turnover,
6. Staff costs/net turnover,
7. Staff costs/value added,
8. Interest charges/net turnover,
9. Interest charges/debt owed to credit institutions,
10. Financial result/net turnover,
11. (Own funds – unpaid share capital)/balance sheet total,
12. Total debt/balance sheet total,
13. Financial debt/balance sheet total,
14. Long-term debt/(long term debt + short term debt),
15. Provisions for liabilities and charges/balance sheet total,
16. Net turnover/total assets.

It can be assumed that the above set of ratios, although much narrower than the group of ratios adopted for the comparative study of the U.S. industrial sectors, is sufficient for characterising the most important analytical areas of corporate activity, but avoids unnecessary repetitions. The analytical tools used in the study include discriminant analysis, multidimensional scaling and cluster analysis. The analyses show that the ratios do differ across sizes of companies, but the way they differ, depends on a country. It can be concluded that profitability does not depend significantly on the size of a company, but that the differences in this area arise in international comparisons. The authors also showed the occurrence of the country effect in Europe and that the size effect may be considered only within each country separately.

Other studies on financial structures of European companies, also using the BACH database, are not fully unambiguous (Gallizo & Salvador, 2002; Rivaud-Danset, Salais, & Dubocage, 2001; Serrano-Cinca, Mar-Molinero,& Gallizo, 2001, 2002). They show the diversity of the results and conclusions drawn by different researchers, which can be explained by the fact that in the studies that focused on the size effect, the country effects were ignored, whereas in the studies of the country effects, the different shares of large and small enterprises in individual countries were not taken into account. Therefore, it can be concluded that these two effects can not be considered separately.

The size effect was also detected in the capital markets (Cooke, 1992; Rees, 1995) and in bankruptcy prediction (Ohlson, 1980; Peel, Peel, & Pope, 1986). Small enterprises are more likely to fail than large businesses. Moreover, it can be expected that roughly half of the small enterprises of the analysed area will go bankrupt within 5 years' time (Storey, Keasey, Watson, & Wynarczyk, 1987). The company size also appears to affect the debt structure (Chung, 1993), the tendency to export (Calof, 1994; Julien, Joyal, Deshaies, & Ramangalahy, 1997), the cost of equity (Archer & Faerber, 1966) and financial structure (Gupta, 1969). Small enterprises have limited access to capital markets – as opposed to large firms, which can raise funding by issuing shares or bonds. The same applies to the banking sector, where credit availability is smaller for small businesses than for large ones (Gatward & Sharpe, 1996).

The above examples of research problems associated with corporate performance diversity reveal the complexity and, above all, the multidimensionality of this issue. The volatility of financial ratios as performance measures is tested from many different points of view, for example, by size, industry or the bankruptcy likelihood. There is also a variety of research methodology applied in this area, where the significant and growing importance of multivariate statistical analysis is notable.

## 2.2 Relative Importance of Country and Industry Effects in Stock Returns in Light of Previous Research

The industry and country effects have been repeatedly tested in different economic areas. One of the still most frequently studied problems is the impact of the national and industrial factors on the behaviour of market rates of return. The industry and country effect in relation to stock returns involve their diversity depending on the industry and country, respectively. Therefore, the industry effect can be defined as the occurrence of certain factors specific for a particular industrial sector and affecting economic entities of that industry in a similar way (Dempsey, Laber, & Rozeff, 1993). The country effect is interpreted likewise.

It has been empirically proven many times that both effects are important from the point of view of returns variability. However, an important theme of many studies is to determine which of the effects is the dominant source of variability in rates of return. Over the past several years many authors, both academics and practitioners, have tried to assess the relative importance of the national and industrial factors. The comparison of these two effects is important above all in terms of investment diversification efficiency. If these are mainly industrial factors which are responsible for rates of return, portfolio managers should use investment strategies based on cross-industry sections. However, the traditional strategy of portfolio diversification by country would be more justified if the returns variability depended mainly on domestic factors. Many attempts to resolve the problem of the relative importance of the country and industry effects have resulted in formulating some suggestions about how to diversify investment portfolios, as well as how to conduct research in the area of finance (Koralun-Bereźnicka, 2009b).

Despite the seemingly rather obvious connection between the relative importance of the country and industry effects and the benefits of portfolio risk reduction, the literature does not state clearly which kind of diversification – cross-industry or cross-country – is more effective (De Moor & Sercu, 2005). This means that even if the industry factors influenced the rates of return stronger than the domestic factors, in some cases international diversification could still provide greater benefits of risk reduction (Adjaouté & Danthine, 2003). The following review of results from different studies in this area will allow to notice the trends in changes of significance of the analysed factors, as well as to organise the conclusions in this regard.

### *2.2.1 Country Effect as the Main Source of Stock Returns Volatility*

As the source of the benefits from international diversification is the countries differentiation, there have been many attempts to establish which country-specific factors are responsible for low levels of correlation of market returns. Finding the factors which influence the covariance in stock returns between countries has long been a challenge both for the theory and practice of portfolio management. Contrary to the natural associations, not all of these factors are directly linked with the degree of international integration of markets. A literature review will reveal the likely underlying causes of their low correlation.

Some studies indicate that this situation is a result of different industrial structures in different countries, which are reflected in the construction of stock indices. Since there is no correlation between different industries, consequently, capital markets, composed of a variety of industries, will also not correlate.

The early research in this area (Grubel, 1968; Levy & Sarnat, 1970; Solnik, 1974) prove a low correlation between returns in different countries and provide arguments that the benefits from international diversification outcome the diversification costs resulting e.g. from higher transaction costs, cultural and regulation differences or political and exchange risk. However the primary reasons for such benefits are not fully explained. Many researchers claim that they result from differences in monetary and fiscal policies, from percentage rate changes, budgetary deficits and economic growth rates. Others believe that the source of regional diversification is the diversity of industrial structures across countries.

A major part of the literature favours the dominance of the country factors over the industrial ones (Beckers, Grinold, Rudd, & Stefek, 1992; Beckers, Connor, & Curds, 1996; Drummen & Zimmermann, 1992; Griffin & Karolyi, 1998; Heston & Rouwenhorst, 1994, 1995; Kuo & Satchell, 2001; Rouwenhorst, 1999). The only exception within this fairly homogenous literature is the study by Roll (1992), who found the industry factors more important. Some broader studies by Beckers et al. (1996) show that the industry factors are more significant if the stocks are classified into 36 different industries than if they are classified into just seven main branches. In each case however, country effects seem to dominate.

However, according to Heston and Rouwenhorst (1994), the impact of pure industry factor is insignificant, unlike country factors, which dominate over industrial ones and any other kinds of influences. With the use of monthly return rates in seven industries and in 12 European countries in the period 1978–1992, they argue that the method of distinguishing industry factors used by Roll includes country effect, which is why it overestimates industry factors. They show that only less than 1 % of domestic indices diversity is explained by the industrial structure reflected in them. According to their model constructed for the purpose of evaluating the importance of industry factors, any return rate can be decomposed into four basic elements: global market factor (common for all stocks), 'pure' country factor, 'pure' industry factor and a specific factor characteristic for a given firm. The term 'pure' is supposed to emphasise that the country and industry factors are free from any other influences. Therefore, the country factor for a given domestic market is the return on the portfolio, which includes investments in that country alone, without taking into account the global or industrial risk. Similarly, the industrial factor is associated with the return on the portfolio restricted to a given industry. This decomposition allows for a clear and direct distinction between global and industry-specific components, which affect asset prices.

Similar conclusions can be drawn from a study concerning developing countries (Serra, 2000), which confirms that market return rates are mainly affected by country factors and that international correlation does not depend on industrial structure of indices. Taking into account the detailed industrial classification shows, however, that the omission of the industry effect leads to a significant loss of diversification benefits. Other studies of the emerging markets also provide similar conclusions about the dominance of the country effect over the industrial ones, in contrast to the developed economies (Phylaktis & Xia, 2006).

A considerable part of differences between countries can be explained by a different level of exposure to general market risk (Ferson & Harvey, 1993). Another potential factor determining the differences in financial results between national stock markets is the market segmentation resulting from investments mainly in domestic markets. In this case different market behaviours result from the variety of preferences and evaluations made by investors from different countries, as the majority of stocks are held by domestic investors. Another reason for market segmentation is the diversity of policy and institutional environment across countries. This might cause economic shocks affecting firms only in one country, as well as global shocks, but affecting various national markets in a different manner.

The occurrence of many different factors of a political, economic, cultural or social character, specific for individual countries makes that the international diversity of market returns remains significant. That is why a strategy of investments diversification based on countries should still be a considerable source of risk reduction.

### *2.2.2 The Importance of Industry Factors for Market Rates of Return*

Industrial factors were first considered as potential determinants of returns in the 60s. A clear significance of these factors is shown in the analysis of American stock returns (King, 1966; Meyers, 1973). In the international context the importance of industries was first revealed by Lessard (1974), whose analyses of stock market indices and industrial indices showed the prevalence of the country effect over the industry effect. Grinold et al. (1989), also confirm these results, although they reveal significant differences depending on country and industry which is expressed in the conclusion that: "Most countries are more important than industries, but the most important industries are more important than less important countries".

According to Roll (1992) the industry factors are of crucial importance. He suggested three dominating factors responsible for the volatility of return from domestic portfolio:

- Technical index construction, which leads to broad and diverse indices (mainly due to a very diverse number of securities included in the national indices)
- Industry structure reflected in the index which may explain some variation;
- Changes in both real and nominal exchange rate influencing the variance of indices denominated in national currencies.

The study involving daily data for 24 domestic indices from April 1988 to March 1991 shows that industry factors explain about 40 % of returns volatility, whereas exchange rates – about 23 %. It is argued however, that these results strongly favour industry effect, as the variables considered constitute industrial return rates (which include influences from outside the given industry), rather than industrial factors (which are the accurate measures of industry-related volatility).

The theory about the relatively low influence of industry factors is also confirmed by other studies (Drummen & Zimmermann, 1992; Grinold, Rudd, & Stefek, 1989; Lessard, 1976), which, however, reveal a more important role of industries. Apart from the differences relating to the analytical periods or range of the research, the identification of a stronger influence of the industry has its origin in the problem, which appeared in the study by Roll, where the industrial index was used as the proxy of the industrial factors and domestic indices replaced country factors. As a result, industrial indices included domestic influences to the same extent as domestic indices – industrial influences.

Using a more detailed industrial classification also revealed interesting differences in the variance of the indices across industries. Namely, in the non-exporting industries, such as media, industrial construction and real estate, domestic factors explain a relatively larger part of the indices volatility due to the high transport costs. However, in the industries producing goods subject to international trade, such as cars, computers, office equipment, pharmaceuticals or semiconductors, the industry-specific factors have a larger share in explaining the variance. Heston and Rouwenhorst (1995), however, speculate that the inclusion of non-European countries would reveal a greater role of the country effects.

A useful way of measuring the relative importance of the country and industry factors is distinguishing between exporting and non-exporting industries. For companies in certain industries the variability in the global industry may be more significant for their returns, since their profitability, cash flow and asset values are more sensitive to the following factors:

- Fluctuations of the prices of production factors used in the industry and traded internationally,
- Fluctuations of the prices of finished goods sold by companies in foreign markets,
- Changes in the competitiveness of foreign firms in relation to domestic exporters and competitive importers.

The coal industry, producing homogeneous goods subject to international trade may serve as an example of such an industry. Supply shocks and conditions of demand for coal are important factors affecting production costs, profitability, as well as current and future operating cash flows of coal extracting companies, which trade it around the world. Similarly, sudden changes in exchange rates affect the relative costs of production factors and prices of coal products, and thus the competitiveness of domestic and foreign coal suppliers.

The distinction between the exporting companies and non-exporters is derived from the industrial economics and exchange rates theory. The early macroeconomic models by Dornbusch (1973, 1987) are based on the hypotheses referring to how the exchange rate changes affect the level of wages, prices of goods and assets in exporting and non-exporting industries. In the case of export goods, for which the exchange rate is the relation of prices of domestic and foreign goods, exchange rate changes impact the cost of production factors and prices of goods, which in turn affects the profitability of the sector.

In the financial literature, the impact of fluctuations in exchange rates on market values and investment decisions of enterprises in exporting and non-exporting industries is modelled by Adler and Dumas (1984), as well as Levi (1994). The empirical studies by Bodnar and Gentry (1993), in turn, provide an industrial analysis of sensitivity to changes in exchange rate and focus mainly on the differences between the exporting and non-exporting industries. Since the exporting industries have a common source of variance, due to the relative changes in costs and prices, the theory predicts that the share prices of these companies are more vulnerable to fluctuations in exchange rates, which is confirmed by empirical studies. Fluctuations in prices of raw materials and goods constitute an industry-specific factor of performance differentiation – more important for companies operating in international markets.

Some more recent studies, e.g. by Weiss (1998), Baca, Garbe, and Weiss, (2000), Cavaglia, Brightman, and Aked (2000), L'Her, Sy, and Tnani (2002), Brooks and Del Negro (2004) or Flavin (2004) show, however, that in recent years, the industry effects match with the regional ones, and sometimes even exceed them, which suggests that the investment strategy combining the international and cross-industry diversification may be more effective in reducing risk than the strategy limited to the traditional international diversification.

### *2.2.3 Impact of Integration on the Relative Importance of Country and Industry Factors*

The influence of the integration process should be particularly evident in the relative importance of the two kinds of factors: the country, where a company operates and the industry in which it holds the main activity. It could be expected that the greater the segmentation of markets, the more significant the impact of national factors. Thus, in the integrated capital markets, the global industrial factors should play a key role (Koralun-Bereźnicka, 2009c). Most practitioners are of the opinion that in the evolution of stock returns the industry specificity is more important than domestic factors.

The recent changes in the relative importance of the country and industry effects may result from the globalisation of companies and integration of financial markets (Koralun-Bereźnicka, 2008b). The activities of many companies over the last decade were focused on the consolidation and rationalisation of operations globally, manifested mainly through international expansion and a series of mergers and acquisitions. For example, the number of cross-border mergers and acquisitions increased from an average of 40 billion dollars a year in the period 1989–1993 to an average of 400 billion dollars in 1994–2000 (Cavaglia, Cho, & Singer, 2001). As a result, companies have become more diversified internationally, which is why they are less sensitive to the country-specific economic shocks affecting their domestic markets. At the same time, however, due to the progress of the integration of global financial markets, they are subject to similar changes (Freimann, 1998; Goetzmann et al., 2005). These developments tend to blur the borders between countries and reduce the importance of the country effect.

The relative importance of the country and industry factors as determinants of international stock returns in the euro area was also a subject of research from the perspective of portfolio performance (Eiling, Gerard, & de Roon, 2005). A study covering the period 1990–2003 shows that significant changes are noticeable in the structure of equity returns in the euro area, although the industrial and national portfolios are indistinguishable in terms of mean, variance and Sharp's indicators. While national returns showed greater variability, but a weaker correlation than the industrial returns in the early 90s of the last century, an inverse relationship was observed at a later stage, i.e. in the second half of the last decade and in the early twenty-first century, which was the period of transition to euro. Furthermore, according to the authors' conclusions, even in a highly-converged group of the economies of the euro area, the international diversification within one industry does not provide such benefits as the total diversification both across countries and across industries.

The earlier mentioned study by Beckers et al. (1996) shows that the industry factors are more significant when the industrial classification is more detailed. Nevertheless, each time the country effect remains predominant. In addition, the researchers conclude that the member states of the European Monetary Union have a much higher level of integration than other countries. Griffin and Karolyi (1998), who also examined both the main division, as well as the more specific classification, draw similar conclusions. The more detailed the industrial classification, the clearer the industry effect. The authors also introduced the distinction between countries belonging to different regions of the world. The inclusion of the major developing countries in the sample showed their lower degree of integration at the international level.

According to a report on the impact of the euro on the European financial markets (Galati & Tsatsaronis, 2003), in 1997 only 20 % of managers acknowledged the superiority of portfolio diversification strategy based on the industries, whereas 50 % found domestic factors as dominant. However, in 2001 these proportions were reversed, with almost 75 % of managers believing that the effectiveness of investment strategy based on the industries is higher than the international one, and only 10 % still believing in the superiority of the country effect. Bolliger (2004) provides further evidence, showing that most banks and brokers decided on the reorganisation of research departments by industries, rather than by countries.

Another confirmation of the changes concerning the relative importance of the two effects is the way of presenting the results of listed companies in the financial press, where most securities are classified by industries, rather than by markets. This tendency is particularly noticeable in Europe. Another example of the radical changes taking place in this area may be the expansion of the international investment funds. The question which remains unanswered is whether the superiority of the industry factors as determinants of returns assumed by practitioners is reflected in the theory. The problem of the relative importance of the country and industry factors was the subject of many studies long before the recent advancement of the financial markets integration. However, there is no clear and convincing evidence to support the practical convictions, as most empirical results show that the domestic influences are stronger than the industrial ones.

The analysis of more than 4,000 securities from 20 developed countries of the years 1997–2000 shows a significant increase of the industrial factors impact on returns (Sonney, 2007, p. 22). In some cases it even exceeds the country effect. The research also provides another conclusion: limiting the sample to the eight member countries of the European Monetary Union reveals a greater impact of the industry effect in comparison with the country effect. One might suppose that this result is a natural consequence of the convergence of economic and fiscal policies in the Community. It appears, however, that this is not the direct cause, as the growing importance of the industry factors was observed in all developed countries. Therefore the shift should be attributed to the increasing globalisation of the world economy rather than to the economic convergence of the euro zone countries. Despite the occurrence of so many factors that integrate financial markets, there are also some forces preventing the total globalisation of this area. Many of them can be observed especially in developing countries. These include, among others, political risk, not complying with corporate governance principles or the poor functioning of national financial systems. The problem remaining in the developed countries, in turn, is the persistence of differences in economic policy, taxation and legal regulations. Despite intensive efforts to harmonise accounting standards, there are still significant differences, even between European countries.

Moreover, despite the clearly marked trend in the recent years among the European companies towards the internationalisation of production and sales, for many of them domestic markets still remain the main area of business. The globalisation process is often curbed by a number of psychological barriers. Although the development of information technology is so advanced that current information virtually from around the world is readily available, investors remain largely not familiarised with foreign markets and the local commercial procedures. Their knowledge about foreign markets is mostly still lower than about the domestic markets, which is why the former may be perceived as more risky. This is particularly true about smaller markets (Kang & Stulz, 1997). Foreign investors also bear the consequences of the distance (Coval & Moskowitz, 2001), different language and culture (Grinblatt & Keloharju, 2001), and even differences in time zones. Even institutional investors, with much greater freedom in economic activity abroad, still have a tendency to remain strongly attached to national markets.

### 2.2.4 Financial Ratios Versus Market Returns

The corporate fundamental analysis can provide a reference point for market rates of return generated by companies. Although not all studies in this area yielded the expected results, most of them proved to be accurate in identifying the relationship between financial ratios and business risk.

There are two main streams distinguishable in the studies of the links between financial ratios and the market rates of return. The first one focuses on the relationship between the stock returns and market ratios, i.e. those ratios which relate to the share price or capitalisation of the company. The most common ratios here are the price-earnings ratio, the dividend yield, which is the relation of the dividend to the share price, and the ratio of book-to-market value. The main objective of this research stream is to identify the possible predictors of these indicators for future rates of return (see e.g. Campbell & Shiller, 1988; DeJong & Whiteman, 1991; Fama & French, 1988; Fama & Schwert, 1977; Goetzmann & Jorion, 1993; Hodrick, 1992; Kothari & Shanken, 1997; Lamont, 1998; Lewellen, 2004; Pontiff & Schall, 1998). Because of the weak link of this research stream with the empirical part of this study, where the above ratios are not analysed, it is not further discussed here.

It is worthwhile, however, to devote some more attention to the other stream within the analysed area of research, which looks for the relationships between financial ratios based on book values and market rates of return. The range of the results concerning the theoretical and empirical links between the accounting and market rates of return is very wide – from the confirmation of a strong and useful correlation (Jacobson, 1987) to the total negation of this relationship (Fisher & McGowan, 1983), although the latter of these extremes is rarely acknowledged in the literature.

For example, the results of research of different industries in the United States and Japan confirm the occurrence of various relationships (mostly nonlinear) between the premium return on equity and financial ratios, which include: return on assets, return on sales, fixed assets and total assets turnover, liquidity ratios, creditors turnover period, stock turnover period, interest cover ratio, debt ratio and equity multiplier (Pahor & Mramor, 2001). Furthermore, the analysis shows that these relationships are largely independent from both industry and country.

Another study, performed on the listed companies in Tehran, aimed at answering the question whether there is a significant relationship between the premium returns and the selected financial ratios (Modares, Abedi, & Mirshama, 2008). The tests indicated that in the analysed periods the variability of ratios including profit category in their construction (return on assets, return on sales and price-earnings ratio) explained changes in premium returns. This in turn proved that in some periods investors, who used the profits for predictive purposes, could achieve premium incomes.

The diversity of the research results indicates that the relationship between the market rates of return and financial ratios based on book values is not obvious. This in turn implies that the inference about the relationship between the drivers of the corporate performance characterised by fundamental financial ratios and the effectiveness of investment portfolio diversification measured by the ratio of risk to the rate of return also does not always have to be clear. As for the use of financial statements analysis for fundamental investments, the results in this area seem to be more promising, since the relationship between accounting values (the accounting amounts, ratios and their increments) and future market returns are confirmed both in theory (Edwards, Kay, & Mayer, 1987) and in practice. A study of the links between the return on equity adjusted for risk and the selected financial ratios for companies in Slovenia in various industries separately, confirmed the occurrence of these relationships. It also revealed, however, that the ratios that determine the rate of return vary across industries (Mramor & Marmor-Kosta, 1997).

Despite the apparent divergence of views in the literature about the relationship between the book and market values, many researchers assume the existence of strong links, for example, between the return on equity and the market rate of return on this capital, although it is not unanimously confirmed. So far, however, there is no better substitute found for the market rate of return, when it is not available.

### 2.2.5 Summary of Studies Review

The review of the previous research on the country and industry effects reveals that up to the early 90s the capital allocation was based largely on the assumption that the country factors are the main source of variability in rates of return. Therefore, the international diversification was generally recognised as the most effective method of reducing the volatility in asset management. The main conclusion emerging from the literature in this area is the dominance of the country factors over the industrial ones as determinants of the returns. However the second half of the last decade of the previous century brings in new results in this area. At present, practitioners are willing to acknowledge the supremacy of global investment strategies based on the industries. The shift is usually explained as a natural consequence of the increasing globalisation and integration of financial markets.

A clear lack of consensus among researchers on the evaluation of the relative importance of the country and industry effects gives rise to further verification of this problem. Some contradictions between the results obtained by different researchers, depending on the method used, the period of study or research sample, prove that it is purposeful and advisable to use alternative methods of resolving the issue and continue exploring the research problem, which particularly concerns the area of integrated Europe.

## 2.3 Empirical Research of the Impact of Country and Industry Factors on Corporate Performance: Aims and Data Description

The main objective of the study is to evaluate the influence of the country and industry factors on corporate performance in the selected European Union countries. The intended result of the analysis should therefore be the identification which factors – national or industrial ones – have a greater impact on financial condition of enterprises. In order to solve the key problem of this research, which can be defined as an assessment of the relative importance of the country and industry effects in corporate performance, a comparative analysis of the diversity of entrepreneurial economic and financial results is applied, both internationally and across industries.

The analysis of the empirical data derived from the aggregated and harmonised financial statements will help to verify hypotheses on the occurrence of the country and industry effects, displayed in the diversification of economic and financial parameters of companies depending on the country and industry, respectively. Consequently, the study will indicate which of these two effects is dominant in affecting the corporate performance.

Therefore, the hypothesis to be verified can be formulated as follows: the country-specific factors have a greater impact on the corporate performance than the industrial factors. If companies belonging to different industries from the same country were more similar than businesses in the same industry, but from different countries, this would mean that there is no reason to reject the hypothesis. If, however, the companies of the same industry from different countries were less diverse than enterprises from different industries of one country, it would mean that the hypothesis is falsified and that these are industrial factors which are more responsible for the corporate performance than the country-specificity. A fairly uniform diversification of corporate performance across industries and across countries would indicate that the impact of the industrial and national factors on the financial condition of enterprises is comparable in terms of strength. In brief, the main research problem can be reduced to the question whether, for example, the performance of companies in the agricultural industry in Italy is more similar to the performance of the Italian companies of the mining industry, or is rather closer to the situation of the agricultural enterprises in Portugal.

Moreover, a number of more specific research problems were formulated. One of them is to verify whether corporate performance parameters differ significantly across industries, as well as internationally. Another issue which requires attention is whether the observed differences are noticeable in case of all industries, countries and ratios, or only some of them. The comparative financial analysis of enterprises across countries and across industries should enable assessing whether and to what extent their performance differs in these two cross-sections, and in which countries and industries the differences are most apparent. It is also interesting which ratios or groups of ratios best reflect these differences. Consequently, one of the subordinate objectives can be formulated as the identification of the ratios with the best discriminatory properties, i.e. the most differentiated in the analysed sections.

Because of the relatively wide range of data characterising many objects, a natural procedure is to organise the elements of the analysed population, i.e. to classify them according to certain criteria. Thus, grouping the objects into categories characterised by a greater within-group similarity is another secondary objective of the analysis.

The final research goal is to simplify the data structure by identifying the major factors determining the corporate performance in the individual countries and industries. The identified factors will then be compared across countries and across industries.

The source of the analytical data is the BACH (Bank for the Accounts of Companies Harmonised) database. The Directorate General for Economic and Financial Affairs of the European Commission collects and harmonises the statistical data of company annual accounting for European countries. The information is published in the BACH database. The data is provided by the institutions that form part of the ECCB (European Committee of Central Balance Sheet Data Offices).

The BACH database is a rich source of information organised by years, countries, industries and size of firm. The harmonised and aggregated data from the annual accounts of non-financial companies was used to calculate 32 financial ratios for each country and industry in each year of a 7-year period 1999–2005. The data from more recent years were not included due to a significant number of missing data at the time of the analysis. The analysed ratios were grouped into three categories, shown in Table 2.1.

The above list of ratios is broader than in the hitherto studies based on the BACH database, but it includes most of the ratios analysed previously. Extending the range of variables is meant to perform a more comprehensive analysis of companies across industries and internationally. The variables in question are all ratios of means and not means of ratios, as only the aggregated data is available (McLeay, 1986). This means that for example the ratio $P_1$ (gross operating profit / turnover) in the Polish agriculture is calculated as the relation of the total of gross operating profits in Polish enterprises for this industry to the total of their turnover, and not as an average value of this ratio for this group of companies. The value of the ratio for Poland should be understood as the aggregated gross operating profits of all enterprises in the country in relation to the turnover of all companies. This is not, however, the mean of ratios $P_1$ for all industries in Poland.

Most of the ratios are stimulants, with the exception of the ratios $P_7$, $P_{11}$, $P_{12}$, $P_{13}$, $L_9$, $L_{10}$, $D_2$, $D_3$, $D_6$, $D_7$ and $D_8$, which were considered as anti-stimulants. Although some of the ratios, e.g. liquidity ratios should not formally be considered as stimulants, they were also treated as variables whose higher values mean a better object evaluation, as practically there is no over-liquidity within the analysed population.

The analysed population includes ten European Union countries: Austria, Belgium, Finland, France, Spain, Holland, Germany, Poland, Portugal and Italy. Nine of them belong to the euro zone, which makes them a group of highly

**Table 2.1** Financial ratios used in the study

| Profitability and turnover ratios | | Liquidity ratios | | Debt ratios | |
|---|---|---|---|---|---|
| $P_1$ | $\frac{\text{Gross operating profit}}{\text{Profit turnover}}$ | $L_1$ | $\frac{\text{Current assets}}{\text{Short-term liabilities}}$ | $D_1$ | $\frac{\text{Gross operating profit}}{\text{Interest}}$ |
| $P_2$ | $\frac{\text{Net operating profit}}{\text{Turnover}}$ | $L_2$ | $\frac{\text{(Currentassets} - \text{stocks)}}{\text{Short-term liabilities}}$ | $D_2$ | $\frac{\text{Long-term debt}}{\text{Assets}}$ |
| $P_3$ | $\frac{\text{Net profit}}{\text{Turnover}}$ | $L_3$ | $\frac{\text{(Cash and cash equivalents)}}{\text{Short-term liabilities}}$ | $D_3$ | $\frac{\text{Long-term debt}}{\text{Equity}}$ |
| $P_4$ | $\frac{\text{Net profit}}{\text{Equity}}$ | $L_4$ | $\frac{\text{Costs of goods sold}}{\text{stocks}}$ | $D_4$ | $\frac{\text{Equity}}{\text{Asets}}$ |
| $P_5$ | $\frac{\text{Net profit}}{\text{Assets}}$ | $L_5$ | $\frac{\text{Turnover}}{\text{Debtors}}$ | $D_5$ | $\frac{\text{Long-term debt}}{\text{Net working capital}}$ |
| $P_6$ | $\frac{\text{Net profit}}{\text{Net working capital}}$ | $L_6$ | $\frac{\text{Cash}}{\text{Assets}}$ | $D_6$ | $\frac{\text{Interest}}{\text{Turnover}}$ |
| $P_7$ | $\frac{\text{Costs of materials and consumables}}{\text{Turnover}}$ | $L_7$ | $\frac{\text{Current assets}}{\text{Assets}}$ | $D_7$ | $\frac{\text{Interest}}{\text{Financial debt}}$ |
| $P_8$ | $\frac{\text{Turnover}}{\text{Assets}}$ | $L_8$ | $\frac{\text{(Current assets} - \text{stocks)}}{\text{Assets}}$ | $D_8$ | $\frac{\text{Provisions}}{\text{Assets}}$ |
| $P_9$ | $\frac{\text{Turnover}}{\text{Fixed assets}}$ | $L_9$ | $\frac{\text{Stocks}}{\text{Net working capital}}$ | | |
| $P_{10}$ | $\frac{\text{Value added}}{\text{Turnover}}$ | $L_{10}$ | $\frac{\text{Stocks}}{\text{Current assets}}$ | | |
| $P_{11}$ | $\frac{\text{Staff costs}}{\text{Turnover}}$ | $L_{11}$ | $\frac{\text{Turnover}}{\text{Net working capital}}$ | | |
| $P_{12}$ | $\frac{\text{Wages and salaries}}{\text{Value added}}$ | | | | |
| $P_{13}$ | $\frac{\text{Financial income}}{\text{Turnover}}$ | | | | |

Source: Author's own compilation

advanced countries in terms of the integration process. The territorial range of the study was deliberately limited to the fairly homogeneous area in order to avoid the possibility of exaggerating the country effect, which could happen if the study covered a wider group of countries, with more diverse levels of development. Including Poland in the study – as the only country excluded from the monetary integration – was meant to compare our country with other countries in the euro area. Accessing the euro zone by Poland is probably a near prospect, so it is purposeful to show the likely gap dividing our country and the partners from the common currency area.

The industrial diversity analysis is performed on the objects, which constitute the economic sectors according to the European Classification of Business Activities (NACE)[1] used in the BACH database. The NACE, developed on the basis of a publication of the European Statistical Office EUROSTAT, provides a structured set of types of socio-economic activities in the national economy. It is used, among others, for the following purposes:

- Collecting and presenting data by type of economic activities in the area of population statistics, production, employment, wages, national income, and other areas of statistics,
- Making international comparisons of uniform categories of activities,
- Classifying businesses for the needs of national register of economic entities – according to the nature of their predominant activity.

[1] *Nomenclatures des Activites de Communite Europeenexx.*

**Table 2.2** Industrial sections by NACE

| NACE | Section | Symbol |
|---|---|---|
| A | Agriculture, hunting and forestry | AGR |
| B | Fishing | FSH |
| C | Mining and quarrying | MIN |
| D | Manufacturing | MNF |
| E | Electricity, gas and water supply | ELE |
| F | Construction | CST |
| G | Wholesale and retail trade | TRD |
| H | Hotels and restaurants | HOT |
| I | Transport, storage and communication | TRS |
| K | Real estate, renting and business activities | RLE |
| L | Public administration and defence | – |
| M | Education | EDU |
| N | Health and social work | HLT |
| O | Other community, social and personal service activities | COM |
| P | Activities of households | – |
| Q | Extra-territorial organisations and bodies | – |

Source: BACH database

There are four levels of activities in the NACE systematics. The types of activities are classified as: sections, divisions, groups and classes. The first level (sections) is embodied in the NACE as an alphabetical code, A to Q, and is further disaggregated in some areas into subsections indicated by 2-digit alphabetical codes. The lowest level comprises four digits. The study includes 13 of the 13 basic sections (one-digit classification). These are the industries where there is the three-letter symbol in the last column of Table 2.2. These symbols are used later in the study in order to facilitate the identification of industries.

Due to the specific nature of the financial statements of enterprises in the financial sector, which largely hinders the direct comparability of common ratios used to diagnose non-financial companies, they were excluded from the study. Several other industries (labelled in NACE as L, P, Q) were also excluded from the analysis due to the very limited data availability.

Summing up, it should be stated that the subject of the empirical research is constituted by the industries in each country, which are described by a variety of financial ratios in a 7-year period. The study involves 32 financial ratios in 13 industries and in 10 countries, which after taking into account the missing observations gives a total of 26,204 data items.

The range of data is four-dimensional including: industries, countries, financial ratios and years. For each country, the range of data thus forms the so called data cube, i.e. the three-dimensional matrix of observation, where the individual dimensions correspond to the industries, annual periods and variables in the form of financial ratios. The scope of the study can therefore be represented as a ten-item series of three-dimensional matrixes, representing individual countries, one of which is shown in Fig. 2.1.

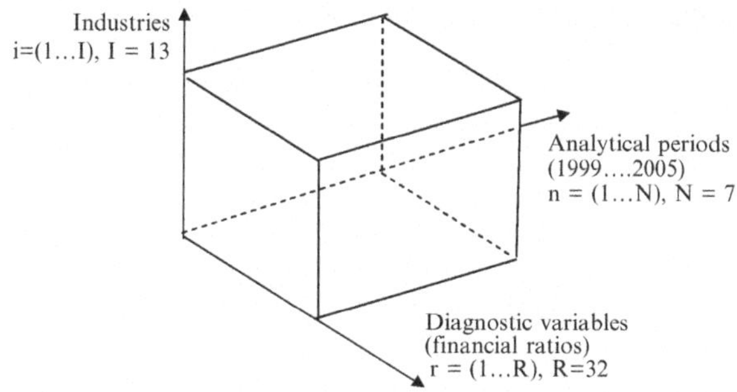


**Fig. 2.1** Data cube analysed in the research (Source: Author's own compilation)

In the above situation, the observational unit is an industry in a country and a given year. The analysis allows identifying the following systems of effects:

- Country and time – when industries are aggregated,
- Industry and time – when countries are aggregated,
- Country and industry – when years are aggregated.

From the above pairs of effects, the last one seems the most interesting, which is why it also constitutes the main object of the study.

The database used in the research provides international and cross-industry comparability of the ratios, as the data available is harmonised and aggregated. On the one hand, the aggregation of data makes it easier to detect certain regularities within the analysed population. On the other hand, however, it causes substantial loss of information, as well as generates some inevitable errors resulting from data generalisation. Inference based on the analyses with the use of the data may also be subject to errors arising from random sampling of enterprises in each industry and country. Although the coverage of the population by the sample size is usually quite high – more than 60 % on average (the detailed data is presented in Table 2.3.), for some objects the rate is much lower, and for others, including Poland – unknown. Therefore, it can certainly be stated that the analyses based on the data are not fully comprehensive and exhaustive.

Consequently, it can be assumed that the variable $x_{ij}$ is a random variable of a given financial ratio for the $i$-th country and $j$-th industry, of normal distribution $x_{ij} \sim N(\mu_{ij}, \sigma_{ij}^2)$ or at least close to normal to the extent enabling multivariate analyses.

## 2.4 Methodology of Corporate Performance Diversity Analysis

The scope of research, both due to the abundance of the data and its multidimensionality, to some extent determines the type of analytical tools employed in the study, i.e. mainly the taxonomic methods. The first part of the name "taxonomic" comes from the Greek word: *taksis* – arrangement, order, while the other part *nomos*

**Table 2.3** Number and share of the companies aggregated in the BACH database (average for 1999–2005)

| | | Country | | | | | | | | | |
|---|---|---|---|---|---|---|---|---|---|---|---|
| Industry | | NL | B | FR | ES | I | A | D | P | FIN | PL |
| AGR | n. | 3509 | 4893 | 2199 | 143 | 325 | 262 | – | 482 | 3131 | 1959 |
| | % | 89 | 100 | 62 | – | 42 | – | – | 26 | 43 | – |
| FSH | n. | 196 | 154 | 116 | 31 | 14 | – | – | 62 | 233 | 58 |
| | % | 90 | 100 | 55 | – | 31 | – | – | 47 | 57 | – |
| MIN | n. | 90 | 219 | 808 | 51 | 137 | 4854 | 146 | 170 | 559 | 235 |
| | % | 98 | 100 | 68 | 29 | 59 | 39 | 90 | 50 | 86 | – |
| MNF | n. | 11840 | 22064 | 39028 | 2698 | 17947 | – | 9630 | 5519 | 16326 | 14546 |
| | % | 93 | 100 | 77 | 21 | 79 | – | 79 | 63 | 97 | – |
| ELE | n. | 89 | 154 | 241 | 171 | 296 | 60 | 527 | 126 | 543 | 870 |
| | % | 100 | 100 | 89 | 76 | 77 | 38 | 62 | 73 | 93 | – |
| CST | n. | 10350 | 25733 | 19734 | 798 | 1925 | 3087 | 3092 | 1839 | 17917 | 4686 |
| | % | 91 | 100 | 68 | 9 | 41 | 29 | 37 | 39 | 85 | – |
| TRD | n. | 31706 | 72103 | 59285 | 1754 | 10860 | 6900 | 9500 | 4587 | 28913 | 14221 |
| | % | 88 | 100 | 73 | 21 | 77 | 23 | 56 | 41 | 90 | – |
| HOT | n. | 3146 | 14131 | 5630 | 315 | 323 | 2626 | – | 305 | 6180 | 660 |
| | % | 84 | 100 | 59 | 12 | 47 | 15 | – | 21 | 81 | – |
| TRS | n. | 5130 | 10521 | 9293 | 425 | 1634 | 1330 | 1499 | 1078 | 12771 | 2029 |
| | % | 92 | 100 | 69 | 47 | 85 | 17 | 80 | 58 | 90 | – |
| RLE | n. | 34020 | 79516 | 26867 | 1789 | 1601 | 2034 | 5739 | 1777 | 25074 | 4904 |
| | % | 88 | 100 | 67 | 21 | 46 | 11 | 42 | 34 | 80 | – |
| EDU | n. | 786 | 626 | 499 | 35 | – | 65 | – | 125 | 998 | 162 |
| | % | 84 | 100 | 29 | 2 | – | – | – | 37 | 71 | – |
| HLT | n. | 3482 | 9359 | 2589 | 50 | – | 181 | – | 165 | 4699 | 708 |
| | % | 85 | 100 | 66 | 8 | – | – | – | 29 | 63 | – |
| COM | n. | 3659 | 8630 | 2826 | 196 | 522 | 779 | – | 226 | 9746 | 880 |
| | % | 87 | 100 | 47 | 19 | 63 | – | – | 46 | 85 | – |

Source: Author's own compilation based on BACH database

means law, rule. Initially, the term 'taxonomy' was introduced by biologists for the classification of plants and animals. The idea of taxonomy was particularly intensively developed in the eighteenth century through the work of a botanist Adanson. In the second half of the nineteenth century numerical methods were used to solve classification problems. The initiator of taxonomic research and application of numerical methods in anthropology was a Polish scientist Czekanowski (1913). The work of Steinhaus (1956) and his team of mathematicians in Wroclaw was also of great importance for the development of the taxonomic methods. The method known as Wroclaw taxonomy is still widely used not only in Poland, but in the world. A commonly used term for numerical taxonomy in Poland is 'taxonometry', which is a scientific discipline dedicated to the principles and procedures of classification (Borys, 1984; Grabiński, 1992; Hellwig, 1988). Further and ongoing development of new taxonomic techniques makes them more and more commonly used in various fields, such as astronomy, geography, linguistics, agriculture, psychology and economics (Siudek, 2006). Hellwig's works were also of crucial importance in the development of the theory of taxonomy in the socio-economic research. They inspired researchers who used quantitative methods in economics (Hellwig, 1968). A taxonomic method with a standard object developed by the same author has created fundamentals for the discipline referred to as multidimensional comparative analysis.

Factor analysis and cluster analysis, applied further in this study, are also the examples of taxonomic methods. Factor analysis, in brief, is to replace a set of independent variables which describe an object, with a less numerous set of new variables, making it easier to characterise this object. Cluster analysis is based on the division of observations into groups with similar objects, where the number of these groups might not be pre-determined. This problem is known in the literature as the taxonomic task or the automatic classification.

The choice of the research methodology can be justified – as mentioned – by the nature of the data, which is a relatively large set of objects (industries, countries and industries in countries) described by a number of diagnostic variables. The methods of multivariate analysis are therefore a natural tool for simplifying the structure of the data and identifying the most important regularities. This does not mean, however, that the application of the taxonomic methods is the only possible approach in this case. The review of the hitherto studies, however, shows that the multivariate statistical analysis often provides an effective solution to similar research problems (Boillat, de Skowronsky, & Tuchschmid, 2002; Cinca et al., 2005; Gupta & Huefner, 1972; Helg, Manasse, Monacelli, & Rovelli, 1995; Leal & Powers, 1997; Sell, 2005).

Due to the fact that the diagnostic variables selected for study are measured with different scales of reference (the ratios vary within different ranges), it is necessary to make them comparable. Eliminating the dimensionality of the variables enables further aggregation of the data. One of the methods of standardising diagnostic variables is the method described by Borys (1978), which makes variables comparable with the use of their spread. One of the attributes of this method is its versatility, thanks to which it can be used for normalisation of variables of any kind, sign, character, size and unit. This kind of transformation of variables brings their values to a fixed range of variation (Domański, Pruska, & Wagner, 1998) – in this case [0,1]. The details of the normalisation procedure are presented in Appendix 1.

Then the classically normalised variables were further analysed. The first stage of the research was to analyse the basic statistics of the financial ratios across industries and across countries. It was meant to initially diagnose the diversity of ratios and detect the basic regularities within the analysed population.

In the case of differences in means of ratios between countries and (or) industries, it is necessary to clarify whether the observed differences are statistically significant, or result from an incidental variation of ratios. For this purpose, the one-way analysis of variance ANOVA was used as a method to test observations, which depend on one or more simultaneous factors. These factors are also known as grouping or classifying factors, or manipulative variables. The analysis of variance, developed in the twenties by Fisher (1954), allows evaluating the significance of differences between many means and explains the probability with which the extracted factors may be the reason for the observed differences between group means. The hypotheses then are as follows: $H_0 : \bigwedge_{i,j} \mu_1 = \mu_2 = \ldots = \mu_t$, against the alternative hypothesis $H_1 : \bigvee_{i,j} \mu_i \neq \mu_j,\ i \neq j$. If the means differ significantly, it can be intuitively concluded that the analysed factors affect the dependent variable. The essence of the analysis of variance is thus the simultaneous examination of the significance of differences between means from multiple groups (populations). The use of ANOVA method involves the fulfilment of assumptions about the measurability of the dependent variables, the normality of their distribution: $N(\mu_i, \sigma_i)$, i = 1, 2, ..., k, and the homogeneity of variance: $\sigma_1^2 = \sigma_2^2 = \ldots = \sigma_t^2$. However, meeting the assumption of normality usually is not indispensable, as the significance tests remain valid. Many empirical examples show that the deviations from normality have little effect on the results of the analysis of variance. In practice, therefore, even significant deviations do not cause large inference errors (see also Domański, 1990, pp. 117–118). Similarly, it can be assumed that some deviations from variance homogeneity are also permissible.

The heterogeneity of the elements of the analysed population, as well as certain similarities detected between them, create a natural need to organise the objects, i.e. to classify them. The classification of objects results from the following premises (Grabiński, Wydymus, & Zeliaś, 1989, p. 10):

- Reducing the accumulated information into just several basic categories, which facilitates the understanding of the variety of phenomena, formulating general conclusions and determining the typology of the analysed items,
- Defining the homogeneous objects of analysis, which facilitates the extraction of the systematic factors and possible cause-result relationships,
- Reducing the time-consumption of the research by limiting the discussion to just a few most common facts, phenomena and objects with relatively low losses of information and not much higher probability of obtaining distorted results of the analysis.

The concept of classification can be interpreted as linking objects into sets or categories based on their properties. This grouping process is the next stage of analysis. One of the many grouping methods, which allows distinguishing the internally coherent groups of objects is the cluster analysis (Borkowski, Dudek, & Szczęsny, 2004; Hartigan, 1975; Jajuga, 1993; Ostasiewicz, 1999; Stanisz, 2000). It aims at classifying the observed data by combining similar objects represented by vectors into certain groups. The higher the level of aggregation, the less similar the objects from different classes of the organised structure.

The need to develop classification schemes, as the first stage necessary for understanding phenomena, is being increasingly recognised in a variety of scientific disciplines, including biology, medicine and marketing (Varadarajan, 1986). As noted by Hunt (1983), categorising elements of a population into mutually exclusive and exhaustive groups can provide the key to the development of the theory. Classification scheme makes it possible to identify the hidden causes of the formation of different categories, as well as to find the characteristic features common for the objects from the same group (Leal & Powers, 1997).

Classification of objects can be based on various characteristics. In this analysis, the criterion is the corporate performance described with the use of ratios. In the applied cluster analysis the following sets of objects are examined: industries, countries and industries in countries. The corporate performance can be compared, if an appropriate measure of similarity or dissimilarity between objects is defined. The algorithm of the agglomeration method used in this case groups the objects according to the square Euclidean distance,[2] which requires prior standardisation of all variables. A characteristic feature of this metric is that it assigns more weight to more distant objects. In order to determine the distances between new clusters formed by the linked objects, i.e. the amalgamation procedure, which determines the degree of similarity of these clusters, the hierarchical Ward's method was chosen (Ward, 1963). It is distinguished by the fact that it uses methods characteristic for the analysis of variance in order to estimate the distances between clusters (Milligan, 1996) and that it tends to form less numerous clusters (Boillat et al., 2002). The method aims at minimising the sum of squares of any two (hypothetical) clusters that can be formed at each stage of the amalgamation. The effectiveness of the Ward's method in detecting data structure is better in comparison with other methods, although it tends to create clusters of small size (Orłowski, 2001; Ward, 1963). Applying Ward's method[3] determined the use of square Euclidean distance as the metric defining the distance between objects.

The variables selected for the cluster analysis should be characterised with large variability and independence. These conditions mean that the variables that do not differentiate the examined objects (industries and countries) should be removed from the initially accepted set of potential characteristics. The possible duplication of the information carried by individual variables should also be eliminated.

The variability of ratios was examined with the use of the variation coefficient.[4] None of the selected variables is a constant one; the standard deviation varies from more than 10 to about a 100 % of the mean. As for the correlation of variables, it is recommended in the literature to leave the smallest possible number of representative variables. However, if the objective of the study is the comprehensive analysis of the corporate performance, it is purposeful to consider many ratios carrying a wide range of information, provided that they meet the statistical requirements for the selection of diagnostic variables (Hellwig, 1981; Nowak, 1990).

---

[2] $d_{(x,y)} = \sum_i (x_i - y_i)^2$.

[3] $D(X,Y) = \frac{m \cdot k}{m+k} \cdot (d(\bar{x},\bar{y}))^2$, where $m$, $k$ – numbers of objects in clusters X and Y.

[4] $V = \frac{\sigma}{\mu}$, where $\sigma$– standard deviation, $\mu$– mean.

The simplest measure is to verify the correlation of the characteristics is the Pearson's correlation coefficient,[5] which measures the strength and direction of the linear relationship between the pairs of variables. The values of the correlation coefficient for all pairs of variables are presented in Appendix 2. The table shows that the pair of the most correlated variables is $P_8$ and $P_9$ ($r = 0.910$). One variable is dependent on the other in 83 % ($r^2$), which means that only 17 % of the information carried by them is different. Usually the variable which is less correlated with other variables should be involved in the study. Since both ratios are related with other variables to a similar extent, it was the ratio $P_8$, which was selected for further analyses, as a more synthetic variable, characterising the turnover of total assets, and not just current assets ($P_9$).

Another pair of highly correlated variables is a pair of liquidity ratios $L_1$, $L_2$ ($r = 0.862$). Since none of the two variables shows a strong relationship with other ratios, the information capacity and analytical usefulness of the ratios were used as the criteria for deciding which of them should be retained in the data set. From this point of view the short-term liquidity ratio ($L_1$) was considered as more important, as it characterises a company's ability to repay creditors in 1 year's time, and not only within about 3 months ($L_2$).

Another value of the correlation coefficient, indicating a relatively strong correlation of variables ($r = 0.835$) was observed in the case of ratios $L_{11}$ and $D_5$. Due to the stronger correlation of the variable $D_5$ with the other ratios, it was removed from the data set. In the case of another pair of highly correlated variables: $P_8$ and $D_6$ ($r = 0.830$) the later of them was eliminated not because of high correlation with the variable $P_9$, which had been previously removed, but due to the similar information content to the ratio $D_7$ which was selected for further analyses.

A similar economic meaning is also carried by the ratios $P_1$ and $P_2$, which is reflected in their high correlation ($r = 0.828$). From this pair of variables, again due to the similar levels of the correlation with other variables, the ratio $P_2$ was selected for further analyses. It was because of the information capacity of this profitability ratio, which takes into account not only the sales, but the total of business operations.

A strong, but inverse relationship can be observed in the case of pairs of profitability ratios $P_{10}$ and $P_{11}$ ($r = -0.824$). The removal of the ratio of staff costs in relation to turnover ($P_{11}$) was determined by a similar content of another ratio ($P_{12}$), which involves the cost of wages and salaries.

Another pair of correlated variables was formed by the ratios $P_3$ and $P_5$ ($r = 0.811$). Despite the slightly higher correlation of the ratio $P_3$ with other ratios, it was retained in the set of diagnostic variables. It was justified by the substantial analysis of the construction of these ratios. In terms of versatility of the analysis, it seems more appropriate to apply a variable measuring the profitability of the total assets, instead of another variable characterising the profitability of turnover.

---

[5] $r_{xy} = \frac{\mathrm{cov}(x,y)}{\sigma_x \sigma_y}$.

Again, a fairly strong inverse relationship can be observed in the case of a pair of liquidity ratios $L_4$ and $L_{10}$ ($r = -0.744$). As none of the two ratios showed significant relationship with the others, the ratio of inventory turnover ($L_4$) was selected for the study instead of the ratio measuring the share of inventory in the current assets. The relative size of the inventory is illustrated by another ratio left for the analysis ($L_9$), which relates inventory to the working capital.

From the last pair of highly correlated variables $L_3$ and $L_6$ ($r = 0.727$) the first one, characterising immediate liquidity (cash solvency ratio), was retained in the target set of variables. It can be assumed that the ratio $L_6$, which is a relation of cash to assets, is much less informative, because, in contrast to the ratio $L_3$, it does not include short-term investments. The balance sheet item 'cash' may often prove quite incidental in terms of value, especially when the cash level is the one from the end of the year.

The remaining ratios were much less correlated with each other ($|r| < 0.68$), so the process of reducing the number of variables was considered as completed. Consequently, ten variables were removed from the initial data set: $P_1$, $P_3$, $P_9$, $P_{11}$, $L_2$, $L_6$, $L_8$, $L_{10}$, $D_5$ and $D_6$, which resulted in reducing the number of diagnostic variables to twenty-two. A detailed list of the variables selected for the cluster analysis is presented in Table 2.4.

Apart from the appropriate selection of variables, the use of cluster analysis in the segmentation research is associated with a decision about the optimum number of the identified clusters. Deciding how many groups to distinguish when dividing an analysed population is one of the fundamental problems that arise in this type of analyses (Migdał-Najman & Najman, 2005). Usually, the knowledge and experience of a researcher allow for such a grouping of objects, that those belonging to a given cluster have as much in common as possible and at the same time bear little resemblance to the objects from outside the group. In many empirical cases, the objects of the analysed populations have certain natural tendencies to be grouped together in relatively homogeneous classes, which greatly facilitates their analysis. When the clusters of objects are intrinsically similar, and there are also clear differences between groups noticeable, it is not difficult to separate these groups and to determine their number (Migdał-Najman & Najman, 2006).

The same applies to the analysed population, where the distinction between internally homogeneous groups of objects is intuitively observable, and therefore relatively easy. In practice, in order to reduce the subjectivity in this area, the graph of linkage distance versus linkage stages can be used. It shows the distances between groups at the moment of their linking. A clear surge of the curve usually indicates the optimal choice of the number of clusters (Dobosz, 2001).

Another, more objective, solution of the problem applied in this study is to determine the number of clusters according to the criterion which is independent from the grouping method. A method called *silhouette index* (SI), proposed by Rousseeuw (1987) is considered as one of the most versatile, simple and effective. The detailed algorithm for calculating the index is presented in Appendix 3.

The silhouette index is a measure that allows determining the optimal number of clusters, i.e. such a configuration which maximises the value of SI (Bolshakova &

**Table 2.4** Financial ratios selected for the study after removal of the correlated variables

| Profitability and turnover ratios | | Liquidity ratios | | Debt ratios | |
|---|---|---|---|---|---|
| $P_2$ | $\frac{\text{Net operating profit}}{\text{Turnover}}$ | $L_1$ | $\frac{\text{Current assets}}{\text{Short-term liabilities}}$ | $D_1$ | $\frac{\text{Gross operating profit}}{\text{Interest}}$ |
| $P_4$ | $\frac{\text{Net profit}}{\text{Equity}}$ | $L_3$ | $\frac{\text{(Cash and cash equivalents)}}{\text{Short-term liabilities}}$ | $D_2$ | $\frac{\text{Long-term debt}}{\text{Assets}}$ |
| $P_5$ | $\frac{\text{Net profit}}{\text{Assets}}$ | $L_4$ | $\frac{\text{Costs of goods sold}}{\text{stocks}}$ | $D_3$ | $\frac{\text{Long-term debt}}{\text{Equity}}$ |
| $P_6$ | $\frac{\text{Net profit}}{\text{Net working capital}}$ | $L_5$ | $\frac{\text{Turnover}}{\text{Debtors}}$ | $D_4$ | $\frac{\text{Equity}}{\text{Asets}}$ |
| $P_7$ | $\frac{\text{Costs of materials and consumables}}{\text{Turnover}}$ | $L_7$ | $\frac{\text{Current assets}}{\text{Assets}}$ | $D_7$ | $\frac{\text{Interest}}{\text{Financial debt}}$ |
| $P_8$ | $\frac{\text{Turnover}}{\text{Assets}}$ | $L_9$ | $\frac{\text{Stocks}}{\text{Net working capital}}$ | $D_8$ | $\frac{\text{Provisions}}{\text{Assets}}$ |
| $P_{10}$ | $\frac{\text{Value added}}{\text{Turnover}}$ | $L_{11}$ | $\frac{\text{Turnover}}{\text{Net working capital}}$ | | |
| $P_{12}$ | $\frac{\text{Wages and salaries}}{\text{Value added}}$ | | | | |
| $P_{13}$ | $\frac{\text{Financial income}}{\text{Turnover}}$ | | | | |

Source: Author's own compilation

Azuaje, 2003). The value of SI provides information about the quality of the resulting group structure. The higher the value of the indicator, the clearer the structure and better grouping (Kauffman & Rousseeuw, 1990).

In cluster analysis, carried out separately for each country and industry, it will be important to compare the results of clustering and to evaluate the similarity of groupings. In order to find out how much alike or how different the groupings of industries are between countries or the groupings of countries between industries, a similarity measure of grouping results can be applied. One of the most common measures used for evaluating similarity of groupings from the many different measures proposed in the literature (Arabie & Boorman, 1973; Fowkles & Mallows, 1983; Goodman & Kruskal, 1979; Gordon, 1987; Rand, 1971; Rohlf, 1974; Wallace, 1983) is the Rand's measure (Najman, 2007), which takes a value of 0 when the two compared groupings are completely dissimilar (in one grouping all objects belong to one group, and in the other, every object is a separate group), and a value of 1 when the groupings are identical. This measure defines the share of pairs of objects convergent between the two groupings in the total number of pairs of objects. The value of this measure tends to increase with the number of groups, whereas the adjusted Rand's measure ($R_{AD}$), applied in this study, is free from this defect (Hubert & Arabie, 1985; Najman, 2007). The calculation method of the measure is presented in Appendix 4.

In order to identify the main factors determining corporate performance in countries and industries, the factor analysis was used. Factor analysis as a statistical method based on examining the interrelationships between variables in a multidimensional space and aims at explaining the reasons for the total variation (for more about factor analysis see e.g. Aczel, 2000; Bolch & Huang, 1974; Dobosz, 2001; Harman, 1967; Morrison, 1990; Tadeusiewicz, 1993).

The factor analysis is based on a linear transformation of variables into new uncorrelated variables (factors), where the sum of variance of the factors is equal to the sum of variance of the original variables. The variance of each new factor explains a number of primary variables and the variation is represented by the eigenvalue. Each consecutive factor (principal component) explains less and less volatility.

Deciding when to stop extracting the factors depends largely on how much random variation remains unexplained by the new factors. The nature of this decision is arbitrary. However, there are several methods which can be used to establish the number of factors, e.g. the Kaiser criterion (Kaiser, 1960), which says that only factors with eigenvalues greater than 1 can be retained, or a graphical method called the scree test proposed by Cattell (1966).

In the context of the main purpose of the study, which is to answer the question about how the country and industry effects influence the corporate performance, the factor analysis will determine whether the extracted factors are the same for countries and industries or whether they differ due to the national and industrial specificity. It should be noted, however, that the factors extracted in the factor analysis are interpreted differently than the country and industry factors. In the case of corporate performance analysis, they are some aspects of the condition of an enterprise, such as liquidity or assets efficiency, characterised by specific ratios. Comparison of the principal components responsible for corporate performance in countries and industries will indicate which groups of variables most affect the efficiency of companies in these two sections and what the similarity is of the factors between countries and industries.

Regardless of the research methodology, aiming to extract the factors specific for countries and industries is greatly hampered by the confluence of these two specificities. The problem with isolating the so-called 'pure' country effect and the 'pure' industry effect is related to the fact that the differences between the mean values of ratios for individual countries may be partly a consequence of the different industrial structures of the economies, and the differences between the mean values of ratios in industries may partly be due to the fact that companies included in an industry are located in different countries.

In the multivariate analysis, where the objects are, by definition, characterised by a large number of variables, it becomes essential to simplify the data structure in order to interpret the relationships within the research area. Apart from the factor analysis (Pluta, 1977, p. 51), a method aiming to extract the underlying factors, which explain the observed similarities or dissimilarities between objects, is the multi-dimensional scaling. The objects are located in a space of a declared number of dimensions in such a way, that the obtained configuration provides the best approximation of the observed distances.

# Chapter 3
# Analysis of the Corporate Performance Diversity in the Selected European Union Countries

## 3.1 Initial Analysis of the Financial Ratios in Industries and Countries

The first stage of the empirical research was to analyse the diversity of financial ratios of enterprises in individual industries. For this purpose, the mean and standard deviation of each ratio in each industry were calculated. The results for the entire data set, i.e. based on the average ratios from the period 1999 to 2005, taking into account all the countries, are presented in the tables in Appendices 5 and 6. The procedure was performed for each country and year separately, although the results of those calculations are not reported here due to their size.

The calculations confirm that there are clear differences in the ratios across industries. Among the profitability ratios, the biggest differences relate to $P_3$ and $P_5$. In the area of liquidity ratios, differences are also significant in case of $L_3$, $L_4$ and $L_{10}$, while the variable $D_3$ is distinguishable among the debt ratios. Even a cursory examination of the tables suggests that ratios $P_4$, $P_8$ or $L_{11}$ have considerably lower discriminatory power. The common element of the profitability ratios, characterised with a high variation across industries, is the net profit which constitutes their numerator. This indicates the intuitively easily explainable variation of profitability between industries. The ratios are relatively high in the mining sector, where the margins are larger than for example in the trade or transport. The wide variation in ratios, which include inventories in their formulas ($L_3$, $L_4$, $L_{10}$), can also be explained through the industrial specificity of companies; relatively low values of these variables were recorded in agriculture, where stocks have a relatively large share in the assets, and therefore their rotation is slower; relatively the highest values of these ratios were observed in transport and education.

It is easy to notice the concentration of extreme values of profitability ratios in two industries. Many of the ratios in this category ($P_2$, $P_3$, $P_5$) take the highest average value in the mining sector, while almost the same set of variables is at the lowest level in the fishing industry ($P_2$, $P_4$, $P_5$) and trade ($P_1$, $P_3$). This phenomenon does not seem to be incidental and indicates the strong dependence of the economic

J. Koralun-Bereźnicka, *Corporate Performance*, Contributions to Management Science,
DOI 10.1007/978-3-319-00345-0_3, © Springer International Publishing Switzerland 2013

viability on the industry. Relatively narrow profit margins are one of the characteristic features of the trade sector, which is also distinguished by high turnover ratios. Wider margins, however, should be expected in industries with a higher share of fixed costs, such as the mining industry. Industries with a developed infrastructure, implementing complex manufacturing processes and offering unique products, tend to show a higher return on sales and a lower asset turnover. An inverse relationship can be observed in industries characterised by standard products, less involved in the manufacturing processes and more similar to commercial activities in terms of activity and assets structure (Mączyńska & Zawadzki, 1997).

The mining sector is also characterised by one of the lowest levels of debt, as evidenced by the relatively high values of ratios $D_1$–$D_4$ converted to stimulants. A definitely high average level of dependence on debt can be observed in the industry of hotels and restaurants. Moreover, a characteristic feature of the education sector is a specific concentration of high values of liquidity ratios, which in turn could be attributed to the fact that the sector is often at least partially subsidised by the state.

Other regularities observed on the basis of the concentration of extreme values of ratios include: the low liquidity in the energy industry, and high in health care, significant assets turnover in trade and a large share of staff costs in the education sector. However, it should be borne in mind that the above observations apply to the aggregated values of ratios for all countries included in the analysis. Examining each of these countries separately would probably reveal more detailed regularities concerning financial ratios, conditioned by such factors as the geographic location or economic policy, which would provide some information on the occurrence of the country effect.

A separate analysis of the basic statistics for each country leads to formulating a few more findings, presented in Table 3.1. These conclusions are based mainly on the analysis of the occurrence of extreme values of ratios in industries.

Summarising the above list, it can be stated that one of the characteristics common to most countries is the good performance of the mining industry. This is especially true about the profitability ratios in such countries as Holland, France, Italy, Germany, Portugal and Poland. Another characteristic feature is the high turnover in the trade sector with simultaneously low profitability, which is the case in France, Italy, Austria, Germany, Portugal, Finland and Poland. An adverse economic and financial situation of the transport industry is also a repetitive symptom which can be observed in particular in the Netherlands, Belgium, France and Italy. Poland stands out from the analysed population because of high liquidity of the education sector. This phenomenon is also characteristic for Finland. Moreover, high debt is symptomatic for the Polish transport sector, which is not observed in other countries.

A similar analysis of the basic descriptive statistics was also performed for the ratios in each industry. The results, i.e. the means and standard deviations based on the average data from the period 1999 to 2005 are presented in Appendices 7 and 8.

The calculations again show the international diversity of financial ratios. Among the profitability ratios the biggest differences appear in the case of $P_{12}$ and $P_{13}$ – the ratios which include labour costs in their formulas. In the area of

**Table 3.1** Conclusions from the analysis of descriptive statistics of country ratios based on average values from 1999 to 2005

| Country | Regularities |
|---|---|
| NL | High concentration of the extreme values of many ratios |
| | High profitability of the mining industry (maximum values of $P_1$–$P_5$) |
| | Low profitability of the transport industry (minimum values of $P_3$–$P_5$, $P_8$) |
| | High liquidity of the health industry (maximum values of $L_1$–$L_3$, $L_6$–$L_8$) |
| | Low liquidity in the mining industry (minimum values of $L_1$–$L_3$, $L_6$) |
| | Low debt burden in the health industry (maximum values of $D_2$–$D_4$) |
| | High debt in transport (minimum values of $D_1$–$D_3$, $D_6$ and $D_7$) |
| | The greatest variability of the ratio $P_8$, the smallest – $P_{13}$ |
| B | Large dispersion of the extreme values of most ratios |
| | High values of profitability and liquidity ratios in the health industry (maximum values of $P_1$, $P_7$, $P_{10}$ and $L_1$–$L_3$, $L_{10}$) |
| | Good performance in all areas of analysis in the energy industry (maximum values of $P_4$–$P_6$, $P_{12}$, $L_5$, $L_{11}$ and $D_1$, $D_5$) |
| | Low profitability of the fishing industry (minimum values of $P_2$, $P_3$, $P_5$, $P_8$) and the real estate activities (minimum values of $P_4$, $P_8$, $P_9$) |
| | High debt in the fishing industry (minimum values of $D_2$–$D_4$) |
| | Low performance of the transport sector (minimum values of $P_6$, $L_{11}$, $D_5$, $D_8$) |
| | The greatest variability of the ratio $L_{10}$, the smallest – $L_{11}$ |
| FR | High profitability of the mining industry (maximum values of $P_1$–$P_3$, $P_5$, $P_{12}$) |
| | High turnover ratios in trade (maximum values of $P_8$, $P_9$, $P_{11}$), but low profitability (minimum values of $P_1$, $P_7$, $P_{10}$) |
| | Good performance of the construction industry in terms of short-term solvency (maximum values of $L_6$–$L_8$) and long-term solvency (maximum values of $D_2$, $D_3$, $D_6$, $D_7$) |
| | High indebtedness of the transport industry (minimum values of $D_2$–$D_4$) |
| | The greatest variability of the ratio $L_{10}$, the smallest – $P_2$ |
| ES | Relatively large dispersion of the extreme values of ratios, except for the negatively distinctive health sector |
| | High values of many ratios in the trade sector: turnover ratios (maximum values of $P_6$, $P_8$, $P_9$), liquidity ($L_5$, $L_{11}$) and debt ($D_3$, $D_6$) |
| | Low profitability level in the health sector (minimum values of $P_1$–$P_3$, $P_5$, $P_6$, $P_{12}$, $P_{13}$) and high debt (minimum values of $D_2$–$D_4$) |
| | Good solvency parameters in the construction industry, both short-term (maximum value of $L_7$ and $L_8$) and long-term (maximum values of $D_2$ and $D_7$) |
| | Low liquidity in the energy sector (minimum values of $L_3$, $L_6$–$L_8$) |
| | The greatest variability of the ratio $L_{10}$, the smallest – $D_5$ |
| I | Definitely the best performance of most ratios in the mining industry (maximum values of $P_1$–$P_6$, $P_{12}$, $P_{13}$, $L_1$–$L_3$, $D_1$, $D_3$, $D_4$) |
| | High values of many ratios in the trade sector: turnover ratios (maximum values of $P_8$, $P_9$, $P_{11}$), liquidity ($L_5$, $L_7$, $L_{11}$) and debt ($D_2$, $D_6$) |
| | Low performance level of the transport industry (minimum values of $P_6$, $P_8$, $P_9$, $L_5$, $L_{11}$, $D_5$, $D_6$, $D_8$) |
| | Low performance level of the fishing industry in terms of profitability and liquidity (minimum values of $P_3$, $P_5$, $P_{13}$, $L_3$, $L_{10}$) |
| | Low performance level of the energy industry in terms of profitability and liquidity (minimum values of $P_4$, $L_1$, $L_7$, $L_8$) |

(continued)

**Table 3.1** (continued)

| Country | Regularities |
|---|---|
| | High debt in the construction industry (minimum values of $D_1$, $D_3$, $D_4$) |
| | The greatest variability of the ratio $L_{10}$, the smallest – $P_4$ |
| | Missing data in the industries of education and health |
| A | High general performance of the real estate sector (maximum values of $P_3$, $P_4$, $P_6$, $L_2$, $L_3$, $D_5$) |
| | Low profitability of the trade sector (minimum values of $P_1$–$P_3$, $P_7$, $P_{10}$), but high turnover ratios (maximum values of $P_8$, $P_9$, $P_{11}$) |
| | Low liquidity in the energy industry (minimum values of $L_3$, $L_6$–$L_8$) |
| | Low indebtedness in the agriculture (high values of $D_2$, $D_4$, $D_5$) |
| | The greatest variability of the ratio $L_{10}$, the smallest – $L_2$ |
| | Missing data in the industries of fishing and manufacturing |
| D | High general performance of the mining industry (maximum values of $P_2$, $P_7$, $P_{10}$, $L_1$–$L_3$, $D_1$, $D_4$) |
| | Low level of many ratios from different areas of analysis in the construction industry (minimum values of $P_2$, $P_3$, $P_5$, $P_{12}$, $L_2$, $L_4$, $L_{10}$) |
| | High turnover ratios in the trade sector (maximum values of $P_8$, $P_9$, $P_{11}$), and high liquidity (maximum values of $L_5$, $L_8$, $L_{11}$), but low profitability (minimum values of $P_1$, $P_7$, $P_{10}$, $P_{13}$) |
| | High profitability in the transport sector (maximum values of $P_3$, $P_5$, $P_6$, $P_{13}$) |
| | High indebtedness of the real estate sector (minimum values of $D_2$, $D_3$, $D_5$, $D_6$) |
| | The greatest variability of the ratio $P_1$, the smallest – $D_7$ |
| | Missing data in the industries of agriculture, fishing, hotels and restaurants, education, health and community activities |
| P | High turnover ratios in the trade sector (maximum values of $P_5$, $P_8$, $P_9$, $P_{11}$), but low profitability ratios $P_7$ and $P_{10}$ |
| | High profitability in the mining industry (maximum values of $P_1$, $P_4$) |
| | Low profitability in the fishing industry (minimum values of $P_1$, $P_2$, $P_{12}$) |
| | High liquidity in the health sector (maximum values of $L_2$, $L_6$, $L_8$) and transport ($L_4$, $L_5$, $L_{10}$), and low in the sectors of energy (minimum values of $L_3$, $L_6$–$L_8$) and agriculture ($L_2$, $L_4$, $L_{10}$) |
| | Low indebtedness of the real estate sector (maximum values of $D_1$, $D_6$), and high of community activities (minimum values of $D_4$, $D_5$) |
| | The greatest variability of the ratio $D_2$, the smallest – $P_3$ |
| | Missing data in the industries of education, health and community activities in 1999 and 2000 |
| FIN | Clear distribution of the extreme values of ratios |
| | The community activities industry the best in terms of profitability (maximum values of $P_1$–$P_5$) and long-term solvency ($D_3$, $D_4$, $D_6$) |
| | The education sector the best in terms of liquidity (maximum values of $L_2$, $L_3$, $L_6$, $L_8$, $L_{10}$) |
| | Low profitability in the trade sector (minimum values of $P_1$–$P_3$, $P_7$, $P_{10}$), but high turnover ratios (maximum values of $P_8$, $P_9$, $P_{11}$) |
| | Low overall performance of the energy industry (minimum values of $P_5$, $P_8$, $P_9$, $L_6$–$L_8$, $D_1$–$D_3$, $D_6$–$D_8$) |
| | Low liquidity in the fishing industry (minimum values of $L_4$, $L_{10}$, $L_{11}$) |
| | The greatest variability of the ratio $D_1$, the smallest – $P_4$ |

(continued)

**Table 3.1** (continued)

| Country | Regularities |
|---|---|
| PL | A relatively good situation of the education sector, particularly in terms of profitability and liquidity (the maximum values of $P_3$, $P_5$, $L_6$, $L_{10}$) and no minimum values |
| | High profitability of the mining industry (maximum values of $P_2$, $P_{10}$, $P_{13}$), but problems with the service of debt (minimum values of $D_7$, $D_8$) |
| | High turnover ratios in the trade sector (maximum values of $P_6$, $P_8$, $P_9$, $P_{11}$), but lower profitability and liquidity (minimum values of $P_1$, $P_4$, $P_7$, $P_{10}$, $L_2$, $L_3$, $L_9$, $L_{10}$) |
| | Low indebtedness of the agriculture sector (maximum values of $D_2$–$D_4$), but also low profitability and liquidity (minimum values of $P_2$, $P_9$, $L_4$, $L_5$) |
| | The greatest variability of the ratio $L_4$, the smallest – $P_3$ |

Source: Author's own compilation based on BACH database

liquidity, by far the most significant spreads can be seen in the ratio $L_5$, illustrating the turnover of debtors, whereas the most diverse debt ratio is $D_6$, which is the relationship of the interest to turnover. The visual analysis of the data also reveals that ratios such as $P_4$, $P_6$ or $L_{10}$ have significantly lower discriminatory power.

A notable characteristic is the concentration of the ratios with extreme values in Finland and Austria. Most of the variables in these two countries take the maximum and minimum value, respectively. High performance of business in Finland, on average across all industries, is reflected particularly in the area of profitability and liquidity. The low level of financial ratios of the Austrian companies is clearly visible in the area of liquidity and debt ratios. The occurrence of such differences between countries with a comparable level of development arises the question about the reasons for these discrepancies. In an attempt to formulate a response, the reasons for differences could be sought for example in the tax system structure, as a specific national factor. The relatively low efficiency of the Austrian companies may result from the level of tax burden in this country, which exceeds the EU average, as well as from the multiplicity of taxes, which companies are obliged to pay (Wach, 2006, pp. 71–83). The level of fiscal stringency, however, does not seem to explain the differences between Austria and Finland, where the tax rates are also high, and the tax system is considered as complicated, although the corporate income tax is linear and paid according to a single rate. It is likely therefore that the reasons for differences between these two, as well as other countries, lie in a number of other factors (discussed in Sect. 3.2.). The multiplicity and the interrelationships of these factors hamper their complete isolation and precise identification of the sources of corporate performance differentiation.

As for Poland, despite the fact that the country does not belong to the euro zone, it is not particularly distinguishable in terms of concentration of extreme negative values, with the exception of the debt ratios. The financial parameters of this category indicate a low degree of debt utilisation by the Polish companies, which may be related to the high costs of debt service compared to other countries.

However, there are other countries that clearly stand out from the rest, namely Portugal, distinguished by low profitability, and the Netherlands with a high average level of liquidity. Other regularities based on the distribution of the extreme values of ratios include a relatively low level of profitability and liquidity in Spain. However, it should be borne in mind that these observations apply to the aggregated value of the ratios for all industries covered by the analysis. Thus it is reasonable to examine each of these industries individually in order to identify more specific patterns in each of them, or find the influences of industry factors. The above procedure was therefore conducted separately for each industry and year, although the results of these calculations are not presented in this study.

Some observations based on the separate analysis of the basic statistics for each industry are presented in Table 3.2. These conclusions are drawn mainly by analysing the distribution of the extreme values of ratios in individual industries.

Summarising the above list, it can be stated that one of the characteristics common to most industries is the good performance in the Netherlands and Finland. This is particularly true about the profitability ratios in such industries as agriculture, fishing, construction, trade, hotels, transport, education, health and community activities in the case of Finland. The Netherlands is positively distinguished in this respect in the industry of fishing, mining, manufacturing, construction, trade, hotels and health. Another characteristic feature for Finland is the low return on equity, despite high values of other profitability ratios, which is observed in the sectors of health, transport, hotels, trade, construction, manufacturing and agriculture. In many cases, it coincides with low levels of corporate debt in this country, which weakens the financial leverage effect, i.e. the increase of the return on equity due to the use of debt in capital structure. According to the tax theories of capital structure, the tax system is a significant determinant of corporate financial structure. The existence of corporate income tax and the related tax shield actually increases the use of debt according to the rule that the higher the tax rate, the higher the leverage (Gajdka, 2002, pp. 295–296). This regularity, however, apparently is not supported by the case of Finland, where tax burdens are high in comparison with other EU countries.

Another repetitive symptom is the adverse economic and financial situation of Portugal (agriculture, fishing, education, community activities) and Austria (energy, hotels, education and health). A characteristic feature for Poland is the lower profitability in many industries, with high liquidity. This is the case for example in the agriculture and community activities.

The relatively large size of the population of objects in terms of industries in countries and the variables describing them, and consequently a multitude of observations and regularities found in the data structure, creates a natural need to reduce the amount of the information by converting it into some more aggregated form, easier to interpret. One of the possible ways of carrying out such aggregation is to use the taxonomic measure of development (TMD). It is characterised by highly transparent and communicative indications, which greatly facilitates the diagnosis of multi-dimensional phenomena. The taxonomic method enables the comparison of multi-attribute objects by means of a synthetic instrument, containing information about all primary variables (Grabiński, 1992; Nowak, 1990; Pluta, 1977).

**Table 3.2** Conclusions from the analysis of descriptive statistics of industry ratios based on average values from 1999 to 2005

| Industry | Regularities |
|---|---|
| AGR | High concentration of maximum values of many ratios in Finland, Poland and Italy |
| | High profitability in Finland (maximum values of $P_1$–$P_3$, $P_5$ and $P_6$) and high liquidity (maximum values of $L_3$ and $L_5$) |
| | Low cost of debt service in Austria (maximum values of $D_6$ and $D_7$) and a high level of indebtedness (minimum value of the indicator $D_1$) with low liquidity parameters (minimum values of $L_6$–$L_8$) |
| | High debt in Belgium (minimum values of $D_3$, $D_4$, $D_6$) |
| | Low labour costs in Italy (maximum values of $P_{11}$ and $P_{12}$) |
| | Low profitability in Poland (minimum values of $P_3$, $P_5$, $P_6$, $P_8$, $P_9$), but high liquidity (maximum values of $L_1$ and $L_2$) |
| | Low liquidity in Portugal (minimum values of $L_2$ and $L_4$) and poor profitability |
| | The greatest variability of the ratio $P_7$, the smallest – $L_{10}$ |
| | Missing data for Germany |
| FSH | Good situation in the Netherlands in terms of profitability (maximum values of $P_1$, $P_6$ and $P_{12}$, and high values of other ratios) and debt (maximum value of $D_5$) |
| | Low liquidity and credit performance in Belgium (the minimum values of $L_1$, $L_2$, $L_7$, $L_8$, $L_{10}$ and $D_1$–$D_7$) |
| | Low debt in Poland and high profitability (maximum values of $D_1$–$D_4$, $D_6$, $P_4$, $P_7$, $P_8$, $P_{10}$) |
| | Good solvency in Spain and Portugal |
| | Low profitability in Portugal (minimum values of $P_1$–$P_3$, $P_8$, $P_{11}$ and $P_{12}$) and Italy (minimum values of $P_6$, $P_7$, $P_8$ and $P_{10}$) |
| | High liquidity and solvency in Finland (maximum values of $P_2$, $P_5$ and $L_1$, $L_3$, $L_6$, $L_{10}$) |
| | The greatest variability of the ratio $P_3$, the smallest – $L_9$ |
| | Missing data for Germany and Austria |
| MIN | High profitability in the Netherlands (maximum values of $P_4$, $P_5$, $P_8$, $P_{11}$, $P_{12}$) and low liquidity (minimum values of $L_1$, $L_3$, $L_9$–$L_{11}$) with high indebtedness (minimum values of $D_3$–$D_5$) |
| | High profitability in Italy (maximum values of $P_1$, $P_3$, and high values of other ratios) |
| | low profitability and liquidity in Spain (minimum values of $P_1$, $P_5$, $P_8$, $P_{11}$, $P_{12}$, $L_4$–$L_6$) |
| | Good performance in Germany, especially in the area of liquidity (maximum values of $L_1$, $L_2$, $L_8$) and debt (maximum values of $D_2$–$D_4$) |
| | High profitability in Poland (the maximum values of $P_2$, $P_7$, $P_{10}$) and high cost of debt (minimum value of $D_7$) |
| | High solvency in Portugal (maximum values of $L_9$, $L_{11}$, $D_5$, $D_8$) |
| | The greatest variability of the ratio $P_3$, the smallest – $D_7$ |
| MNF | High performance in the Netherlands in terms of profitability (maximum values of $P_3$, $P_5$, $P_6$, $P_{12}$, $P_{13}$) and Poland ($P_4$, $P_7$, $P_8$, $P_{11}$) |
| | High value of many profitability and liquidity ratios in Finland (maximum values of $P_1$, $P_2$, $P_{10}$, $L_1$, $L_2$) |
| | Low level of debt in Germany (maximum values of $D_2$–$D_4$) and low profitability (minimum values of $P_1$, $P_2$, $P_{11}$) |

(continued)

**Table 3.2** (continued)

| Industry | Regularities |
|---|---|
| | The lowest performance level of the industry in Italy, especially in terms of profitability and liquidity (minimum values of $P_3$, $P_5$, $P_6$, $P_{13}$, $L_3$, $L_5$, $D_4$) |
| | Favourable liquidity characteristics in Poland (maximum values of $L_5$, $L_6$, $L_9$–$L_{11}$) |
| | The greatest variability of the ratio $D_1$, the smallest – $D_3$ |
| | Missing data for Austria |
| ELE | High general performance in Belgium (maximum values of $P_4$–$P_6$, $L_3$, $L_5$, $L_9$, $L_{11}$, $D_5$) |
| | High liquidity in Germany (maximum values of $L_2$, $L_7$, $L_8$) |
| | High profitability in Spain (maximum values of $P_2$, $P_3$, $P_{11}$) and low liquidity (minimum values of $L_3$, $L_5$, $L_6$) |
| | Low profitability and liquidity in Austria and high indebtedness (minimum values of $P_4$, $P_5$, $P_8$, $P_9$, $P_{11}$, $P_{13}$, $L_1$, $L_2$, $L_7$, $L_8$, $D_1$, $D_4$) |
| | High debt in Finland (minimum values of $D_2$, $D_3$, $D_6$, $D_7$) |
| | Low profitability in Poland (minimum values of $P_2$, $P_3$) |
| | The greatest variability of the ratio $D_3$, the smallest – $P_4$ |
| CST | High liquidity and profitability in the Netherlands (maximum values of $L_1$–$L_4$, $L_6$, $P_3$, $P_4$) |
| | High profitability and low indebtedness in Finland (maximum values of $P_1$, $P_2$, $P_5$, $P_6$, $P_8$, $D_1$, $D_4$) |
| | High solvency in Austria (maximum values of $D_6$, $D_7$) |
| | Low profitability in Italy (minimum values of $P_8$–$P_{10}$), but low labour costs (maximum values of $P_{11}$ and $P_{12}$) and high debt level (minimum values of $D_2$–$D_4$, $D_6$) |
| | Low profitability and liquidity in Germany (minimum values of $P_1$–$P_3$, $P_5$, $P_6$, $L_2$, $L_4$, $L_8$, $D_5$, $D_8$) |
| | Low labour costs in Poland (maximum value of $R_7$ and high $P_{11}$) |
| | The greatest variability of the ratio $L_1$, the smallest – $P_4$ |
| TRD | Large dispersion of the extreme values of ratios |
| | High return on sales and assets, as well as liquidity in Finland (maximum values of $P_2$, $P_3$, $P_5$, $L_1$–$L_3$) |
| | Low profitability in Germany (minimum values of $P_1$–$P_3$, $P_5$, $P_6$) with high assets turnover (maximum values of $P_8$, $P_9$) |
| | Rather low profitability in Poland, with the exception of low labour costs (maximum values of $P_{11}$ and $P_{13}$) |
| | Low liquidity in Spain (minimum values of $L_1$, $L_6$–$L_8$), but high solvency (maximum values of $D_1$, $D_5$) |
| | The greatest variability of the ratio $D_3$, the smallest – $P_4$ |
| HOT | High concentration of extreme values of ratios in Finland and Austria |
| | High profitability and liquidity in Finland (maximum values of $P_5$, $P_6$, $P_8$, $P_9$, $L_1$–$L_3$, $L_5$, $L_6$, $L_9$, $L_{11}$), but low return on equity (minimum value of $P_4$) |
| | High return on sales in the Netherlands and high cost of debt (minimum values of $D_6$–$D_8$) |
| | Low profitability in Belgium (minimum values of $P_2$, $P_3$, $P_5$, $P_7$, $P_{10}$) |
| | Low liquidity in Austria (minimum values of $L_1$, $L_2$, $L_4$, $L_7$, $L_8$) |
| | Low profitability in Portugal (minimum values of $P_7$, $P_8$) |

(continued)

**Table 3.2** (continued)

| Industry | Regularities |
|---|---|
| | Uncharacteristic situation in Poland (maximum values of $P_4$, $P_{13}$, $D_2$, $D_4$ and minimum of $P_6$, $L_9$, $L_{11}$) |
| | The greatest variability of the ratio $P_{12}$, the smallest – $D_1$ |
| | Missing data for Germany |
| TRS | Low profitability in the Netherlands (minimum values of $R_3$, $R_5$, $R_{13}$), but high liquidity (maximum values of $L_1$–$L_3$, $L_6$, $L_{11}$) |
| | High indebtedness in France (minimum values of $D_2$–$D_4$), but good liquidity (maximum values of $L_7$–$L_9$) |
| | Low liquidity in Austria (minimum values of $L_7$, $L_8$, low $L_4$) |
| | High profitability in Finland (maximum values of $P_3$, $P_5$, $P_8$, $P_9$), but low return on equity (minimum ratio $P_4$) and good solvency (maximum values of $D_1$, $D_4$) |
| | Relatively good condition in Poland (maximum values of $P_4$, $P_7$, $P_{11}$, $L_{10}$, $D_8$) |
| | The greatest variability of the ratio $P_{12}$, the smallest – $P_{13}$ |
| RLE | Clearly poor profitability and liquidity in Poland (minimum values of $P_3$, $P_5$, $L_7$, $L_8$) |
| | High turnover ratios in Italy (maximum values of $P_8$, $P_9$) |
| | High profitability in Austria (maximum values of $P_4$, $P_6$) |
| | Low labour costs in Germany (minimum values of $P_{11}$, $P_{12}$) |
| | Low profitability in Portugal (minimum values of $P_2$, $P_8$, $P_9$) |
| | High liquidity and low indebtedness in Italy (maximum values of $L_7$–$L_{11}$, $D_1$, $D_2$) |
| | Low liquidity in Germany (minimum values of $L_1$, $L_2$, $L_9$, $L_{11}$) |
| | Good solvency in Austria (maximum values of $D_5$–$D_7$) |
| | The greatest variability of the ratio $D_2$, the smallest – $L_9$ |
| EDU | High concentration of the extreme values of ratios in Finland, Austria and Poland |
| | High profitability in Poland (maximum values of $P_1$–$P_6$, $P_{13}$) |
| | High profitability, liquidity and solvency in Finland (maximum values of $P_7$, $P_8$, $L_1$–$L_3$, $L_5$, $L_6$, $D_1$, $D_4$) |
| | Low liquidity in Austria (minimum values of $L_1$–$L_4$, $L_9$) |
| | Low profitability, liquidity and solvency in Portugal (minimum values of $P_2$, $P_6$, $P_{11}$, $P_{12}$, $L_7$, $L_8$, $L_{11}$, $D_5$, $D_6$) |
| | Low profitability in Spain (minimum values of $P_5$, $P_8$, $P_9$) |
| | High concentration of the extreme values of ratios in Belgium, both the minimum ($P_3$, $P_7$, $P_{10}$, $D_3$, $D_7$) and maximum ($P_{11}$, $L_4$, $L_9$, $L_{11}$, $D_5$) |
| | The greatest variability of the ratio $P_{12}$, the smallest – $D_5$ |
| | Missing data for Italy and Germany |
| HLT | High concentration of the extreme values of ratios in the Netherlands, Spain and Austria |
| | Definitely the best performance parameters in the Netherlands (maximum values of $P_2$, $P_3$, $P_{10}$, $P_{12}$, $P_{13}$, $L_1$–$L_3$, $L_6$–$L_8$, $D_2$–$D_4$) |
| | High profitability in Finland (maximum values of $P_5$–$P_8$), but low return on equity (minimum value of $P_4$) |
| | Low profitability and liquidity in Spain (minimum values of $P_1$–$P_3$, $P_5$, $P_{11}$, $P_{12}$, $L_3$, $L_6$) |
| | Low liquidity and profitability in Austria (minimum values of $P_6$, $P_9$, $P_{13}$, $L_4$, $L_9$, $L_{11}$) |
| | Low liquidity in Poland (minimum values of $L_1$, $L_2$, $L_7$, $L_8$) |
| | The greatest variability of the ratio $P_8$, the smallest – $P_4$ |
| | Missing data for Italy and Germany |

(continued)

**Table 3.2** (continued)

| Industry | Regularities |
|---|---|
| COM | High concentration of the extreme values of ratios in Finland, Portugal, Austria and Poland |
| | Definitely the best performance parameters in Finland (maximum values of $P_1$–$P_5$, $P_9$, $P_{11}$, $L_5$–$L_7$, $L_{10}$, $D_1$, $D_3$, $D_4$) |
| | Clearly the worst performance in Portugal (minimum values of $P_2$, $P_3$, $P_5$, $P_8$, $P_9$, $P_{12}$, $L_1$–$L_4$, $L_8$, $D_2$–$D_4$, $D_7$) |
| | Low profitability and liquidity in Austria (minimum values of $P_1$, $P_4$, $P_6$, $P_{10}$, $P_{13}$, $L_7$, $L_9$, $L_{11}$) |
| | High liquidity in Poland (maximum values of $L_1$–$L_3$) |
| | The greatest variability of the ratio $L_6$, the smallest – $P_3$ |
| | Missing data for Germany |

Source: Author's own compilation based on BACH database

Therefore, in order to reduce the dimensionality of the data which would enable visualising the analysed phenomena, the taxonomic measure of development was calculated for each object (industry in country) in each year. The results of these calculations are shown in Appendix 9. They were the basis for the graphical presentation of the synthetic level of development of different industries and countries in the form of maps of Europe in Appendices 10 and 11. The size of graphs representing each country corresponds to the potential of a country measured by the size of corporate assets in all industries. The radius of each circle is proportional to the square root of the assets value. The share of each industry corresponds to the taxonomic measure of development (average for the whole period) in relation to other industries in the group. In order to maintain the clarity of the graphs, the industries were divided into two groups represented on separate maps. For the same reason the detailed information on the industries for Austria were omitted and the graph representing Poland was enlarged.

The occurrence of the country and industry effects, which are the main focus of the analyses, can be measured, inter alia, by the means of dispersion measures (Kutlaca & Radosevic, p. 4). For the preliminary comparison of the impact of these effects, the variation coefficient[1] was used, which was calculated in two sections: across countries and across industries. The results are shown in Table 3.3. The presented calculations show that the dispersion of a slight majority of ratios is larger between industries than between countries. This is evidenced by the variation coefficient – usually higher for industries than for countries, which in the table was marked by bolding the appropriate values. It proves therefore a little more impact of the industry effect on the selected set of financial ratios, compared with the country effect.

It may seem likely that the country effect in the analysed population is naturally enhanced by the inclusion of an atypical object, i.e. Poland, which is the only country not yet a member of the common currency area. It can therefore be assumed

[1] $v = \frac{\sigma}{\mu}$, $\mu \neq 0$, where $\sigma$ – standard deviation, $\mu$ – mean.

**Table 3.3** Variation coefficient of corporate financial ratios across industries and across ten countries (higher values in bold)

| Ratio | Country | Industry | Ratio | Country | Industry | Ratio | Country | Industry |
|---|---|---|---|---|---|---|---|---|
| $P_1$ | 0.384 | **0.556** | $L_1$ | **0.640** | 0.413 | $D_1$ | **1.200** | 0.530 |
| $P_2$ | **0.690** | 0.502 | $L_2$ | **0.817** | 0.539 | $D_2$ | 0.215 | **0.370** |
| $P_3$ | **1.108** | 0.423 | $L_3$ | **0.554** | 0.508 | $D_3$ | **0.335** | 0.210 |
| $P_4$ | **1.059** | 0.120 | $L_4$ | 0.662 | **0.813** | $D_4$ | **0.631** | 0.369 |
| $P_5$ | **0.784** | 0.321 | $L_5$ | 0.231 | **0.408** | $D_5$ | **0.767** | 0.137 |
| $P_6$ | **0.699** | 0.135 | $L_6$ | 0.426 | **0.558** | $D_6$ | 0.228 | **0.275** |
| $P_7$ | 0.180 | **0.459** | $L_7$ | 0.240 | **0.609** | $D_7$ | **0.330** | 0.305 |
| $P_8$ | 0.414 | **0.644** | $L_8$ | 0.396 | **0.556** | $D_8$ | 0.170 | **0.221** |
| $P_9$ | 0.417 | **0.921** | $L_9$ | 0.294 | **0.317** | | | |
| $P_{10}$ | 0.308 | **0.470** | $L_{10}$ | 0.149 | **0.526** | | | |
| $P_{11}$ | 0.248 | **0.502** | $L_{11}$ | **1.025** | 0.194 | | | |
| $P_{12}$ | 0.426 | **0.597** | | | | | | |
| $P_{13}$ | **2.722** | 0.827 | | | | | | |

Source: Calculations based on BACH database

**Table 3.4** Variation coefficient of corporate financial ratios across industries and across nine countries (Poland excluded, higher values in bold)

| Ratio | Country | Industry | Ratio | Country | Industry | Ratio | Country | Industry |
|---|---|---|---|---|---|---|---|---|
| $P_1$ | 0.373 | **0.553** | $L_1$ | **0.600** | 0.430 | $D_1$ | **1.109** | 0.502 |
| $P_2$ | **0.634** | 0.490 | $L_2$ | **0.762** | 0.572 | $D_2$ | 0.222 | **0.392** |
| $P_3$ | **1.219** | 0.476 | $L_3$ | **0.523** | 0.517 | $D_3$ | **0.335** | 0.223 |
| $P_4$ | **0.990** | 0.159 | $L_4$ | 0.722 | **0.825** | $D_4$ | **0.634** | 0.378 |
| $P_5$ | **0.808** | 0.321 | $L_5$ | 0.229 | **0.410** | $D_5$ | **0.873** | 0.155 |
| $P_6$ | **0.781** | 0.169 | $L_6$ | 0.413 | **0.543** | $D_6$ | 0.222 | **0.267** |
| $P_7$ | 0.192 | **0.486** | $L_7$ | 0.230 | **0.587** | $D_7$ | **0.369** | 0.335 |
| $P_8$ | 0.413 | **0.642** | $L_8$ | 0.376 | **0.539** | $D_8$ | 0.175 | **0.221** |
| $P_9$ | 0.399 | **0.901** | $L_9$ | 0.292 | **0.319** | | | |
| $P_{10}$ | 0.303 | **0.475** | $L_{10}$ | 0.148 | **0.519** | | | |
| $P_{11}$ | 0.244 | **0.498** | $L_{11}$ | **1.147** | 0.227 | | | |
| $P_{12}$ | 0.450 | **0.623** | | | | | | |
| $P_{13}$ | **2.948** | 0.846 | | | | | | |

Source: Calculations based on BACH database

that excluding Poland from the analysis would reduce the intensity of the country effect, whereas the industry effect would be enhanced in a more homogeneous population of countries. To verify this question, the above calculations were carried out again on the same set of ratios, but only for nine countries – without Poland. The results are shown in Table 3.4.

Comparison of the results in Tables 3.3 and 3.4 shows that the intensity of the impact of the country effect is not particularly dependent on the inclusion of Poland in the analysis. Although the exclusion of our country results in a natural decrease of the variation coefficient for a number of ratios (especially in the area of liquidity), both across industries and across countries, the number as well as the composition of the group of ratios which demonstrated greater cross-industry variation remained unchanged.

## 3.2 Cross-Industry Analysis of Ratios Variance

In the event of differences in means of ratios between countries and (or) industries, it is necessary to verify whether the observed differences are statistically significant, or whether they result from an incidental diversity of ratios. For this purpose, the one-way analysis of variance was employed. The discriminatory power of ratios was evaluated with the use of the F-statistic, whose value for the entire data set, as well as for individual countries, are shown in Appendix 12. The cases, for which there was no reason to reject the null hypothesis about the equality of means across industries were highlighted by shading the appropriate boxes of the table.

The calculations show that most of the ratios considered for all countries together are characterised with good discriminatory properties. The exceptions are four ratios ($P_4$, $P_6$, $D_3$ and $D_5$), for which there is no reason to reject the hypothesis about equal means of ratios in industries. Moreover, it can be seen that both the number and range of non-discriminating ratios vary between countries, which indicates the occurrence of the country effect in the corporate performance. For example, the ratio $P_4$ considered separately for each country does not have the differentiating properties only in four countries (Spain, Austria, Finland and Poland). A similar phenomenon can be observed in the case of the debt ratio $D_5$, where the absence of significant differences occurred in only five countries: Belgium, Spain, Italy, Germany and Portugal. However, as for the ratio $P_6$, it appears not to differentiate between industries in all the analysed countries except France, where, all ratios vary significantly across industries. The countries with the biggest number of non-discriminating ratios were Portugal, Poland and Spain, although the ratios do not coincide exactly between these countries.

Finding some non-discriminating diagnostic variables in the dataset should be the basis for their possible removal from further analysis. Thus, it would be justified to eliminate the ratio $P_6$. Other ratios demonstrate rather significant cross-industry differences either in each country separately or in all of them together. Therefore their exclusion would contribute to a significant narrowing of the study. Before deciding on the composition of the target set of the diagnostic variables, the ratios should also be submitted to the analysis of variance with regard to the industries. If the deficiencies of discriminatory power occurred in the same ratios, it would be a sufficient basis to remove them. The issue in question is discussed in the Sect. 3.3.

If the analysis of variance does not show significance of differences between the analysed groups, i.e. there is no reason to reject the null hypothesis, the further testing of the differentiation is pointless. However, when the null hypothesis is rejected in the analysis of variance, as in most of the variables considered, the question arises which of the compared populations are responsible for rejecting the null hypothesis, namely which of the means differ significantly from each other. It requires a detailed study of differences between the means of the individual industries with the use of the *post-hoc* tests, also known as multiple comparisons tests. The name of test results from the fact that they are applied after finding the lack of equality between the means. These tests are also called homogeneous grouping tests, because once applied, they can create groups of means. The means of the same group do not differ significantly, in contrast to the means of different groups.

Of the many available tests the most often recommended Tukey's test was used, which enables grouping of means. The details of the test are shown in Appendix 13. This test was performed for all variables which demonstrate significant cross-industry variation either in all countries or at least in one country. The results of these analyses are presented in the tables in Appendices 14–16. Because of the abundance of information resulting from the *post-hoc* analysis and the need to synthesise it, the presentation of the results is limited only to the most important facts. Therefore, in the first place the number of identified homogeneous groups of objects is given for each ratio. A larger number of groups usually indicates a greater variation of the variable. The lines marked with a '+' contain objects which are positively distinguishable in terms of the variable, i.e. the objects located in the group with the highest mean. However, only those objects are listed, which did not belong to another homogeneous group at the same time. In the study population inseparable groups were often formed, which means that a given object could belong to several groups simultaneously. The occurrence of separable groups is marked in the table by bolding the number of groups. It often happens in the case of variables which differentiate the characterised objects very well, i.e. with high values of the F-statistics. The order of objects in the analysed table is consistent with the values of the variable, i.e. the best industries are listed first. The lines marked with a '–' contain objects negatively distinguishable, that is the objects with the least favourable values of the variable, starting from worst. A crossed out box means that the variable did not demonstrate significant differences, so the *post-hoc* analysis was not performed.

The above discussed results partially overlap with the conclusions from the analysis of the basic statistics of ratios in industries and countries, but also provide more detailed information about the degree of variables differentiation between the objects. In addition, the *post-hoc* analysis more accurately illustrates the situation of a given industry in each country in terms of each ratio. As for the objects not listed in any of the groups in the table, it can be concluded that the level of a given ratio is uncharacteristic – neither very good nor bad.

However, the conclusions from the *post-hoc* analysis do not need to be fully consistent with the regularities observed on the basis of the basic statistics analysis. Certain discrepancies in the distribution of extreme values of ratios are due to the transformation algorithms used on the primary data. In the case of the initial ratio analysis (basic statistics), the data was transformed according to the normalisation method within each country separately. The analysis of variance was performed on the basis of variables normalised for all countries together, which results in slightly different values of the transformed data and, consequently, sometimes different distribution of extremes. An example of such a situation may be the Polish agricultural industry, whose indebtedness appeared favourably according to the analysis of basic statistics (Table 3.1.), but the analysis of variance showed that it

**Table 3.5** Probabilities of the post-hoc Tukey's test for the aggregated profitability ratio in industries, p = 0.05 (significant differences are highlighted)

| No. | Industry | 1 | 2 | 3 | 4 | 5 | 6 | 7 | 8 | 9 | 10 | 11 | 12 |
|---|---|---|---|---|---|---|---|---|---|---|---|---|---|
| 1 | AGR | | | | | | | | | | | | |
| 2 | FSH | 1.000 | | | | | | | | | | | |
| 3 | MIN | 0.030 | 0.063 | | | | | | | | | | |
| 4 | MNF | 0.960 | 0.976 | 0.776 | | | | | | | | | |
| 5 | ELE | 0.578 | 0.683 | 0.000 | 0.010 | | | | | | | | |
| 6 | CST | 0.000 | 0.000 | 0.653 | 0.005 | 0.000 | | | | | | | |
| 7 | TRD | 0.000 | 0.000 | 0.000 | 0.000 | 0.000 | 0.000 | | | | | | |
| 8 | HOT | 0.921 | 0.950 | 0.869 | 1.000 | 0.006 | 0.010 | 0.000 | | | | | |
| 9 | TRS | 0.992 | 0.995 | 0.000 | 0.206 | 0.998 | 0.000 | 0.000 | 0.144 | | | | |
| 10 | RLE | 0.578 | 0.686 | 0.987 | 1.000 | 0.000 | 0.039 | 0.000 | 1.000 | 0.018 | | | |
| 11 | EDU | 0.000 | 0.000 | 0.000 | 0.000 | 0.000 | 0.005 | 0.990 | 0.000 | 0.000 | 0.000 | | |
| 12 | HLT | 0.000 | 0.000 | 0.349 | 0.002 | 0.000 | 1.000 | 0.000 | 0.004 | 0.000 | 0.016 | 0.143 | |
| 13 | COM | 1.000 | 1.000 | 0.002 | 0.561 | 0.976 | 0.000 | 0.000 | 0.455 | 1.000 | 0.124 | 0.000 | 0.000 |

Source: Calculations based on BACH database

was characterised by much worse parameters, as a kind of derivative of the ratios level in the agriculture of other countries.

The detailed results of the *post-hoc* analysis for profitability and turnover ratios are presented in Appendix 14. However, a certain synthetic summary of the analysis of variance in relation to the ratios of this category may be the application of the ANOVA procedure for the mean of all the ratios from this group. The use of such means obviously is a considerable simplification of the whole data structure, but may help identify the most important regularities arising from the analysis of individual ratios separately, as in many cases these conclusions are quite similar. The one-way analysis of variance for the aggregated profitability ratio, which is the mean of the variables $P_1$–$P_{13}$, showed significant cross-industry differentiation for all countries together ($F = 33.49$, $p = 0.000$), which gave rise to the further *post-hoc* analysis. The probabilities for the Tukey's test are shown in Table 3.5.

The above results confirm the distinctness of the trade industry, which significantly differs from most other industries. The relative position of industries on the profitability scale is illustrated in Fig. 3.1, which exhibits the high average profitability of the trade in all countries. This is mainly due to the positively distinguishable turnover ratios ($P_8$ and $P_9$) and a low ratio of staff costs to turnover ($P_{11}$), as the other ratios in this category stand out rather negatively in comparison to other industries.

The identified differences also allow for the formation of homogeneous groups of industries in which objects do not differ significantly from each other in terms of the broadly defined profitability. The composition of these groups is presented in Table 3.6.

The trade sector, which in the analysis of individual variables has repeatedly appeared in the group of objects with the lowest values of ratios, this time is in the group with the best parameters. This is due to definitely the highest turnover ratios included in this category which influence the overall average.

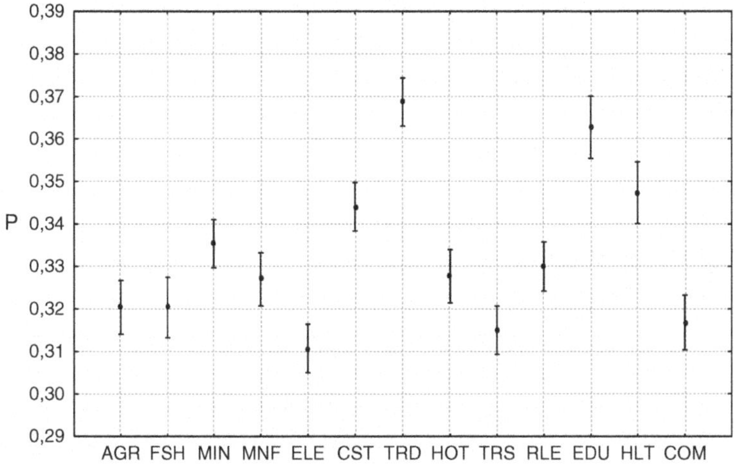


**Fig. 3.1** Plot of marginal means and confidence limits (95 %) of the aggregated profitability ratio for industries (Source: Calculations based on BACH database)

**Table 3.6** Homogenous groups of industries based on the aggregated profitability ratio

| Industry | P mean | 1 | 2 | 3 | 4 | 5 | 6 | 7 |
|---|---|---|---|---|---|---|---|---|
| ELE | 0.311 | X | | | | | | |
| TRS | 0.315 | X | X | | | | | |
| COM | 0.317 | X | X | X | | | | |
| AGR | 0.320 | X | X | X | | | | |
| FSH | 0.320 | X | X | X | X | | | |
| MNF | 0.327 | | X | X | X | | | |
| HOT | 0.328 | | X | X | X | | | |
| RLE | 0.330 | | | X | X | | | |
| MIN | 0.335 | | | | X | X | | |
| CST | 0.344 | | | | | X | | |
| HLT | 0.347 | | | | | X | X | |
| EDU | 0.363 | | | | | | X | X |
| TRD | 0.369 | | | | | | | X |

Source: Calculations based on BACH database

The second category of analytical variables ($L_1$–$L_{11}$) includes liquidity ratios, all of which have good discriminatory power in relation to the whole group of countries, and most of which also in relation to individual countries separately. The detailed results of the *post-hoc* analyses are presented in Appendix 15.

Some of the detected patterns in this category of ratios are intuitively easy to explain by the specificity of the industry. An example is the elasticity of assets ($L_7$), i.e. the ratio of the current to total assets. This ratio divides the industries in all countries into six homogeneous groups, where the industries of trade and construction are in the best position, while the energy industry – in the worst. The specificity of the trade and construction allows us to expect a high share of current assets, particularly in the form of stocks of goods and materials. Much greater

**Table 3.7** Probabilities of the post-hoc Tukey's test for the aggregated liquidity ratio in industries, p = 0.05 (significant differences are highlighted)

| No. | Industry | 1 | 2 | 3 | 4 | 5 | 6 | 7 | 8 | 9 | 10 | 11 | 12 |
|---|---|---|---|---|---|---|---|---|---|---|---|---|---|
| 1 | AGR | | | | | | | | | | | | |
| 2 | FSH | 1.000 | | | | | | | | | | | |
| 3 | MIN | 0.001 | 0.017 | | | | | | | | | | |
| 4 | MNF | 1.000 | 1.000 | 0.009 | | | | | | | | | |
| 5 | ELE | 0.000 | 0.000 | 0.000 | 0.000 | | | | | | | | |
| 6 | CST | 0.000 | 0.000 | 0.000 | 0.000 | 0.000 | | | | | | | |
| 7 | TRD | 0.000 | 0.000 | 0.000 | 0.000 | 0.000 | 0.998 | | | | | | |
| 8 | HOT | 0.000 | 0.000 | 0.000 | 0.000 | 0.114 | 0.000 | 0.000 | | | | | |
| 9 | TRS | 0.000 | 0.000 | 0.000 | 0.000 | 0.560 | 0.000 | 0.000 | 1.000 | | | | |
| 10 | RLE | 0.000 | 0.000 | 0.990 | 0.000 | 0.000 | 0.000 | 0.000 | 0.013 | 0.000 | | | |
| 11 | EDU | 0.364 | 0.206 | 0.000 | 0.106 | 0.000 | 0.000 | 0.002 | 0.000 | 0.000 | 0.000 | | |
| 12 | HLT | 0.968 | 0.862 | 0.000 | 0.746 | 0.000 | 0.000 | 0.000 | 0.000 | 0.000 | 0.000 | 0.999 | |
| 13 | COM | 0.289 | 0.704 | 0.934 | 0.682 | 0.000 | 0.000 | 0.000 | 0.000 | 0.000 | 0.222 | 0.000 | 0.007 |

Source: Calculations based on BACH database

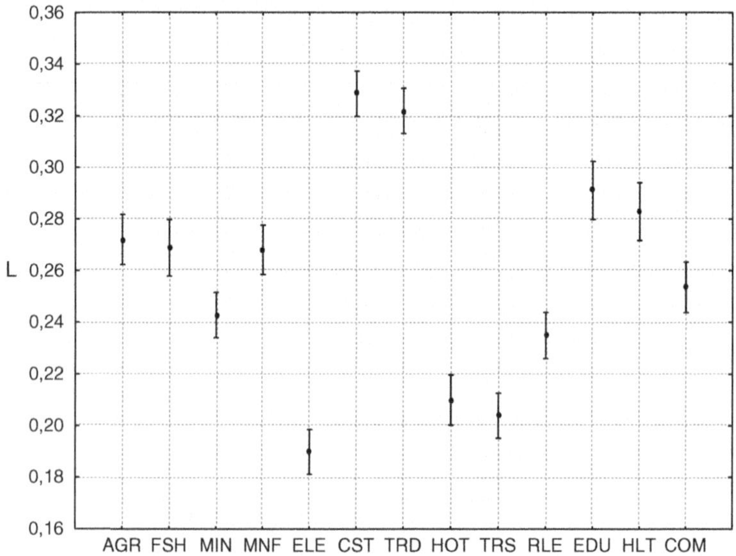


**Fig. 3.2** Plot of marginal means and confidence limits (95 %) of the aggregated liquidity ratio for industries (Source: Calculations based on BACH database)

immobilisation of assets, as evidenced by a high share of the fixed assets, is the typical phenomenon for the energy industry. The industrial specificity of the energy sector is also clearly revealed by similar values of the ratio of current to total assets ($L_7$) and the ratio illustrating the share of more liquid assets (i.e. excluding inventory) in the total assets ($L_8$). The similarity of these ratios can be associated with the characteristic feature of energy supply companies, which are unable to preserve inventories, at least when it comes to the finished products.

**Table 3.8** Homogenous groups of industries based on the aggregated liquidity ratio

| Industry | L mean | 1 | 2 | 3 | 4 | 5 |
|---|---|---|---|---|---|---|
| ELE | 0.190 | X | | | | |
| TRS | 0.204 | X | | | | |
| HOT | 0.210 | X | | | | |
| RLE | 0.235 | | X | | | |
| MIN | 0.243 | | X | | | |
| COM | 0.254 | | X | X | | |
| MNF | 0.268 | | | X | X | |
| FSH | 0.269 | | | X | X | |
| AGR | 0.272 | | | X | X | |
| HLT | 0.283 | | | | X | |
| EDU | 0.291 | | | | X | |
| TRD | 0.322 | | | | | X |
| CST | 0.329 | | | | | X |

Source: Calculations based on BACH database

The summary of the analysis of variance in terms of liquidity ratios, i.e. the one-way ANOVA procedure for the aggregated liquidity ratio, which is the average of all variables in this category ($L_1$–$L_{11}$), shows significant cross-industry differences for all countries ($F = 86{,}80$, $p = 0.000$). The probabilities of the *post-hoc* analysis are shown in Table 3.7.

The relative position of industries on the liquidity scale is also illustrated by Fig. 3.2, which reaffirms a low capacity for timely payment of creditors in the energy and transport industry, and high liquidity in the trade and construction.

The composition of homogeneous industry groups formed on the basis of the identified similarities in terms of liquidity is shown in Table 3.8.

When interpreting these results, it should be borne in mind that the above classification of objects is not the same for every country, since it is created for the aggregated group of all countries, and thus is considerably generalised.

The results of the post-hoc analysis for the last category of ratios – debt ratios – is shown in Appendix 16. One of the regularities worth noting concerns the ratio of long-term debt to total assets ($D_2$). Considering this ratio, the industries of trade and construction are usually positively distinguishable. Poland is the only country in the reference population where the agricultural sector has the leading position in terms of low long-term debt. This may be due to the difficult access to external capital for Polish companies in this sector compared with other EU countries. Another regularity for our country, uncharacteristic for the other EU members, is a relatively low value of the interest (financial costs) share in turnover (ratio $D_6$ converted into a stimulant) in the health sector. This means that a relatively high proportion of revenues is absorbed by the interest, which may be related to its considerable debt.

The one-way analysis of variance for the aggregated debt ratio, which is the average of the ratios $D_1$–$D_8$, shows significant cross-industry differences for all countries, but the smallest of all three categories of ratios ($F = 9.28$; $p = 0.000$). The probabilities of the *post-hoc* analysis are shown in Table 3.9.

**Table 3.9** Probabilities of the post-hoc Tukey's test for the aggregated debt ratio in industries, p = 0.05 (significant differences are highlighted)

| No. | Industry | 1 | 2 | 3 | 4 | 5 | 6 | 7 | 8 | 9 | 10 | 11 | 12 |
|---|---|---|---|---|---|---|---|---|---|---|---|---|---|
| 1 | AGR | | | | | | | | | | | | |
| 2 | FSH | 0.436 | | | | | | | | | | | |
| 3 | MIN | 0.001 | 0.000 | | | | | | | | | | |
| 4 | MNF | 0.992 | 0.988 | 0.000 | | | | | | | | | |
| 5 | ELE | 0.242 | 0.000 | 0.883 | 0.004 | | | | | | | | |
| 6 | CST | 0.307 | 1.000 | 0.000 | 0.982 | 0.000 | | | | | | | |
| 7 | TRD | 0.654 | 1.000 | 0.000 | 1.000 | 0.000 | 1.000 | | | | | | |
| 8 | HOT | 0.726 | 1.000 | 0.000 | 1.000 | 0.000 | 1.000 | 1.000 | | | | | |
| 9 | TRS | 1.000 | 0.063 | 0.010 | 0.695 | 0.697 | 0.022 | 0.108 | 0.165 | | | | |
| 10 | RLE | 0.997 | 0.024 | 0.042 | 0.455 | 0.909 | 0.007 | 0.040 | 0.069 | 1.000 | | | |
| 11 | EDU | 1.000 | 0.272 | 0.026 | 0.940 | 0.719 | 0.181 | 0.445 | 0.517 | 1.000 | 1.000 | | |
| 12 | HLT | 1.000 | 0.156 | 0.053 | 0.841 | 0.857 | 0.090 | 0.272 | 0.339 | 1.000 | 1.000 | 1.000 | |
| 13 | COM | 1.000 | 0.069 | 0.037 | 0.682 | 0.857 | 0.028 | 0.123 | 0.176 | 1.000 | 1.000 | 1.000 | 1.000 |

Source: calculations based on BACH database

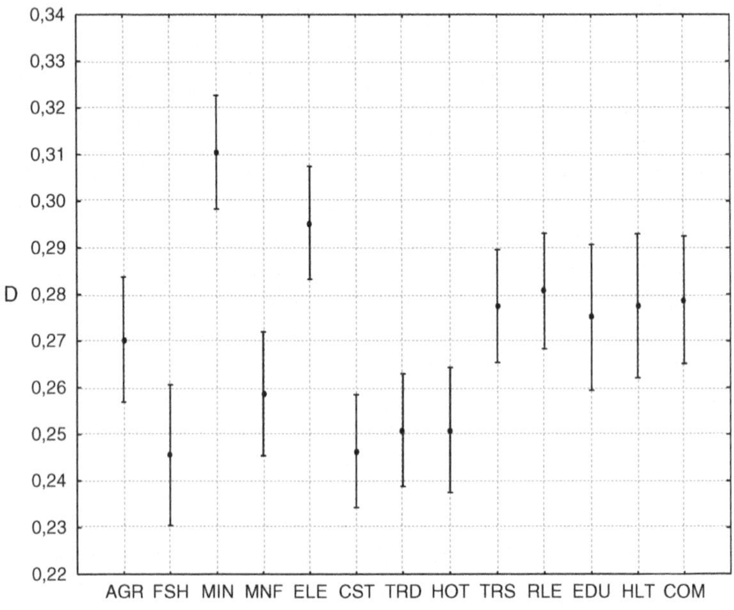


**Fig. 3.3** Plot of marginal means and confidence limits (95 %) of the aggregated debt ratio for industries (Source: Calculations based on BACH database)

Figure 3.3, illustrating the relative position of industries on the solvency scale, mainly confirms the high level of debt in the construction industry, fisheries, trade and hotels, but good solvency of the mining and energy industry.

Table 3.10. contains the composition of homogeneous groups of industries based on the identified differences in solvency.

The analyses performed above clearly indicate the existence of the industry effect in case of most of the financial ratios. The intensity of this effect, however,

**Table 3.10** Homogenous groups of industries based on the aggregated debt ratio

| Industry | D mean | 1 | 2 | 3 | 4 | 5 |
|---|---|---|---|---|---|---|
| FSH | 0.246 | X | | | | |
| CST | 0.246 | X | | | | |
| TRD | 0.251 | X | X | | | |
| HOT | 0.251 | X | X | X | | |
| MNF | 0.259 | X | X | X | | |
| AGR | 0.270 | X | X | X | X | |
| EDU | 0.275 | X | X | X | X | |
| TRS | 0.277 | X | X | X | X | |
| HLT | 0.278 | X | X | X | X | X |
| COM | 0.279 | | X | X | X | X |
| RLE | 0.281 | | | X | X | X |
| ELE | 0.295 | | | | X | X |
| MIN | 0.311 | | | | | X |

Source: Calculations based on BACH database

varies depending on the character of the diagnostic variables, as well as on the country. The cross-industry differentiation of ratios is thus not uniform across countries, which in turn implies the need to analyse the international diversity of ratios in order to detect the country effect.

## 3.3 Cross-Country Analysis of Ratios Variance

The analogous procedure of the variance analysis was also conducted across countries. In this case the grouping factor was the country. The F-statistic values and the probability p for the entire data set, as well as for individual industries are shown in Appendix 17.

As with the cross-industry analysis of variance, most of the ratios examined for all industries together have good discriminatory power. The only exceptions are ratios $P_4$, $P_6$, $L_9$, $L_{11}$ and $D_2$, but it is worth noting that this is a little different and a broader set of ratios than in the case of cross-industry differentiation. The similarities are reflected in the course of the examination of individual industries separately. Although the ratios which do not show discriminatory characteristics are different between industries, it must be noticed that there are ratios which show no significant variation both across industries and countries, e.g. $P_4$ and $P_6$. It is also characteristic that the ratio of long-term debt to assets ($D_2$), not showing significant international differences for all industries jointly, reveals the discriminatory properties in all industries examined individually, except the mining.

There is also a reverse kind of regularity, namely that the ratios showing cross-country discriminatory power in the case of all industries lose these properties when individual industries are considered separately. Examples include sales profitability ratio $P_3$, interest coverage $D_1$ and the ratio of long-term debt to working capital $D_5$.

As in the cross-industry analysis of variance there were countries where all the ratios differentiated between industries, in the analysis of international diversification there are also industries where all the ratios differ significantly across countries. These are the construction and trade sector. As for the industries in which a relatively large number of ratios do not differ significantly between countries, they include transport and fisheries.

As mentioned in the Sect. 3.2, one of the purposes of the analysis of variance is the initial verification of the discriminatory properties of variables, which aims to identify the target composition of the examined features. The indication for the removal of a variable may be its poor ability to differentiate. The cross-industry analysis of variance indicated that the variable – candidate for exclusion from further analysis is the ratio $P_6$. However, the international analysis of variance does not confirm these suggestions, as this ratio shows good differentiation properties with respect to most industries. Comparison of tables in Appendices 12 and 17 does not allow distinguishing any overlapping sets of ratios that would not have the desired differentiating properties in both sections. Removing one set of ratios for country and another for industry analysis would hamper the comparability of these two sections. Therefore it is purposeful and reasonable to use all of the initially accepted ratios in the final set of variables, despite the inaccurate fulfilment of the condition concerning the discriminating abilities by some of them.

The demonstrated significance of international diversification of most ratios, makes it expedient to deepen the study, by specifying which countries are most distinguishable, and in what respects. The results of the *post-hoc* analysis in the international context are presented in Appendices 18–20, although – as in the cross-industry *post-hoc* analysis – the presentation of information was limited to the extreme objects with respect to each ratio.

As for the profitability and turnover ratios (Appendix 18), the profitability of sales ($P_3$) deserves particular attention, due to its low value in Poland in many industries (agriculture, fisheries, mining, manufacturing and energy). Similar regularities can be observed with reference to the ratio of cost of sales to turnover ($P_7$). Analysing the classification based on this ratio reveals that Poland is among countries with the lowest values of most ratios (with often the discreditable last rank). Frequent adverse distinction of Polish industries is also the case in the case of the ratios of the labour cost share in the turnover ($P_{11}$) or the relationship of profit from financial activities to turnover ($P_{13}$).

However, there are also cases where the performance of Polish industries is quite favourable in comparison with other countries. This refers e.g. to the ratio of assets turnover ($P_8$). A positive situation of the Polish sector of education evidenced by the relationship of operating profit and net profit to turnover (ratios $P_2$ and $P_3$) and the ratio of net profit to working capital ($R_6$) is also worth noting.

The analysis of the relationship of wage costs to the added value ($P_{12}$) also shows that Poland is again one of the best countries. According to this criterion, Poland is at the forefront in two industries: agriculture and energy. Analysis of this ratio in relation to Poland confirms the competitive advantage of this country in terms of labour costs. This feat, however, is not strong enough to make the overall

**Table 3.11** Probabilities of the post-hoc Tukey's test for the aggregated profitability ratio in countries, p = 0.05 (significant differences are highlighted)

| No. | Country | NL | B | FR | ES | I | A | D | P | FIN | PL |
|---|---|---|---|---|---|---|---|---|---|---|---|
| 1 | NL | | | | | | | | | | |
| 2 | B | 0.391 | | | | | | | | | |
| 3 | FR | 0.000 | 0.077 | | | | | | | | |
| 4 | ES | 0.003 | 0.806 | 0.947 | | | | | | | |
| 5 | I | 0.995 | 0.049 | 0.000 | 0.000 | | | | | | |
| 6 | A | 1.000 | 0.205 | 0.000 | 0.001 | 1.000 | | | | | |
| 7 | D | 1.000 | 0.560 | 0.000 | 0.017 | 0.999 | 1.000 | | | | |
| 8 | P | 0.992 | 0.951 | 0.001 | 0.079 | 0.653 | 0.937 | 0.995 | | | |
| 9 | FIN | 0.025 | 0.990 | 0.573 | 1.000 | 0.001 | 0.009 | 0.086 | 0.334 | | |
| 10 | PL | 1.000 | 0.222 | 0.000 | 0.001 | 0.999 | 1.000 | 1.000 | 0.960 | 0.008 | |

Source: Calculations based on BACH database

profitability of Polish enterprises clearly better than the profitability of competing operators in the euro area. On the contrary – as demonstrated by the analysis of other ratios – Poland is often ranked in the category of countries with the weakest performance.

The summarising one-way analysis of variance for the aggregated profitability ratio, which is the average of the variables $P_1$–$P_{13}$, shows significant cross-industry differences for all countries examined as a total ($F = 9.07$; $p = 0.000$), which gave rise to the further *post-hoc* analysis. The probabilities for the Tukey's test are shown in Table 3.11.

These results confirm the distinctness of mainly France, Finland, Netherlands and Poland, which are significantly different from many countries. However, it is important to note that compared to cross-industry analysis of variance, the variation of ratios between countries is much less intense, though still considerable. This is reflected among others in a smaller number of dissimilar pairs of objects, as well as a smaller number of homogeneous groups, although this fact might be also associated with the smaller number of objects classified. This may prove a stronger impact of the industry effect of the corporate financial ratios in comparison with the country effect. The relative position of countries on the profitability scale is also illustrated by the graph in Fig. 3.4, which exposes the high profitability of enterprises in France, Spain and Finland, while relatively low in Italy and also Poland.

The identified differences also allow for the formation of homogeneous groups of countries in which the objects do not differ significantly in terms of the broadly defined profitability. This is presented in Table 3.12.

Countries, most favourably distinctive from the rest in terms of the aggregated profitability are France, Spain, Finland and Belgium. Italy is ranked last in this classification. The above table shows that the reason for the significant dissimilarity of Poland from several other countries is the relatively low average level of profitability of Polish companies.

The second category of analytical variables, i.e. liquidity ratios ($L_1$–$L_{11}$), is a group where only two variables do not have the discriminatory power for the entire

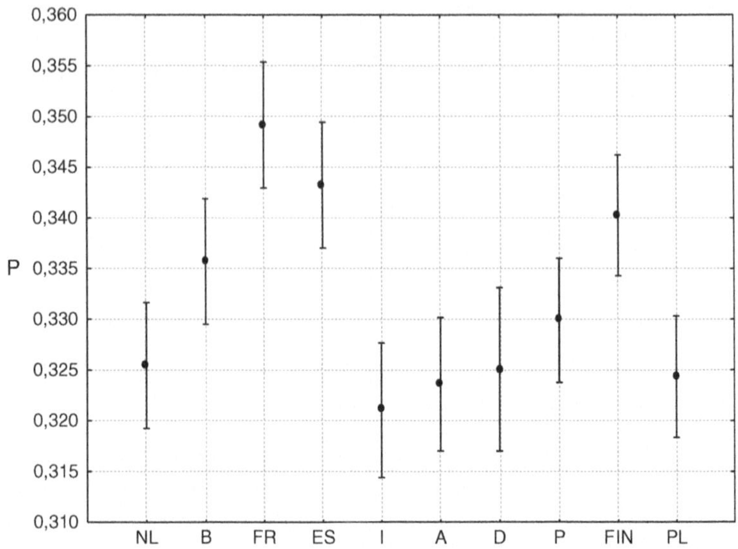


**Fig. 3.4** Plot of marginal means and confidence limits (95 %) of the aggregated profitability ratio for countries (Source: Calculations based on BACH database)

**Table 3.12** Homogenous groups of countries based on the aggregated profitability ratio

| Country | P mean | 1 | 2 | 3 | 4 | 5 |
|---|---|---|---|---|---|---|
| I | 0.321 | X | | | | |
| A | 0.324 | X | X | | | |
| PL | 0.324 | X | X | | | |
| D | 0.325 | X | X | X | | |
| NL | 0.325 | X | X | X | | |
| P | 0.330 | X | X | X | X | |
| B | 0.336 | | X | X | X | X |
| FIN | 0.340 | | | X | X | X |
| ES | 0.343 | | | | X | X |
| FR | 0.349 | | | | | X |

Source: Calculations based on BACH database

population of industries. Most of them also show significant international variability in relation to each industry separately.

The results of the *post-hoc* analysis for this group of ratios are shown in Appendix 19. One of the conclusions that arise in the analysis of these results is the relatively large numerical superiority of the elements of groups with low liquidity, which indicates that the majority of enterprises, in principle, regardless of the country of origin, experiences difficulties in managing financial liquidity.

Poland is often classified into groups of countries with lower levels of liquidity, which is especially noticeable in the case of ratios $L_7$ and $L_8$, and proves relatively low flexibility of the assets structure of Polish enterprises.

**Table 3.13** Probabilities of the post-hoc Tukey's test for the aggregated liquidity ratio in countries, p = 0.05 (significant differences are highlighted)

| No. | Country | NL | B | FR | ES | I | A | D | P | FIN | PL |
|---|---|---|---|---|---|---|---|---|---|---|---|
| 1 | NL | | | | | | | | | | |
| 2 | B | 0.004 | | | | | | | | | |
| 3 | FR | 0.995 | 0.095 | | | | | | | | |
| 4 | ES | 0.000 | 1.000 | 0.017 | | | | | | | |
| 5 | I | 0.850 | 0.481 | 1.000 | 0.173 | | | | | | |
| 6 | A | 0.000 | 0.486 | 0.000 | 0.839 | 0.001 | | | | | |
| 7 | D | 0.977 | 0.465 | 1.000 | 0.187 | 1.000 | 0.002 | | | | |
| 8 | P | 0.000 | 0.935 | 0.001 | 0.998 | 0.017 | 0.998 | 0.025 | | | |
| 9 | FIN | 1.000 | 0.017 | 1.000 | 0.002 | 0.977 | 0.000 | 0.999 | 0.000 | | |
| 10 | PL | 0.001 | 1.000 | 0.035 | 1.000 | 0.282 | 0.656 | 0.289 | 0.984 | 0.005 | |

Source: Calculations based on BACH database

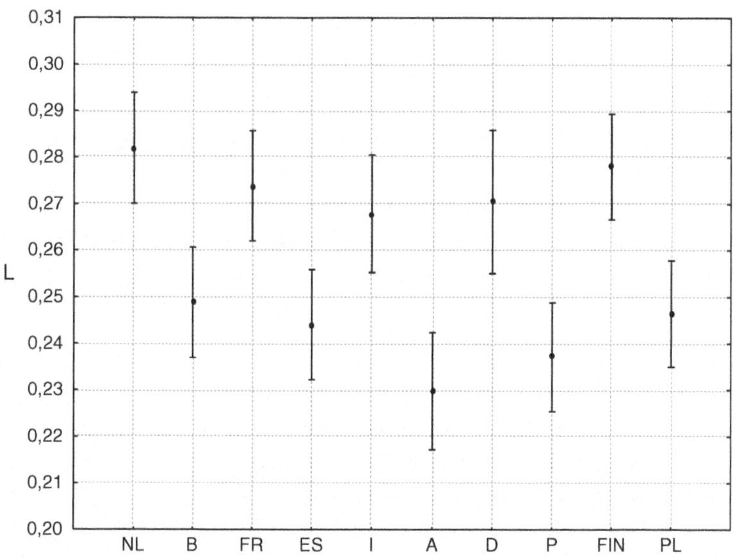


**Fig. 3.5** Plot of marginal means and confidence limits (95 %) of the aggregated liquidity ratio for countries (Source: Calculations based on BACH database)

Application of the summarising procedure of the one-way analysis of variance for the aggregated liquidity ratio L shows significant international differences for the total of all industries (F = 9.20; p = 0.000), very similar in intensity to the previous category of aggregated ratios. The probabilities of the post-hoc analysis are shown in Table 3.13.

The above data reaffirms the significant dissimilarity of the Netherlands and Finland from other countries, which, as shown by a separate analysis of individual ratios, results from the usually much higher values of the financial parameters, which is also shown in the Fig. 3.5., illustrating the relative position of countries on

**Table 3.14** Homogenous groups of countries based on the aggregated liquidity ratio

| Country | L mean | 1 | 2 | 3 | 4 |
|---|---|---|---|---|---|
| A | 0.230 | X | | | |
| P | 0.237 | X | | | |
| ES | 0.244 | X | X | | |
| PL | 0.246 | X | X | | |
| B | 0.249 | X | X | X | |
| I | 0.268 | | X | X | X |
| D | 0.270 | | X | X | X |
| FR | 0.274 | | | X | X |
| FIN | 0.278 | | | | X |
| NL | 0.282 | | | | X |

Source: Calculations based on BACH database

the liquidity scale. That chart also confirms the relatively low capacity for timely payment of creditors by Polish companies, only little better than in Austria – the weakest country in this respect.

The composition of homogeneous groups of countries based on the identified similarities in terms of liquidity is shown in Table 3.14.

Although the above results are considerably generalised, as the analysis was performed for a total of all industries, they provide a clear summary of the detailed analyses.

The results of the cross-country *post-hoc* analysis for the last category of variables – debt ratios – are presented in Appendix 20. Considering this group of variables, Poland stands out positively in terms of just two parameters: the self-financing ratio ($D_4$) and consequently the relation of interest to financial debt ($D_7$). In general, the low level of long-term debt in financial structure probably does not result from conservative capital structure strategy, but rather may indicate that the access to this type of financing is still relatively limited or difficult for Polish companies. On the one hand, the relatively high share of self-financing in Polish enterprises in many industries provides a higher level of their safety in terms of long-term solvency. On the other hand, however, it might indicate firms' aversion to more aggressive financial strategies or lack of sufficient knowledge to efficiently use external sources of capital. At the same time, however, many Polish industries stand out negatively in terms of the relationship of long-term debt to assets ($D_2$) or to equity ($D_3$).

The one-way analysis of variance for the aggregated variable D also shows significant cross-industry differences in all countries together ($F = 21.72$; $p = 0.000$). The probabilities of the *post-hoc* analysis are shown in Table 3.15. The case of Austria is omitted here due to the missing data for many ratios of this category.

The table confirms that the most distinctive country from the others is Germany. Figure 3.6, illustrating the relative position of the countries on the scale of debt, indicates that this dissimilarity is due to Germany's favourable values of ratios in this area, which prove little dependence on external sources of financing.

Table 3.16. contains the composition of homogeneous groups of countries, formed on the basis of the identified similarities in debt ratios.

**Table 3.15** Probabilities of the post-hoc Tukey's test for the aggregated debt ratio in countries, p = 0.05 (significant differences are highlighted)

| No. | Country | NL | B | FR | ES | I | D | P | FIN | PL |
|---|---|---|---|---|---|---|---|---|---|---|
| 1 | NL | | | | | | | | | |
| 2 | B | 0.017 | | | | | | | | |
| 3 | FR | 0.109 | 0.999 | | | | | | | |
| 4 | ES | 0.180 | 0.996 | 1.000 | | | | | | |
| 5 | I | 0.039 | 1.000 | 1.000 | 0.999 | | | | | |
| 6 | D | 0.000 | 0.000 | 0.000 | 0.000 | 0.000 | | | | |
| 7 | P | 0.007 | 1.000 | 0.996 | 0.982 | 1.000 | 0.000 | | | |
| 8 | FIN | 0.793 | 0.000 | 0.000 | 0.001 | 0.000 | 0.000 | 0.000 | | |
| 9 | PL | 0.380 | 0.000 | 0.000 | 0.000 | 0.000 | 0.000 | 0.000 | 0.999 | |

Source: Calculations based on BACH database

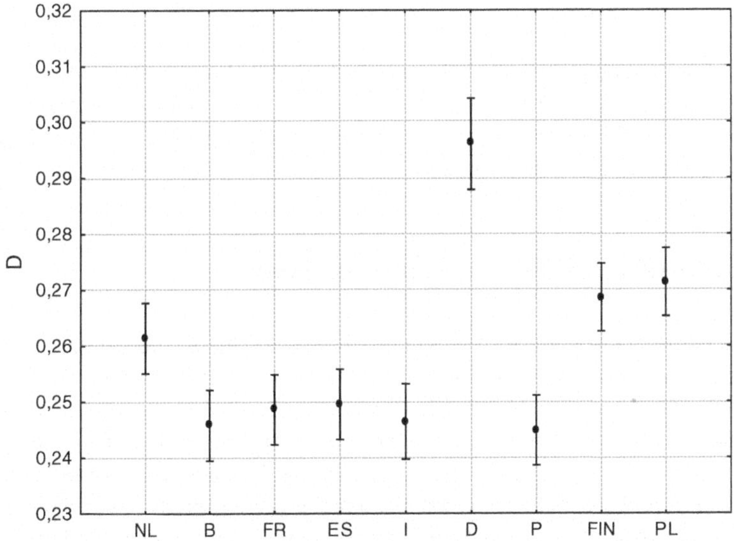


**Fig. 3.6** Plot of marginal means and confidence limits (95 %) of the aggregated debt ratio for countries (Source: Calculations based on BACH database)

**Table 3.16** Homogenous groups of countries based on the aggregated debt ratio

| Country | D mean | 1 | 2 | 3 | 4 |
|---|---|---|---|---|---|
| P | 0.245 | X | | | |
| B | 0.246 | X | | | |
| I | 0.246 | X | | | |
| FR | 0.249 | X | X | | |
| ES | 0.249 | X | X | | |
| NL | 0.261 | | X | X | |
| FIN | 0.269 | | | X | |
| PL | 0.271 | | | X | |
| D | 0.296 | | | | X |

Source: Calculations based on BACH database

**Table 3.17** One-way analysis of ratios variance over time (all countries and industries): F-statistic and p values, p = 0.05 (significant differences are highlighted)

| Ratio | F | p | Ratio | F | p | Ratio | F | P |
|---|---|---|---|---|---|---|---|---|
| $P_1$ | 0.364 | 0.902 | $L_1$ | 0.296 | 0.939 | $D_1$ | 1.244 | 0.282 |
| $P_2$ | 0. 647 | 0.693 | $L_2$ | 0.277 | 0.948 | $D_2$ | 0.858 | 0.525 |
| $P_3$ | 5.687 | 0.000 | $L_3$ | 0.564 | 0.759 | $D_3$ | 1.140 | 0.337 |
| $P_4$ | 0.784 | 0.583 | $L_4$ | 0.844 | 0.536 | $D_4$ | 0.375 | 0.895 |
| $P_5$ | 1.184 | 0.313 | $L_5$ | 0.695 | 0.653 | $D_5$ | 0.205 | 0.975 |
| $P_6$ | 0.712 | 0.633 | $L_6$ | 0.157 | 0.988 | $D_6$ | 0.711 | 0.640 |
| $P_7$ | 2.688 | 0.014 | $L_7$ | 0.081 | 0.998 | $D_7$ | 1.660 | 0.128 |
| $P_8$ | 0.262 | 0.954 | $L_8$ | 0.105 | 0.996 | $D_8$ | 0.297 | 0.938 |
| $P_9$ | 0.125 | 0.993 | $L_9$ | 0.614 | 0.719 | | | |
| $P_{10}$ | 0.263 | 0.954 | $L_{10}$ | 0.348 | 0.911 | | | |
| $P_{11}$ | 0.325 | 0.924 | $L_{11}$ | 0.174 | 0.984 | | | |
| $P_{12}$ | 0.150 | 0.989 | | | | | | |
| $P_{13}$ | 0.739 | 0.618 | | | | | | |

Source: calculations based on BACH database

The cross-country diversity of ratios, identified through the above analyses clearly indicates the occurrence of the country effect in most of financial ratios. The impact of this effect, however, varies depending both on the diagnostic variables, as well as on the industry.

## 3.4 Analysis of Ratios Variance in Time

The procedure of the analysis of variance was also conducted, taking the criterion of time as a qualitative predictor. Therefore, the year was the grouping factor in this case. This was to verify whether the means of individual ratios vary considerably over time, i.e. between individual research periods. The results of the analysis of ratios variance over time are important for further research methodology, as significant differences between years mean that it is appropriate to carry out various analytical procedures for each year separately. If the analysis of variance across time showed no significant diversity of variables, the time average of the ratios could be considered as a typical level of phenomena during the 7-year period. The results of this analysis are presented in Table 3.17, where the distinguished F-statistic and p values indicate significant differentiation of a variable over time.

The calculations show that the vast majority of ratios does not reveal significant differences in time, as the means of ratios statistically are not significantly different in individual years. The exceptions include only two profitability ratios. With respect to these variables the Tukey's test was performed in the *post-hoc* analysis, to determine the reasons for their diversity. It indicates whether the source of discrepancies between the ratio values is an identifiable increasing or decreasing trend, or whether the deviations result from some random fluctuations over time. Analysis of plots of marginal means for the two distinguished variables, shown in Fig. 3.7, shows that in the case of the ratio $P_3$ a slight, but fairly steady growth can

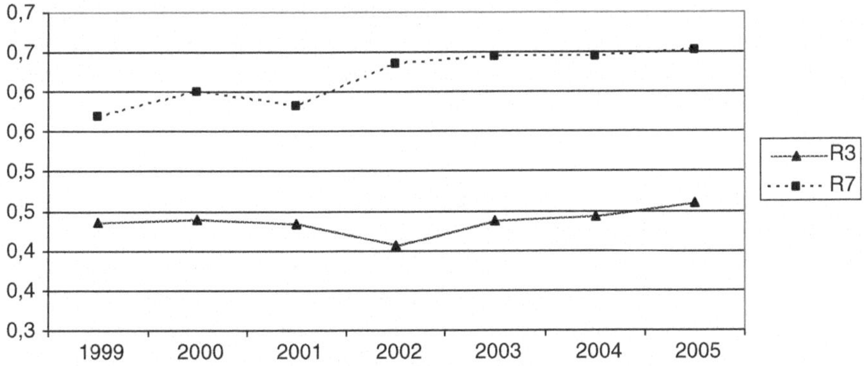


**Fig. 3.7** Plot of marginal means of ratios with significant variation in time (Source: Calculations based on BACH database)

be identified. However, in the case of the other variable $P_7$ the source of significant differentiation in time is rather random behaviour of the ratio, which takes an unusually low value in 2002.

In view of the fact that most diagnostic variables do not demonstrate significant differentiation in time, and those ratios whose means are significantly different between periods are only exceptions, it can be assumed that the time means of ratios will sufficiently represent a typical level of corporate performance during the analytical period. Therefore, most of further analyses will be based on means of variables, thus excluding the time factor.

## 3.5 Industry and Country Effect Through Two-Way Analysis of Ratios Variance

In the previous sections the analysis of variance was presented, where the number of categorising variables was limited to a single factor – industry, country or time. However, the analysis of equality of means is also used when there are more qualitative factors, e.g. when comparing the effect of several different features categorised in one or more measurable characteristics. In the present study the combined impact of the country and industry specificity on financial ratios may be particularly interesting.

It is clear from the analyses in the previous sections the majority of diagnostic variables is influenced by both the industry and the country. However, the one-way analysis of variance does not respond the question which of these two factors influences the level of ratios more, because it does not reveal the total impact of the industrial and national factor. However, the multivariate analysis of variance proves to be helpful here as a statistical technique which allows studying such complex interactions.

The assumptions of the multivariate analysis of variance are analogous to the previously discussed conditions for the one-way analysis. The two-way analysis applied in this study is the simplest variant of this method. Therefore, there are two categorising features, namely industry and country, and measurable characteristics (ratios) examined separately, whose values are likely to depend on the membership to specific categories. The total variability of the observed features (dependent variables) is attributed to the influence of the categorising characteristics (independent variables) and the random error. It is assumed that, if there is some influence of the independent features on the dependent variables, the variability in the groups is smaller than the variability between groups. Therefore the null hypothesis is subject to testing, which holds that there is no difference between groups, against the alternative hypothesis according to which such a difference exists. Finding no differences between groups gives no rise to further analysis. A positive test result provides the basis to seek answers to more specific questions about the nature of the relationship between the categorising features and the independent variables. The results of the two-way analysis of variance are presented in Table 3.18, where the symbols C, I, and CI denote the analysis carried out only for the features of the 'country', 'industry' and for both of these attributes.

The presented calculations show that the significant interaction of industry and country occurs in the case of all the studied ratios except for the variable $D_3$. This interaction, however, in the vast majority of the variables, is weaker than the effect of the country and (or) the industry considered separately. The only exceptions are the variables $P_6$, $L_{11}$ and $D_5$, for which the combined effect is stronger. Furthermore, a comparison of the influence of both effects based on the values of the F-statistics shows that in most cases the dominant factor is the industry effect. Only for about one third of the variables the opposite situation was observed, i.e. the greater importance of the country than of the industry. In some of these cases (highlighted in the table) the industry effect proved to have no significant impact on a ratio.

The overall conclusion is that the most typical situation for the analysed variables is the one, where the industry has the greatest impact on the value of a ratio, then the country, and finally the interaction of both factors combined. The dominance of the industry effect is especially striking in the case of variables from the category of profitability and turnover, particularly ratios $P_8$–$P_{11}$. The industrial specificity of corporate performance is particularly revealed in the trade industry, where the ratios of total assets turnover ($P_8$) and fixed assets turnover ($P_9$) take the maximum values almost regardless of the country. At the same time this sector is often characterised by the lowest ratio of added value to turnover, which can be also observed in many countries under analysis.

A considerably stronger impact of the industry than of the country is also visible in the case of assets elasticity, illustrated with the ratio of current to total assets ($L_7$). This time, the industry with the best value of the parameter in most countries is, in addition to trade, the construction industry, while the smallest elasticity is usually characteristic for the energy sector.

Similarly, the two-way analysis of variance was also conducted for the other two combinations of qualitative factors, namely for the following pairs: country – year and industry – year. This was to verify the significance of the time factor, combined

**Table 3.18** Two-way analysis of ratios variance – the country effect (C), the industry effect (I) and the combined effect (CI): values of F-statistic and p, p = 0.05 (deficiencies of significance are highlighted)

| Ratio | Effect | F | p | Ratio | Effect | F | p | Ratio | Effect | F | p |
|---|---|---|---|---|---|---|---|---|---|---|---|
| | C | 7.3 | 0.000 | | C | 21.0 | 0.000 | | K | 19.4 | 19.4 |
| $P_1$ | I | 208.6 | 0.000 | $L_1$ | I | 17.2 | 0.000 | $D_1$ | S | 11.5 | 11.5 |
| | CI | 8.4 | 0.000 | | CI | 4.9 | 0.000 | | KS | 3.5 | 3.5 |
| | C | 32.6 | 0.000 | | C | 21.3 | 0.000 | | K | 6.4 | 0.000 |
| $P_2$ | I | 65.8 | 0.000 | $L_2$ | I | 17.7 | 0.000 | $D_2$ | S | 0.1 | 0.996 |
| | CI | 4.9 | 0.000 | | CI | 5.2 | 0.000 | | KS | 3.6 | 0.000 |
| | C | 7.6 | 0.000 | | C | 58.2 | 0.000 | | K | 0.4 | 0.865 |
| $P_3$ | I | 23.5 | 0.000 | $L_3$ | I | 10.4 | 0.000 | $D_3$ | S | 0.7 | 0.639 |
| | CI | 3.3 | 0.000 | | CI | 6.1 | 0.000 | | KS | 0.6 | 1.000 |
| | C | 2.6 | 0.019 | | C | 42.8 | 0.002 | | K | 62.3 | 0.000 |
| $P_4$ | I | 0.0 | 1.000 | $L_4$ | I | 116.9 | 0.000 | $D_4$ | S | 157.3 | 0.000 |
| | CI | 1.3 | 0.037 | | CI | 12.0 | 0.000 | | KS | 15.2 | 0.000 |
| | C | 11.3 | 0.000 | | C | 12.5 | 0.000 | | K | 1.4 | 0.205 |
| $P_5$ | I | 0.7 | 0.650 | $L_5$ | I | 0.0 | 1.000 | $D_5$ | S | 0.3 | 0.919 |
| | CI | 2.9 | 0.000 | | CI | 7.0 | 0.000 | | KS | 1.3 | 0.021 |
| | C | 0.9 | 0.479 | | C | 273.6 | 0.000 | | K | 9.7 | 0.000 |
| $P_6$ | I | 0.8 | 0.538 | $L_6$ | I | 126.5 | 0.000 | $D_6$ | S | 43.1 | 0.000 |
| | CI | 1.3 | 0.047 | | CI | 13.0 | 0.000 | | KS | 9.9 | 0.000 |
| | C | 130.4 | 0.000 | | C | 114.7 | 0.000 | | K | 16.1 | 0.000 |
| $P_7$ | I | 127.4 | 0.000 | $L_7$ | I | 1,592.7 | 0.000 | $D_7$ | S | 17.1 | 0.000 |
| | CI | 4.2 | 0.000 | | CI | 25.0 | 0.000 | | KS | 3.1 | 0.000 |
| | C | 146.8 | 0.000 | | C | 168.6 | 0.000 | | K | 177.1 | 0.000 |
| $P_8$ | I | 1,590.7 | 0.000 | $L_8$ | I | 756.3 | 0.000 | $D_8$ | S | 285.9 | 0.000 |
| | CI | 28.7 | 0.000 | | CI | 28.9 | 0.000 | | KS | 58.1 | 0.000 |
| | C | 112.9 | 0.000 | | C | 2.8 | 0.010 | | | | |
| $P_9$ | I | 2,301.8 | 0.000 | $L_9$ | I | 45.7 | 0.000 | | | | |
| | CI | 37.9 | 0.000 | | CI | 3.3 | 0.000 | | | | |
| | C | 16.7 | 0.000 | | C | 86.7 | 0.000 | | | | |
| $P_{10}$ | I | 51.4 | 0.000 | $L_{10}$ | I | 722.9 | 0.000 | | | | |
| | CI | 7.9 | 0.000 | | CI | 26.5 | 0.000 | | | | |
| | C | 82.4 | 0.000 | | C | 1.4 | 0.193 | | | | |
| $P_{11}$ | I | 483.7 | 0.000 | $L_{11}$ | I | 2.1 | 0.061 | | | | |
| | CI | 32.6 | 0.000 | | CI | 1.5 | 0.001 | | | | |
| | C | 319.4 | 0.000 | | | | | | | | |
| $P_{12}$ | I | 189.0 | 0.000 | | | | | | | | |
| | CI | 12.6 | 0.000 | | | | | | | | |
| | C | 8.9 | 0.000 | | | | | | | | |
| $P_{13}$ | I | 68.8 | 0.000 | | | | | | | | |
| | CI | 13.3 | 0.000 | | | | | | | | |

Source: Calculations based on BACH database

with the effect of country and industry. There is a possibility that, although the time factor examined alone proved insignificant in relation to most ratios (as shown by one-way analysis of variance), it could prove significant in conjunction with the factor of country and (or) industry.

From the results of the described analyses, it can be concluded that the interaction of time factor, both in combination with the industry and the country effect is significant only in few of the studied variables. The results of the calculations – as not directly related to the country and industry effect – are presented in Appendices 21 and 22. Simplifying, it can be assumed that – at least within the research period – the time factor does not differentiate corporate performance significantly.

# Chapter 4
# Cross-Industry and Cross-Country Comparative Cluster Analysis

## 4.1 Cluster Analysis of Industries

Graphical creation of clusters can be presented in the form of a tree diagram. The result of applying the agglomerative algorithm for industries based on the average ratios for all countries in the whole research period is a hierarchical tree, shown in Fig. 4.1.

The earlier described silhouette index, as a tool used to determine the optimum number of clusters, was calculated for different numbers of hypothetical clusters in this grouping of industries (as well as in subsequent groupings). The results of these calculations are presented in Table 4.1.

The index takes the highest value when the population is divided into two groups. Increasing the number of clusters deteriorates the grouping quality, resulting in a gradual decline of the index. In practice, most often the optimal grouping is achieved when the 'branches' of the tree diagram are intersected in the place where they are the longest (Sagan, 2009). Thus, the most homogeneous, distinct groups are obtained by cutting the tree diagram e.g. around the 14th linkage distance. Then the surveyed population can be divided into clearly separated clusters. In the first one there are seven industries: mining, energy, real estate, hotels, transport, education and health. All the six remaining industries are in the other cluster. The resulting clusters can thus be described as agro-trade-manufacturing and mining-energy-service companies. The graph also shows that the diversity of objects within the clusters is quite similar, though slightly larger in the first cluster, as evidenced by longer linkages.

The number of clusters determined on the basis of the silhouette index, however, should not be treated as the only feasible option of dividing the population. Empirical research shows that sometimes such a way of grouping makes it impossible to find common characteristics of objects (Migdał-Najman & Najman, 2006). Decreasing or increasing the number of clusters in this case may help detect some shared features and interpret them according to the knowledge of the examined phenomenon.

J. Koralun-Bereźnicka, *Corporate Performance*, Contributions to Management Science, DOI 10.1007/978-3-319-00345-0_4, 

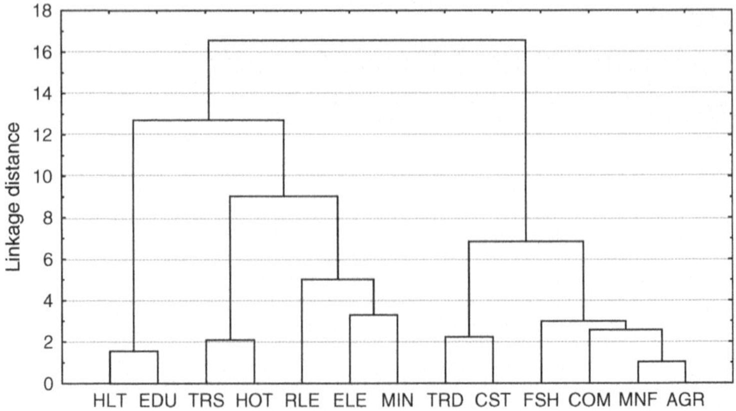


**Fig. 4.1** Tree diagram based on average ratios from 1999 to 2005 for ten countries; Ward method, square Euclidean distance (Source: Calculations based on BACH database)

**Table 4.1** Silhouette index for different numbers of industry clusters

| Number of clusters | 2 | 3 | 4 |
|---|---|---|---|
| SI value | 0.410 | 0.369 | 0.345 |

Source: Calculations based on BACH database

Therefore, in order to make a more detailed classification of the analysed industries, the division could be continued until the linkage distance is about ten, which would lead to extracting three clusters, two of which form one larger at an earlier cessation of division. It seems, however, that the division of industries into just two clusters results in a more distinct and clear grouping, especially given the relatively low number of the objects being grouped.

Analysis of the basic statistics for each industry, presented in Table 4.2, shows that the industries from the first cluster (mining-energy-services) are characterised by slightly higher average performance parameters in all countries. This concerns mainly the industry of education, mining and health care. The weakest ratios are noted in transport, hotels and fishing.

The above cluster analysis allows detecting similarities between the classified objects. However, it does not reveal the specific reasons for linking certain objects into groups. It is therefore important to detect the common characteristic of objects in the same cluster.

One way of recognising the nature of the obtained clusters, i.e. identifying the features shared by the industries from the same group, is the analysis of means of each of them in various dimensions. Therefore, the means of ratios characterising industries from both clusters were calculated. The plot of means for each cluster of industries in all countries is shown in Fig. 4.2.

Comparing the plots of means shows that the first cluster, containing the industries of mining, energy, real estate, hotels, transport, education and health, on average is characterised by slightly better performance parameters, as evidenced

**Table 4.2** The mean and standard deviation of ratios in industries for 1999–2005

| | Industries | | | | | | | | | | | | |
|---|---|---|---|---|---|---|---|---|---|---|---|---|---|
| Content | AGR | FSH | MIN | MNF | ELE | CST | TRD | HOT | TRS | RLE | EDU | HLT | COM |
| $\mu$ | 0.448 | 0.408 | 0.604 | 0.469 | 0.480 | 0.476 | 0.499 | 0.372 | 0.375 | 0.485 | 0.643 | 0.603 | 0.575 |
| $\sigma$ | 0.261 | 0.306 | 0.319 | 0.272 | 0.333 | 0.325 | 0.406 | 0.321 | 0.310 | 0.304 | 0.304 | 0.335 | 0.224 |

Source: Calculations based on BACH database

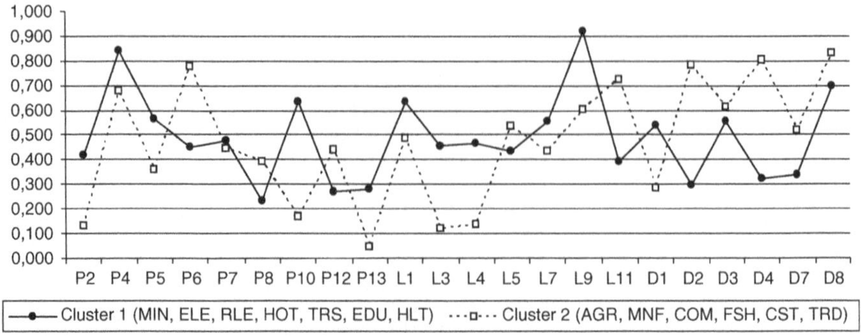


**Fig. 4.2** Plot of means of the selected ratios for each cluster of industries in all countries (Source: Calculations based on BACH database)

by higher mean values of most variables. This is particularly clear in the case of the profitability and liquidity ratios, as the variables characterising debt are less powerful in terms of discriminating between the two clusters.

Within the profitability ratios, the supremacy of objects from the first cluster occurs in the case of six variables ($P_2$, $P_4$, $P_5$, $P_7$, $P_{10}$, $P_{13}$), but only for two of them the difference is statistically significant (at 5 %). Although the remaining ratios in fact take higher values for the industries from the other cluster, the statistical significance of the difference is only noted for one variable ($P_6$).

The situation is similar in terms of liquidity ratios, where five of them have better values in the first cluster ($L_1$, $L_3$, $L_4$, $L_7$, $L_9$), two of which are significantly higher ($L_4$, $L_9$). However, only one of the other ratios ($L_{11}$) is significantly higher in the second cluster.

The mutual relations between clusters in the area of debt ratios are quite different, as most of the ratios were higher in the second cluster ($D_2$, $D_3$, $D_4$, $D_7$, $D_8$), but in none of the cases the difference was statistically significant. The first cluster prevailed only in one case ($D_1$), which however was not statistically significant, either.

To summarise this analysis, it can therefore be concluded that most of the ratios (12 of 22) have a higher mean in the first cluster, four of which are significantly higher. The first five-item cluster is characterised by higher profitability of industries and better liquidity parameters, but also higher level of debt compared to the other.

The above reasoning shows that not all variables have equally good discriminatory abilities for creating clusters. The analysis of ratios variance shows which of them is significantly different between groups of industries in each country, as presented in Table 4.3.

The table shows that among the profitability and turnover parameters, the ratios which most often differentiate between the clusters of industries include: operating profitability of sales ratio ($P_2$), cost of sales to turnover ($P_7$) and the ratio of added value to turnover ($P_{10}$). Among the ratios characterising short-term solvency, the

**Table 4.3** Ratios significantly different between clusters of industries ($p < 0.05$)

| Country | Number of ratios | Ratios | | |
|---|---|---|---|---|
| | | Profitability | Liquidity | Debt |
| NL | 16 | $P_2$, $P_4$, $P_5$, $P_8$, $P_{12}$ | $L_1$, $L_3$, $L_4$, $L_7$ | $D_1$, $D_2$, $D_3$, $D_4$, $D_6$, $D_7$, $D_8$ |
| B | 14 | $P_4$, $P_5$, $P_6$, $P_7$ | $L_1$, $L_3$, $L_4$, $L_5$, $L_{11}$ | $D_1$, $D_2$, $D_3$, $D_4$, $D_7$ |
| FR | 8 | $P_2$, $P_4$, $P_5$, $P_6$ | $L_7$, $L_{11}$ | $D_1$, $D_2$ |
| ES | 8 | $P_2$, $P_7$, $P_8$, $P_{10}$ | $L_5$, $L_7$ | $D_2$, $D_7$ |
| I | 13 | $P_2$, $P_4$, $P_5$, $P_7$, $P_{10}$, $P_{13}$ | $L_1$, $L_3$, $L_4$, $L_7$, $L_9$ | $D_1$, $D_4$ |
| A | 7 | $P_2$, $P_7$ | $L_1$, $L_7$, $L_9$ | $D_2$, $D_8$ |
| D | 3 | $P_2$ | $L_7$, $L_9$ | – |
| P | 8 | $P_7$, $P_8$, $P_{10}$ | $L_1$, $L_7$, $L_9$ | $D_7$, $D_8$ |
| FIN | 8 | $P_5$, $P_7$, $P_{10}$ | $L_1$, $L_3$, $L_5$ | $D_1$, $D_4$ |
| PL | 11 | $P_2$, $P_7$, $P_{10}$, $P_{13}$ | $L_1$, $L_3$, $L_5$, $L_7$ | $D_2$, $D_3$, $D_4$ |
| **All** | **10** | $P_2$, $P_5$, $P_{10}$, $P_{13}$ | $L_1$, $L_3$, $L_7$ | $D_1$, $D_2$, $D_4$ |

Source: Calculations based on BACH database

variables significantly differentiating between the clusters are the short-term liquidity ratio ($L_1$), the share of current assets in the assets ($L_7$) and the cash ratio ($L_3$).

The debt ratios have relatively the weakest discriminatory abilities, but it should be mentioned that this is the category with the smallest number of variables. In terms of the significance of between-group variation it is worth noting the interest coverage ratio ($D_1$), the long-term debt ratio ($D_2$) and equity to assets ratio ($D_4$). Germany is the only country from the analysed population, where none of the debt ratios differs significantly between the clusters.

In the next stage of the study the structure of clusters in each year of the period were analysed, although the results are not presented as graphs. Comparing the structure of clusters obtained separately for each year of the period reveals great similarity of these classifications. In most years the population was divided again into two groups, whose detailed composition is shown in Table 4.4.

The table shows that in all studied years, except 2001, the number of clusters was the same, although their size and composition varied. In the first 2 years of the research period, the structure of clusters showed some volatility over time. Nevertheless, there are easily identifiable similarities between the groupings. A characteristic feature of the first cluster is the concentration mostly around four industries: mining, real estate, education and health, which remain in the same group, irrespective of the period. These elements, like all others belonging to the same cluster throughout all six periods, have been bolded in the table.

The fixed elements of the other cluster include the following industries: agriculture, fisheries, manufacturing, construction and trade, which constitute a kind of core of the group. Thus, only four other industries are assigned to different clusters depending on the period. The stability of the composition of the two clusters is characteristic for the last 4 years of the research period. This confirms the conclusions of the analysis of ratios variance in time. A similar structure of clusters in the sub-periods proves little variation of the diagnostic variables across years.

**Table 4.4** Cluster analysis results based on average ratios for all countries (permanent elements of clusters are bolded)

| | Elements of the clusters | |
|---|---|---|
| Year | Cluster 1 | Cluster 2 |
| 1999 | **MIN**, ELE, HOT, TRS, **RLE**, **EDU**, **HLT**, COM, | **AGR**, **FSH**, **MNF**, **CST**, **TRD** |
| 2000 | **MIN**, ELE, **RLE**, **EDU**, **HLT** | **AGR**, **FSH**, **MNF**, **CST**, **TRD**, HOT, TRS, COM |
| 2002 | **MIN**, **RLE**, **EDU**, **HLT**, COM | **AGR**, **FSH**, ELE, **MNF**, **CST**, **TRD**, HOT, TRS |
| 2003 | **MIN**, **RLE**, **EDU**, **HLT**, COM | **AGR**, **FSH**, ELE, **MNF**, **CST**, **TRD**, HOT, TRS |
| 2004 | **MIN**, **RLE**, **EDU**, **HLT**, COM | **AGR**, **FSH**, ELE, **MNF**, **CST**, **TRD**, HOT, TRS |
| 2005 | **MIN**, **RLE**, **EDU**, **HLT**, COM | **AGR**, **FSH**, ELE, **MNF**, **CST**, **TRD**, HOT, TRS |

Source: Calculations based on BACH database

The specification of the elements of the clusters from 2001 was deliberately omitted in the above table due to their unusual composition, considerably different from the other years. In this year, as the only one in the entire study period, three clusters were distinguished as a result of the agglomerative procedure. The clusters included the following industries:

- Cluster 1: TRD,
- Cluster 2: RLE, EDU, MIN,
- Cluster 3: AGR, FSH, MNF, ELE, CST, HOT, TRS, HLT, COM.

Despite some notable similarities to other sub-periods, such as the proximity of agriculture, fisheries, manufacturing and construction or mining and real estate, there are also clear differences, such as the separation of the health and mining industry, and especially the trade from other industries. A closer look at the raw data from this period reveals that the formation of a separate single-element cluster by the trade in this year was not due to unusual values of the ratios in this sector, which were very similar to the previous and the following year. The distribution of extreme values of ratios in the trade sector in 1999–2001 was also almost identical. Therefore it can be assumed that it was the performance of other industries which was responsible for the unusual grouping results in 2001.

It is also worth performing cluster analysis separately for each of the three categories of ratios. Both the number and structure of the cluster is in fact slightly different when considering performance, liquidity and solvency ratios individually. The results are shown in Figs. 4.3, 4.4 and 4.5. Cluster analysis, in which only the profitability ratios were adopted as the grouping variables (average for the whole period for all countries), again resulted in identifying two distinct groups. In addition, the internal structure of each of the clusters is very close to the grouping results obtained with the use of all selected variables.

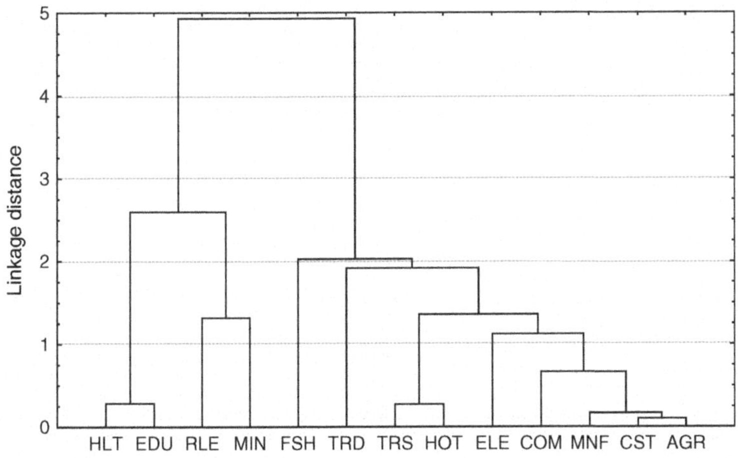


**Fig. 4.3** Tree diagram based on average profitability ratios from 1999 to 2005 for ten countries; Ward method, square Euclidean distance (Source: Calculations based on BACH database)

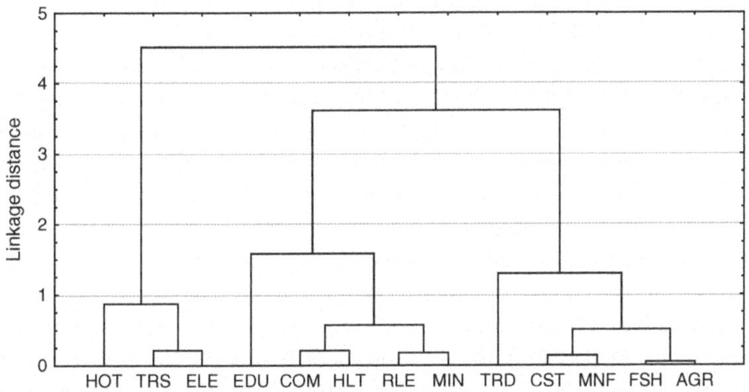


**Fig. 4.4** Tree diagram based on average liquidity ratios from 1999 to 2005 for ten countries; Ward method, square Euclidean distance (Source: Calculations based on BACH database)

The above grouping is different from the one performed for all variables mainly due to the location of the community services, which in terms of profitability shows no similarity to the sectors of health, mining, real estate and education, but is close to the manufacturing, agriculture and construction. Moreover, when considering the profitability ratios, the location of the trade and fisheries is different, as these industries are far away from other objects in the cluster due to their relatively low performance in this area. In general, however, the similarity of the compared structures is due to the fact that the profitability ratios are the largest group of diagnostic variables, and therefore have the greatest influence on the formation of clusters based on the ratios of all three analytical areas.

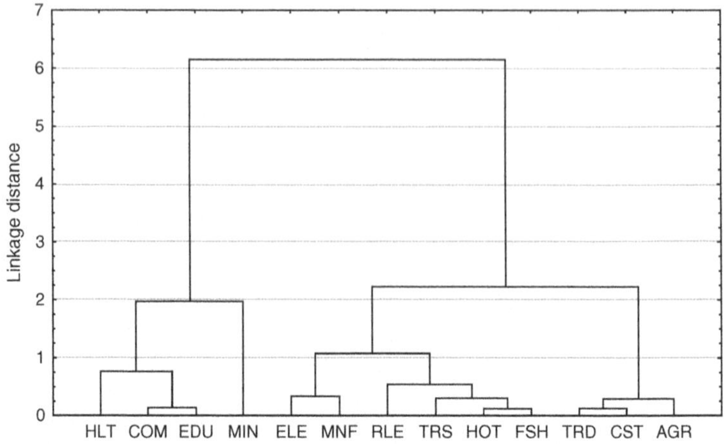


**Fig. 4.5** Tree diagram based on average debt ratios from 1999 to 2005 for ten countries; Ward method, square Euclidean distance (Source: Calculations based on BACH database)

A little more different arrangement of objects in clusters results when only the liquidity ratios are applied, as shown in Fig. 4.4.

Although the industries of health, education, mining, real estate and community services still form the separate cluster of high performance in terms of liquidity, the other industries are now two distinct groups, the larger of which is characterised with the lowest average short-term solvency ratios. Markedly separated from other objects are the industries of transport, energy and hotels, which is associated with their predominantly low liquidity parameters. A split into two clusters is again a result of the use of the debt ratios as grouping variables, as shown Fig. 4.5.

This time, the first cluster, which contained five elements in the case of the cluster analysis based on all ratios, was reduced to just four items. In this case the real estate sector due to its relatively low debt burden is closer to the transport, hotels and fishing industry. The common feature of the objects in the less numerous cluster is the relatively good solvency.

The above cluster analyses were based on the aggregated variables, as they were means of ratios both in time and in terms of countries, which undoubtedly makes the inference very generalised, and much of the information is lost due to the synthesis. Hence, it is also purposeful to carry out similar analyses separately for each country, in order to detect similarities and differences between the industries on an international level. This is discussed in the Sect. 4.2.

## 4.2 Comparative Cluster Analysis of Industries Across Countries

When interpreting the results of the analyses discussed in the Sect. 4.1., it should be kept in mind that these procedures were based on the average performance of industries in all countries. To identify the differences between countries, a similar procedure was conducted separately for each of them. The purpose of this study was to conduct a comparative cluster analysis of the industries between the examined countries. The object of comparison is the nature of industry clusters, both in terms of their number, size and internal structure. Consequently, the study also aimed at identifying the characteristics of the formed groups and to detect the country effect, as a factor influencing the financial ratios of enterprises. This time, bearing in mind the previously detected significant similarities between the different research periods, the time means of ratios were applied. The results of the analyses are presented graphically in Appendix 23.

These graphs show that the inclusion of country specificity in grouping industries allows identifying significant differences in the formation of clusters. These differences refer both to the number of the distinguished clusters and their internal structure. In a separate consideration of countries the number of isolated clusters ranged between 2 and 5. The composition of each cluster is also often clearly dependent on the country. The observed differences, however, did not relate equally to all industries. In the analysed population, there are industries insusceptible to the country effect, such as trade and construction, which in all countries are in the same cluster, usually characterised with lower values of variables. Moreover, these industries often exhibit a high level of mutual similarity, as evidenced by often short-distance linkages between them.

The comparative analysis of clusters structure in the international context reveals the following patterns:

- The only countries, where the industries of education and health are not in the same cluster are the Netherlands, France and Portugal (with the exception of Italy and Germany, where there are missing data for these industries),
- The Netherlands, France, Italy and Austria are the only countries where the mining and real estate industries belong to different clusters; only in Austria mining is more similar to the trade and construction,
- Mining is a self-contained, one-item cluster in three countries (the Netherlands, France and Italy),
- The trade and construction industries, typically occurring close to each other, are usually accompanied by the agriculture, with the exception of the Netherlands and Germany (in the second case due to the lack of data for the agricultural sector),
- Agriculture and fisheries are in the same cluster in all countries except Belgium, France and Portugal, where fishing is in the cluster with the energy, mining and

service sectors (except Austria and Germany, which there are missing data for these industries),
- In Finland, Poland and Benelux countries, the hotels sector is more similar to the trade and construction or agriculture and fisheries, whereas in the other countries it is closer to the real estate industry,
- Germany is the only country (except Austria, due to the lack of data), where the manufacturing industry is linked with the energy and mining, and does not belong to the cluster of the agriculture, trade and services,
- In most countries, the transport sector is similar to the energy and (or) real estate, except in Belgium, where it is linked with the trade and construction.

Moreover, the most obvious division of industries into two groups is in Poland, where the clusters demonstrate the highest internal homogeneity, as evidenced by the relatively short linkage distances. The above mentioned similarities and differences indicate the occurrence of the country effect in the analysed set of corporate financial ratios, but the impact of this effect is different depending on the industry.

For a more formal assessment of the similarity of the obtained groupings, the earlier mentioned adjusted Rand's measure $R_{AD}$ can be used, as presented in Table 4.5.

When interpreting the above values of the similarity index, it is clear that in most cases the groupings of industries bear little resemblance between countries. Moreover, the grouping results are often very different, as evidenced by the negative values of the measure. Only in two cases, namely Spain – Italy, and Italy – Austria, there is a moderate similarity of the clustering results, as the values are greater than 0.5. As for Poland, the industry grouping results are quite similar to the classification obtained for Finland. It is also worth noting that both countries are characterised with the largest dissimilarity of grouping results from other countries, as evidenced by the largest number of the negative $R_{AD}$ values. Confronting these observations with the tree diagrams confirms the existence of the earlier discussed common features between the two countries.

## 4.3 Cluster Analysis of Countries

Apart from the industries, the objects which can also be submitted to clustering procedure are countries. Classification of countries is a method aimed at discovering the mutual similarities between them and, consequently, at facilitating further inference. The result of the agglomeration algorithm based on average ratios for all industries in the 7 years' period is the hierarchical tree shown in Fig. 4.6.

The above tree diagram reveals clear separation of Poland and Finland from the rest of the objects, which makes the pair of countries a two-item cluster. Cutting the branches of the tree diagram near the eighth distance leads to identifying two clusters, the other of which consists of all the other countries analysed. In search for the reasons for such a large distance of Poland and Finland from other countries,

**Table 4.5** Similarity evaluation of industry clusters in countries – adjusted Rand's measure

| Country | NL | B | FR | ES | I | A | D | P | FIN |
|---|---|---|---|---|---|---|---|---|---|
| B | 0.109 | | | | | | | | |
| FR | 0.082 | 0.330 | | | | | | | |
| ES | −0.111 | 0.012 | 0.015 | | | | | | |
| I | 0.186 | 0.166 | 0.219 | 0.533 | | | | | |
| A | −0.076 | −0.076 | 0.023 | 0.561 | 0.367 | | | | |
| D | 0.013 | 0.039 | 0.067 | 0.086 | 0.093 | 0.013 | | | |
| P | −0.008 | 0.012 | 0.118 | 0.436 | 0.325 | 0.250 | 0.086 | | |
| FIN | 0.066 | 0.088 | −0.025 | −0.020 | 0.170 | −0.077 | 0.186 | −0.071 | |
| PL | 0.199 | 0.220 | −0.037 | 0.230 | 0.221 | −0.060 | −0.019 | −0.026 | 0.439 |

Source: Calculations based on BACH database.

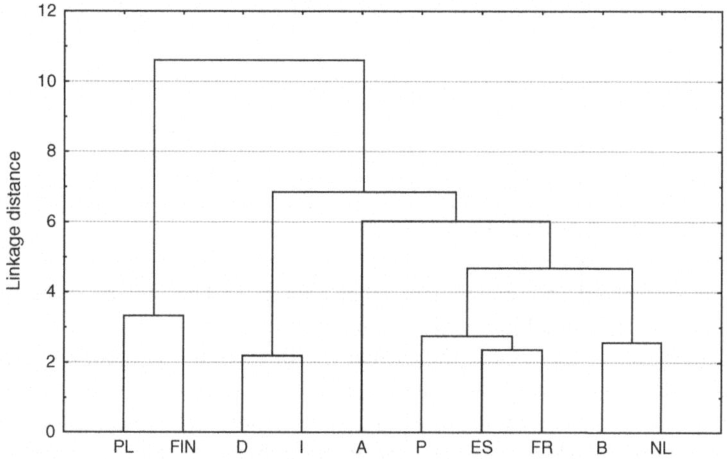


**Fig. 4.6** Tree diagram based on average ratios for all industries from 1999 to 2005; Ward method, square Euclidean distance (Source: Calculations based on BACH database)

the basic statistics characterising individual objects can be used. A glance at the means and standard deviations in Table 4.6., shows that Finland and Austria are extreme objects in terms of mean values. Poland comes the second in terms of mean of all the selected ratios in all industries. Taking into account the standard deviation – it is an object characterised with the highest cross-industry differentiation, which resulted in the above formation of clusters.

The procedure, involving the identification of cluster centres, applied for countries in individual industries, allows detecting the characteristics of groups of countries. In this case, also the average ratios were calculated for the two clusters of countries. The graph confirms the previously observed contrasts in the economic and financial characteristics of the Polish industries, some of which are characterised with very high values of certain ratios (e.g. education) with at the same time very weak performance in other sectors. The result is a favourable

**Table 4.6** The mean and standard deviation of ratios in countries for 1999–2005

| | Countries | | | | | | | | | |
|---|---|---|---|---|---|---|---|---|---|---|
| Content | NL | B | FR | ES | I | A | D | P | FIN | PL |
| $\mu$ | 0.543 | 0.428 | 0.478 | 0.440 | 0.428 | 0.391 | 0.487 | 0.401 | 0.708 | 0.571 |
| $\sigma$ | 0.263 | 0.312 | 0.284 | 0.347 | 0.336 | 0.342 | 0.318 | 0.319 | 0.294 | 0.376 |

Source: Calculations based on BACH database

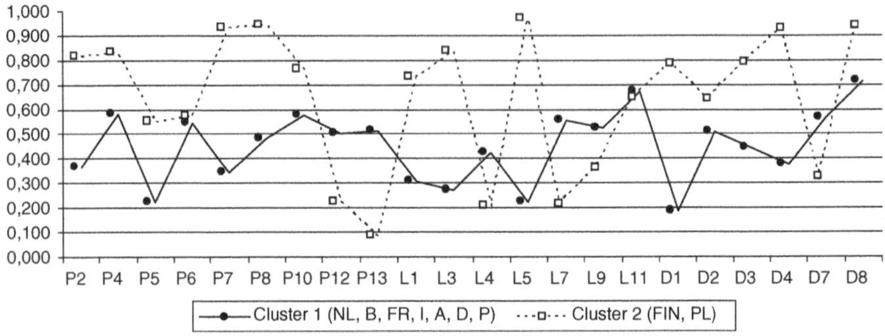


**Fig. 4.7** Plot of means of the selected ratios for each cluster of countries in all industries (Source: Calculations based on BACH database)

placement of Poland as compared to other countries. The plot of means for the clusters of countries in all industries is shown in Fig. 4.7.

A comparison of the means shows that the first cluster, containing eight euro area countries, on average is characterised by slightly worse performance parameters, as evidenced by lower mean values of most variables. This applies to all categories of variables, i.e. the area of profitability, liquidity and debt. Some superiority of the objects from the first cluster can only be seen in the case of variables $P_{12}$, $P_{13}$, $L_4$, $L_7$, $L_9$, $L_{11}$ and $D_7$. Generally, however, the differences between the means of these ratios in the clusters are statistically insignificant. Significant differentiation (at 5 %) occurred only in four cases (variables $P_2$, $L_3$, $L_5$, $D_4$).

Summarising the analysis, it can be concluded that most of the ratios (15 of 22) are better in the second cluster, but only four of them are significantly different. Finland and Poland are therefore characterised by a clearly better operating profitability, short-term liquidity, debtors turnover and self-financing.

Since not all of the variables are characterised by equally good discriminatory power, it should be analysed in which analytical areas there are really important differences between the clusters. For this purpose the analysis of ratios variance between groups of countries in different industries was performed. The results of this analysis, presented in Table 4.7, show which of the ratios differ substantially between clusters of countries.

The table shows that within the parameters of profitability and turnover, the ratios most commonly occurring as differentiating the clusters of countries include:

**Table 4.7** Ratios significantly different between clusters of industries ($p < 0.05$)

| | | Ratios | | |
|---|---|---|---|---|
| Industry | Number of ratios | Profitability | Liquidity | Debt |
| AGR | 4 | $P_{13}$ | $L_1$, $L_3$, $L_9$ | – |
| FSH | 5 | $P_6$, $P_8$ | $L_4$, $L_7$, $L_{11}$ | – |
| MIN | 15 | $P_2$, $P_5$, $P_6$, $P_7$, $P_{10}$, $P_{12}$, $P_{13}$ | $L_4$, $L_7$, $L_{11}$ | $D_2$, $D_3$, $D_4$, $D_7$, $D_8$ |
| MNF | 6 | $P_5$, $P_6$, $P_8$, $P_{13}$ | $L_7$ | $D_2$ |
| ELE | 8 | $P_8$, $P_{10}$ | $L_5$ | $D_2$, $D_3$, $D_4$ |
| CST | 4 | – | $L_3$, $L_4$, $L_9$ | $D_8$ |
| TRD | 3 | $P_6$ | $L_9$, $L_{11}$ | – |
| HOT | 12 | $P_6$, $P_7$, $P_8$, $P_{13}$ | $L_3$, $L_5$, $L_9$ | $D_1$, $D_2$, $D_3$, $D_4$, $D_7$ |
| TRS | 6 | $P_6$ | $L_1$, $L_7$ | $D_2$, $D_3$, $D_4$ |
| RLE | 11 | $P_2$, $P_7$, $P_{10}$, $P_{12}$, $P_{13}$ | $L_1$, $L_3$, $L_7$ | $D_2$, $D_3$, $D_4$ |
| EDU | 11 | $P_2$, $P_7$, $P_{10}$, $P_{13}$ | $L_1$, $L_3$, $L_4$, $L_7$ | $D_2$, $D_3$, $D_4$ |
| HLT | 6 | $P_7$, $P_{10}$, $P_{13}$ | $L_7$ | $D_2$, $D_4$ |
| COM | 12 | $P_2$, $P_7$, $P_{10}$, $P_{12}$, $P_{13}$ | $L_1$, $L_3$, $L_7$ | $D_2$, $D_3$, $D_4$, $D_8$ |
| **All** | **8** | $P_2$, $P_7$, $P_{10}$, $P_{13}$ | $L_7$ | $D_2$, $D_3$, $D_4$ |

Source: Calculations based on BACH database

the relationship of the financial profit to turnover ($P_{13}$), and – as with the analysis of ratios variance between the clusters of industries – the ratio of costs of sales to turnover ($P_7$) and the ratio of value added to turnover ($P_{10}$).

The construction industry is the only industry, for which none of the profitability ratios shows significant differentiation between clusters of countries. Similarly, the trade and transport sectors do not differ significantly in terms of profitability between clusters of countries, which confirms the similarity of industry factors in different countries.

The liquidity ratios significantly different between the clusters include: the ratio of current assets to total assets ($L_7$), the ratio of short-term liquidity ($L_1$) and immediate liquidity ($L_3$). Ratios $L_1$ and $L_3$ also showed the most significant between-group variability in the analysis of variance for the clusters of industries.

When it comes to the debt ratios, in the analysis of variance they show significantly better discriminatory properties for the clusters of countries than for industries. In terms of the significance of between-group differences, the remarkable ratios are: long-term debt ($D_2$), long-term debt relative to equity ($D_3$) and self-financing ratio ($D_4$). Only in the agriculture, fisheries and trade, none of the debt ratios differs significantly between the clusters.

The above grouping process was based on the time means of ratios for the entire study period, which obviously deprives the analysis of one important dimension. However, a similar procedure of cluster analysis performed separately for each year leads to extracting each time the same number of groups and of similar composition. Thus, the uniqueness of Finland was characteristic in each of the 7-year study period. The internal structure of the clusters was quite stable, as shown in Table 4.8.

The clearly visible separateness of Finland and Poland from other countries in almost all years of the research period raises the natural question whether this is due

**Table 4.8** Cluster analysis results based on average ratios for all industries (permanent elements of clusters are bolded)

| Year | Cluster 1 | Cluster 2 |
|---|---|---|
| 1999 | PL, **FIN**, A | **I**, **ES**, **FR**, **P**, **B**, **D**, NL |
| 2000 | **FIN** | PL, A, **P**, **ES**, **FR**, **B**, **D**, **I**, NL |
| 2001 | PL, **FIN** | A, **ES**, **FR**, **P**, **B**, **D**, **I**, NL |
| 2002 | PL, **FIN** | **D**, **I**, A, **ES**, **P**, **B**, **FR**, NL |
| 2003 | PL, **FIN** | **D**, A, **FR**, **P**, **ES**, **B**, **I**, NL |
| 2004 | PL, **FIN**, NL | **D**, **I**, A, **P**, **ES**, **FR**, **B** |
| 2005 | PL, **FIN**, NL | **B**, **ES**, **P**, **FR**, **I**, **D**, A |

Source: Calculations based on BACH database

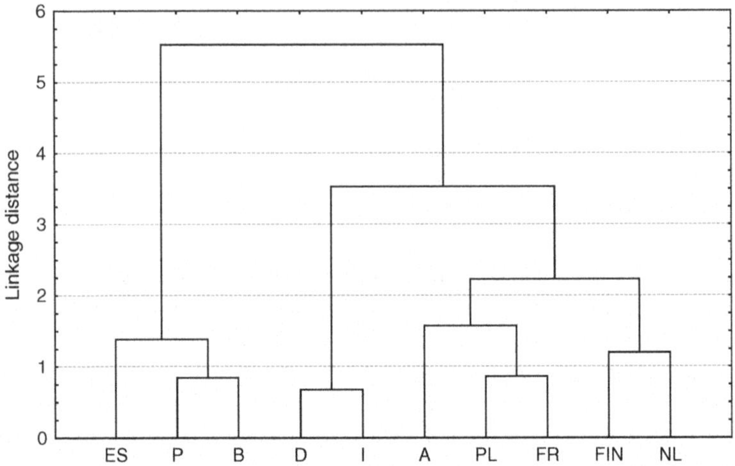


**Fig. 4.8** Tree diagram based on average profitability ratios from 1999 to 2005 for all industries; Ward method, square Euclidean distance (Source: Calculations based on BACH database)

to the difference of ratios of enterprises in these countries in all analytical areas, or whether it is caused by untypical parameters in certain categories of variables. Therefore, it is also expedient to examine separately the formation of clusters in the three categories of ratios. Cluster analysis based on the ratios from only one area (average for the whole period for all industries) does not always have to isolate Polish and Finnish enterprises. The composition and the detailed structure of the resulting groups are shown in Figs. 4.8, 4.9 and 4.10.

Using only the profitability and turnover ratios divides the analysed population of countries into two groups, the first of which (Spain, Portugal and Belgium) is characterised by lower values of ratios. The other cluster, linking the remaining seven countries, is characterised by a slightly higher profitability level, partly because of Finland and Poland, where the highest concentration of maximum values of ratios is recorded. At the same time, however, it is also Poland where there is a number of ratios with the lowest values, such as $P_3$, $L_7$, $L_8$, $D_7$.

The cluster analysis carried out for liquidity ratios leads to distinguishing three clusters of objects, one of which links Poland with Finland. The long distance of the

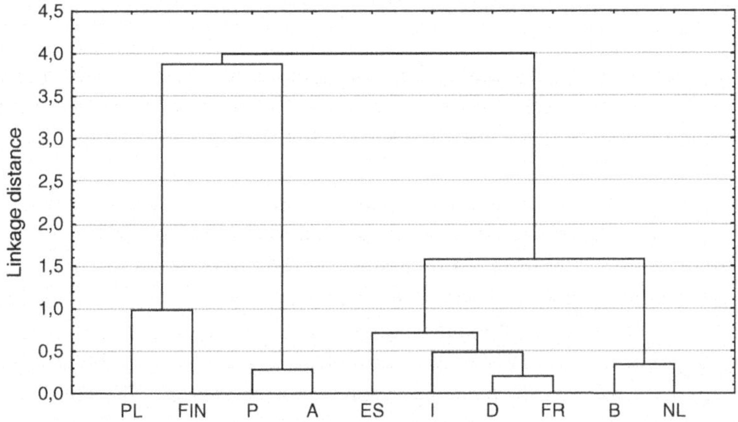


**Fig. 4.9** Tree diagram based on average liquidity ratios from 1999 to 2005 for all industries; Ward method, square Euclidean distance (Source: Calculations based on BACH database)

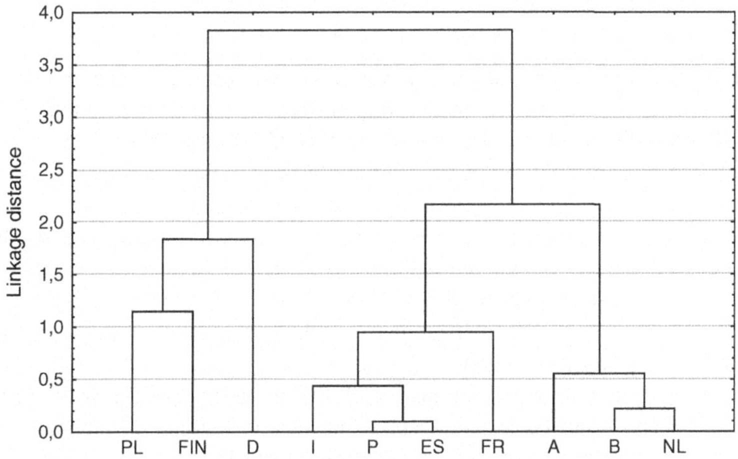


**Fig. 4.10** Tree diagram based on average debt ratios from 1999 to 2005 for all industries; Ward method, square Euclidean distance (Source: Calculations based on BACH database)

two countries from the rest of the objects is undoubtedly associated with high values of most ratios in this category. In Poland the extreme values of ratios fall on $L_5$ (maximum), as well as $L_7$ and $L_8$ (minimum). $L_1$ and $L_3$ take the maximum values in Finland, which means that Finnish companies hold the largest liquidity reserves.

The opposite of Finland in this respect is the Austria, where these ratios usually take the lowest values in the group, which also is confirmed by the largest remoteness of these countries from each other on the graph. The relatively low short-term solvency parameters in Portugal are the reason for which this country is linked directly with Austria.

The separation of Poland, Finland and Germany from other countries revealed in cluster analysis based on the debt ratios is due to unusually high values of the debt ratios in these countries. This means that the Polish, Finnish and German companies are on average the least indebted. However, the use of debt is the most costly in the Polish case. Austria, in turn, is characterised by the low long-term solvency parameters which determines its distant location in relation to Poland.

The high aggregation of ratios (averaged both in time and across industries) in the above analyses allows to draw general conclusions, but also significantly reduces the information about the individual industries. Therefore, in order to detect the similarities and differences between countries in terms of individual industries, similar analyses were performed separately for each sector. This constitutes the content of the Sect. 4.4.

## 4.4 Comparative Cluster Analysis of Countries Across Industries

The main objective of the study described in this section is to conduct a comparative cluster analysis of the selected European Union countries in industries. The object of comparison is the formation of clusters of countries both in terms of their number, size and internal structure. The analysis is meant to detect the industry effect as a factor influencing the financial ratios of companies.

To identify the differences between individual industries, a similar procedure of the cluster analysis was conducted separately for each of them. This time, due to the existence of significant similarities between the different sub-periods of the research, the time means of ratios were used. The results of the analyses are presented graphically in Appendix 24.

The graphs show that the inclusion of the industry specificity in grouping countries reveals significant differences in the formation of clusters. These differences refer both to the number of resulting clusters, which is more volatile than with the cluster analysis for the total of all industries for different years, as well as their internal structure, clearly dependent on the industry.

However, the scale of the observed differences varies depending on the country. In the study population there are countries which are relatively resistant to the industry effect, such as France and Belgium, which remain in the same cluster in most industries, usually characterised by high values of the variables. In contrast to the conclusions from the cluster analysis for all industries – separate consideration of each industry shows a smaller number of two-item clusters formed by Poland and Finland. Such a situation occurred only in the education sector. The reason for a clear separation of the two countries from the rest of the population is the particularly favourable situation in terms of the profitability parameters in Poland and liquidity ratios in Finland. A similar situation is also the case in the agricultural sector, where the cluster formed by Finland and Poland also includes Austria. This time the reason for isolation of these countries is the high profitability in Finland and favourable liquidity and credit parameters in Poland. In other industries, both the cluster structure and location of Poland are much more diverse.

In each of the industries, where there is a characteristic separation of one object from the rest of the countries, it is worth finding the reasons for such a formation of clusters. In the fisheries sector, in which a one-item cluster is formed by Belgium, it is strongly associated with the weakest liquidity and debt parameters in this country (the lowest values of $L_1$, $L_7$ and all debt ratios except $D_8$).

In the mining industry it is the Netherlands that is a separated object. The formation of a one-item cluster by this country also has to do with some of the lowest liquidity and debt ratios. At the same time, however, the country is characterised by significant contrasts in its financial and economic parameters. There is an unusual accumulation of extreme values of the profitability ratios – both maximum (return on equity, return on assets, assets turnover and the ratio of staff costs to added value) and minimum (return on working capital, operating profitability and the ratio of added value to turnover).

Another industry with an unusual structure of the clusters is the hotels sector, in which the distinguished object is Austria. The isolation of this country can be attributed to particularly adverse liquidity characteristics compared to other objects (the lowest short-term liquidity, inventories turnover and the least flexible structure of assets). The country is also characterised by relatively high profitability of the industry, as well as high debt. Very similar economic and financial parameters can also be seen in the education sector, where they are also the reason for the formation of a one-item cluster by Austria.

As for the health sector, the Netherlands owes its isolation in this area to very favourable ratios in all analytical areas. This sector is characterised by high liquidity, low debt, and some of the most favourable parameters of profitability.

Turning now to the structure of other clusters, which – as mentioned – have a much greater variation between industries, it is worth paying attention to certain recurring phenomena. They concern for example frequent occurrence of Spain and Portugal in the same cluster. This is the case in eight industries, which – due to the geographical neighbourhood of these countries – can point to the influence of certain territorial factors affecting economic and financial situation of many industries. A similar effect can be observed in the neighbouring Netherlands and Belgium, which also belong to the same clusters in the agriculture, manufacturing, construction, retail, hotels, education and community services, or Germany and Belgium (mining, energy and trade). It is likely, however, that the location of countries close in geographical terms in the same clusters is an accidental phenomenon, as evidenced by frequent coexistence in the same clusters of the following countries:

- France and Finland (fisheries, mining, energy, construction, trade, real estate),
- Spain and Italy (agriculture, mining, manufacturing, energy, hotels, community services),

- Austria and Finland (agriculture, mining, energy, trade, real estate, community services),
- Italy and Germany (manufacturing, trade).

In order to obtain the information about the similarity of the groupings of countries between industries, the adjusted Rand's measure ($R_{AD}$) was used, the results of which are presented in Table 4.9.

When interpreting the above values of similarity index, it is clear that in most cases, the groupings of countries show little similarity between the industries. A large number of negative values of the measure shows considerable variation of the clustering results. Only in two cases, there is a moderate similarity of the grouping results, which applies to the following pairs: community services and education, community services and health care. Similarly, only two pairs of industries (education and health, agriculture and hospitality) show high similarity of the cluster analysis results, as evidenced by $R_{AD}$ values close to or higher than 0.9.

The biggest dissimilarity of the groupings between industries can be observed in the case of the manufacturing industry and transport, where the adjusted Rand measure is most often negative. It is also confirmed by visual analysis of the tree diagrams for these industries.

## 4.5 Relative Importance of Country and Industry Effect in the Light of Cluster Analysis

So far, the cluster analysis carried out separately for the countries and industries provided relevant information on the similarities of cluster structures in these two sections. However, it did not allow for a fully objective assessment of the relative importance of the country effect and the industry effect. The identification of natural clusters formed by objects, which include the information on both the country of origin and the industry of activity, should provide some information about the dominance of one of the considered effects.

If different industries of the same country tended to be grouped together in the same cluster, it would suggest a greater impact of the country of origin on the business performance than of the industry. At the same time one would expect that the same industry in different countries would be located in different clusters. In other words, the clusters would be more similar to national than industrial division of objects.

If however it is the industry which has a greater impact on business performance than the country, companies from one industry, but form different countries should be assigned to the same cluster, and companies from the same country, regardless of the industry, should be located in different clusters. This would mean that the resulting clusters are closer to the industrial breakdown of the reference population than to the national division.

Clusters, in which it would be difficult to identify the dominant element of a country or an industry, would suggest that it cannot be determined which of the

**Table 4.9** Similarity evaluation of country clusters in industries – adjusted Rand's measure

| Industry | AGR | FSH | MIN | MNF | ELE | CST | TRD | HOT | TRS | RLE | EDU | HLT |
|---|---|---|---|---|---|---|---|---|---|---|---|---|
| FSH | 0.043 | | | | | | | | | | | |
| MIN | −0.111 | 0.048 | | | | | | | | | | |
| MNF | −0.019 | 0.043 | 0.127 | | | | | | | | | |
| ELE | 0.123 | 0.157 | −0.111 | −0.140 | | | | | | | | |
| CST | 0.112 | −0.057 | −0.124 | 0.019 | −0.093 | | | | | | | |
| TRD | −0.050 | 0.030 | −0.129 | −0.134 | 0.048 | −0.162 | | | | | | |
| HOT | 0.857 | 0.082 | −0.148 | 0.095 | 0.174 | 0.129 | 0.027 | | | | | |
| TRS | −0.154 | 0.067 | 0.130 | 0.135 | −0.127 | −0.126 | −0.082 | −0.169 | | | | |
| RLE | 0.071 | −0.004 | 0.054 | −0.018 | −0.113 | 0.028 | −0.074 | −0.059 | −0.014 | | | |
| EDU | 0.234 | −0.082 | −0.154 | −0.306 | 0.248 | 0.277 | 0.128 | 0.182 | −0.231 | −0.154 | | |
| HLT | 0.286 | 0.004 | −0.140 | −0.250 | 0.290 | 0.240 | 0.073 | 0.239 | −0.165 | −0.111 | 0.955 | |
| COM | 0.500 | 0.093 | −0.111 | −0.250 | 0.455 | 0.055 | 0.164 | 0.400 | −0.105 | −0.119 | 0.609 | 0.647 |

Source: Calculations based on BACH database

considered effects has a greater impact on the corporate performance within the analysed population.

The agglomerative cluster analysis is an analytical tool which can be used to solve this research problem. It is performed on the objects formed by the industries in countries, making it possible to determine the nature of clusters as groups of either national or industrial character. The results of the cluster analysis for the two-item objects are shown in Appendix 25. Due to the missing data, the analysis includes a total of 120 cases – excluding the fisheries of Austria and Germany, the education and health care in Italy and Germany, manufacturing in Austria and the agriculture, hotels and community services in Germany.

In order to relatively easily identify the dominant effect in individual clusters, the division of the reference population should be carried out in such a way that the clusters were similar in terms of size and were not too numerous. The greater the number of objects in a cluster, the greater the within-group diversity and thus the more difficult it is to identify the predominant factor. Since the cluster analysis is supposed to form the basis for identifying each group of objects as an industry-dominated or a country-dominated, a natural division seems to be the one in which the number of clusters corresponds either to the number of the analysed countries (10) or industries (13).

With this in mind, as well as the fact that the division of population into ten groups would result in significant differences in their size, the branches of the tree diagram were intersected where the linkage distance is about 9, which resulted in isolating 13 clusters of similar homogeneity and size. Thus, the number of clusters corresponds to the number of industries included in the analysis.

The first cluster from the top is definitely the cluster of a national character, because it houses seven different economic industries, most of which come from three countries: the Netherlands, Belgium and France. In the second cluster, it is also the country effect which is more pronounced, as the group is concentrated mainly around Finland, the Netherlands and Belgium. It is a little more difficult to define the character of the third cluster, which has two dominant types of objects – both as a country (Italy) and an industry (hotels). This is shown by comparison of the number of objects from the same countries and from the same industries, as presented in Table 4.10. The slight numerical superiority of the Italian industries over the hotels industry indicates the national nature of the cluster. However, closer analysis of the sequence of linkages in the cluster suggests that industrial factors are more important here because of the immediate vicinity of the hotel industries from different countries. Given the above, it can be concluded that the cluster in question shows no clear industrial or national character.

The fourth cluster is definitely of an industrial character, dominated by the energy and transport industry. Despite the close presence of different industries from Portugal within the cluster, a closer examination of linkages between these objects shows that the same industries from different countries exhibit greater mutual similarity. For example, the Portuguese energy industry is closer to the Italian energy sector than to the Portuguese transport industry. Similarly, the energy

**Table 4.10** The number of different industries and countries in clusters of industries in countries

| Content | | Number of cluster | | | | | | | | | | | | |
|---|---|---|---|---|---|---|---|---|---|---|---|---|---|---|
| | | **1** | **2** | **3** | **4** | **5** | **6** | **7** | **8** | **9** | **10** | **11** | **12** | **13** |
| Industry | AGR | 1 | 2 | 1 | – | – | – | – | – | 2 | – | – | 1 | 2 |
| | FSH | 2 | 1 | 2 | – | – | – | – | – | 2 | – | – | – | 1 |
| | MIN | – | 1 | – | 1 | 1 | – | 3 | 3 | – | – | – | 1 | – |
| | MNF | – | 3 | 1 | – | – | – | – | – | 1 | – | – | 1 | 3 |
| | ELE | 1 | – | – | 6 | 2 | – | – | 1 | – | – | – | – | – |
| | CST | – | – | 2 | – | – | – | – | – | – | – | 2 | 2 | 4 |
| | TRD | – | – | – | – | – | – | – | – | – | – | 8 | 2 | – |
| | HOT | 3 | – | 4 | – | 2 | – | – | – | – | – | – | – | – |
| | TRS | 2 | – | – | 3 | 4 | – | – | – | – | 1 | – | – | – |
| | RLE | 1 | 2 | – | – | – | – | 2 | – | 3 | 1 | – | – | 1 |
| | EDU | – | 1 | – | – | – | 4 | 1 | – | – | 2 | – | – | – |
| | HLT | 1 | – | – | – | – | 3 | 3 | – | – | 1 | – | – | – |
| | COM | – | 2 | 1 | – | 1 | 1 | – | 1 | – | 2 | – | – | 1 |
| Country | NL | 4 | 4 | 1 | – | 1 | – | 1 | – | – | – | 2 | – | 1 |
| | B | 2 | 3 | – | – | 1 | 1 | 2 | 1 | 1 | – | 1 | – | – |
| | FR | 2 | – | 1 | – | 1 | 2 | 1 | 1 | – | – | 1 | – | 4 |
| | ES | 1 | – | – | – | 4 | 1 | 2 | – | 1 | – | 1 | – | 3 |
| | I | – | – | 5 | 1 | 1 | 1 | – | 1 | – | – | 1 | – | 1 |
| | A | – | – | 1 | 1 | – | – | 1 | – | 1 | 4 | – | 3 | – |
| | D | 1 | – | – | 2 | – | – | 1 | – | 1 | – | 1 | – | 1 |
| | P | – | – | 1 | 2 | 1 | – | 1 | 1 | 2 | 1 | – | 4 | – |
| | FIN | – | 5 | 1 | 1 | – | 2 | – | 1 | – | – | 2 | – | – |
| | PL | 1 | – | 1 | 3 | 1 | 1 | – | – | 2 | 2 | 1 | – | 2 |

Source: Calculations based on BACH database

sector in Germany is more similar to the energy sector in Poland than to the German transport industry.

The dominance of the industry impact is also revealed in the fifth cluster, in which the most frequent industry item is the sector of transport. An equally frequent country item in the group is Spain, which could indicate the influence of domestic factors of similar intensity, but this effect is marked only with respect to the Spanish transport and energy sectors. The prevalence of the national influences, however, is debatable in this case, because a substantial similarity of these two industries was also seen in the previous cluster between other pairs of countries.

Again, the dominance of industrial factors is exemplified by the sixth cluster, which could be called a cluster of education and health due to the most frequent occurrence of these two sectors. This demonstrates the low significance of the country of origin of these sectors for their economic and financial characteristics. The dominance of the industry specificity over the country specificity can be seen for example in the case of Spain, where the education sector is more similar to the French education sector than to any other industry in Spain.

Greater compliance with the industrial than territorial division is also observed in the seventh cluster, which links mainly the industries of health and mining. There is also an obvious dispersion in terms of countries here. The linkages of individual objects within the cluster do not reveal any influence of domestic factors, except from Spain, whose specificity is exhibited by the proximity of the real estate and the mining industry.

A similar phenomenon occurs in the eighth cluster, which is also characterised by the fact that it coincides more with the industrial division of the population than the national one. The dominant industry item here is the mining sector, which also determines the industrial nature of this group. Representation of five different countries in the cluster, without the domination of any of them again suggests the greater importance of industrial factors for the companies in this sector. This cluster is also characterised by the smallest size and the lack of items from the same country.

The industry effect is a little less clear in the ninth cluster, but in this case it is still easier to identify the dominant element in the form of an industry (real estate) than a country. At the same time the cluster links the agriculture and fisheries. The only exception which proves the existence of certain national influences is the case of Poland, where the real estate sector is similar to the Portuguese one, although less similar than to the Polish agricultural sector.

The tenth cluster exhibits different nature. Because of the domination of the Austrian industries, it can be defined as a group of objects revealing the country specific factors.

The 11th cluster, in turn, is again a clearly industrial one, limited only to two types of sectors. It includes the trade sectors of all countries except Austria and Portugal, as well as the construction in Finland and the Netherlands. The absence of any other industries in the group and the simultaneous presence of representatives of the majority of the countries analysed, prove the susceptibility of companies from these two sectors to the industrial factors. However, even in such a clearly industrial cluster, one can also discern some national influences, demonstrated by the bigger mutual similarity of the Dutch trade and construction sectors than their similarity to the corresponding industries in other countries, respectively.

The 12th cluster is a combination of objects of five different industries, but from only two countries – Austria and Portugal. It can therefore be concluded that it is the country effect which has the dominant role in this case. Also, the analysis of linkage sequence of objects within the cluster seems to indicate that its elements are more similar between countries than between industries. It is worth noting that the countries which make the core of the group are characterised by generally poorer economic and financial characteristics, which determine their separation.

The last – the 13th – cluster is another grouping, in addition to the third one, of indeterminate nature. This is because it is a compilation of the impact of both industrial and national factors. In terms of industries the cluster can be defined as a constructing and manufacturing due to the quantitative predominance of these two industries. However, the presence of two countries: France and Spain, is equally strong. To determine which factor has the dominant character a thorough analysis of the linkages within the cluster should be performed. It shows for example that the mutual similarity of the agriculture and manufacturing is higher in France and Spain respectively than between the same industries in both countries. A different phenomenon can be seen in the case of the construction industry, where the objects tend to be linked first by industry, and only then – by country.

To sum up the nature of each cluster in order to evaluate the relative importance of the industry and country factors, it can be concluded that the similarity of objects is determined by country of origin of the company only in 4 of the 13 identified clusters. In most other clusters (7) the industry effect is more prominent. In two remaining clusters the intensity of national and industrial factors is similar, making it impossible to unambiguously determine their nature. At the same time, however, some national influences can be traced in the clearly industrial clusters. Similarly, the industrial specificity can also be observed in the clusters dominated by countries.

Cluster analysis of industries in countries can also be used to indicate which objects are particularly susceptible to the analysed effects. As for the countries, the domestic effects are most pronounced in the case of Finland, the Netherlands, Spain, France and Italy. The industry effect is most readily observable in the trade and construction, and also in the education, mining, real estate, health care and energy.

The largest scattering of industries into various clusters, proving a relatively lower impact of common industry factors concerns such sectors as the community services, agriculture, fisheries and manufacturing. The countries which least marked their character in clusters include Belgium, Austria and Germany. In the last two cases, however, it may be due to the incompleteness of the data and the need to exclude certain industries of these countries from the analysis.

The combination of the two qualitative features of objects, i.e. their industrial and national specificity, has allowed to reclassify these, taking into account both of these parameters simultaneously and to identify the dominant effect in each cluster. The analysis of the composition of individual clusters identified as a result of the agglomerative method shows that the industry effect outweighs the country effect in most of them.

The results of the above analyses create a natural need to find the reasons responsible for the diverse intensity of the impact of national and industrial factors in individual clusters. Using the previous research achievements in the analysed area (discussed earlier in Sect. 2.2), it can be hypothesised that the domestic factors exert a stronger influence on corporate performance in the industries which do not produce export goods, while the industrial factors exert a greater influence in sectors which do produce such goods. With regard to the identified clusters, one would therefore expect that the clusters of a typical industrial character should group the exporting sectors. Similarly, one would expect that the industries of non-exporters are scattered in different clusters and are subject to the domestic factors to a greater extent.

The analysis of the nature of clusters nature in this context only in some cases shows some convergence with the hypothetical expectations regarding the relationship between exporting and susceptibility to the industry factors. The industries which produce export goods, and at the same time are affected by the industry factors more than by the national ones include the mining industry (the eighth cluster), the energy industry (the fourth cluster) and the trade (the 11th cluster). In turn, the group of non-exporting industries (at least not on a large scale) under the influence of domestic factors (equal to or greater than the industrial ones), include the construction (the 13th cluster), the hotels (the third cluster) and the community services (the industry scattered into different clusters).

At the same time, however, the analysis results provide examples, which do not confirm the relationship between exporting and industry specificity. The industries which do not produce typical export goods, but show strong industrial characteristics are in fact: transport (the fifth cluster), real estate (the ninth cluster), education and health (the sixth cluster). In contrast, the typically exporting industries, such as agriculture and fisheries, do not reveal these industrial characteristics.

Summarising the above discussion, it is clear that the hypothesis of a greater impact of industry factors in the sectors producing export goods is not directly and unequivocally confirmed by the conclusions derived from the cluster analysis.

The next stage of the research is aimed at finding the characteristics of individual clusters, whose detailed composition in terms of industries in countries is shown in Table 4.11. It is worth noting that the results of the analysis of variance carried out in relation to clusters of industries in countries show significant between-group differentiation for all the analysed ratios, as shown in Table 4.12.

Since with such a large number of variables the plot of means would be difficult to read, a tabular summary of these values was used instead in order to identify the characteristics of the various clusters (Table 4.13.). The extreme values for each variable were marked: the maximum – bolded, and the minimum – shaded.

The table confirms, inter alia, the following regularities:

- Concentration of the minimum values of profitability and debt ratios in the first cluster, created mainly by the Benelux countries,
- Concentration of a number of minimum values of ratios in the fourth cluster – the energy cluster,
- High financial and economic performance of education and health sectors, forming mainly the sixth cluster,
- Maximum value of many ratios in the eighth cluster of the mining character mainly,
- Concentration of a number of extreme values (both maximum and minimum) in the 11th cluster, dominated by the trade sector.

The characteristic features of the clusters can also be considered separately in the individual areas of analysis. Thus, taking into account the average value of all the ratios from the category of profitability and turnover, the best clusters are successively: the mining cluster no. 8), the mining and health cluster no. 7) and the Austrian cluster no. 10). The worst in this respect is the first cluster of a national level (dominated by the Netherlands and Belgium), the trade cluster no. 11) and the Dutch-Finnish cluster no. 2).

In terms of liquidity, the Austrian cluster no. 10) ranks in the first place, the cluster of the education and health no. 6) comes the second, and the mining cluster

**Table 4.11** Composition of clusters of industries in countries

| Clusters | | | | | | | | | | | | |
|---|---|---|---|---|---|---|---|---|---|---|---|---|
| 1 | 2 | 3 | 4 | 5 | 6 | 7 | 8 | 9 | 10 | 11 | 12 | 13 |
| NL_AGR | NL_MNF | NL_FSH | I_ELE | NL_MIN | B_EDU | NL_HLT | B_ELE | B_RLE | A_TRS | NL_CST | A_MIN | B_CST |
| NL_HOT | FIN_MNF | P_COM | P_ELE | FR_ELE | FR_EDU | D_MIN | P_MIN | P_RLE | A_RLE | NL_TRD | A_CST | FR_CST |
| NL_TRS | NL_COM | I_AGR | P_TRS | ES_ELE | ES_EDU | B_MIN | FR_MIN | PL_AGR | A_EDU | B_TRD | A_TRD | ES_CST |
| B_FSH | FIN_MIN | I_MNF | D_ELE | ES_TRS | FR_HLT | P_EDU | FIN_COM | PL_RLE | A_COM | FIN_TRD | P_AGR | I_RLE |
| B_HOT | NL_RLE | I_FSH | PL_ELE | ES_HOT | PL_HLT | B_HLT | I_MIN | ES_FSH | PL_COM | FIN_CST | P_CST | PL_FSH |
| NL_ELE | NL_EDU | I_CST | A_ELE | P_HOT | I_COM | A_HLT | | D_MNF | P_HLT | FR_TRD | P_MNF | D_CST |
| PL_HOT | B_AGR | PL_CST | PL_TRS | ES_COM | FIN_EDU | FR_RLE | | A_AGR | PL_EDU | I_TRD | P_TRD | PL_MNF |
| FR_FSH | B_MNF | FR_HOT | FIN_ELE | B_TRS | FIN_HLT | ES_RLE | | P_FSH | | D_TRD | | FR_AGR |
| ES_HLT | B_COM | I_HOT | D_TRS | I_TRS | | ES_MIN | | | | ES_TRD | | FR_MNF |
| FR_TRS | FIN_AGR | FIN_HOT | PL_MIN | FIN_TRS | | | | | | PL_TRD | | FR_COM |
| D_RLE | FIN_FSH | A_HOT | | | | | | | | | | ES_AGR |
| | FIN_RLE | | | | | | | | | | | ES_MNF |

Source: Calculations based on BACH database

**Table 4.12** Analysis of variance of selected ratios in relation to clusters of industries in countries

| Profitability and turnover ratios | | | Liquidity ratios | | | Debt ratios | | |
|---|---|---|---|---|---|---|---|---|
| Variable | F | p | Variable | F | p | Variable | F | P |
| $P_2$ | 12.83 | 0.000 | $L_1$ | 10.86 | 0.000 | $D_1$ | 8.291 | 0.000 |
| $P_4$ | 5.240 | 0.000 | $L_3$ | 13.77 | 0.000 | $D_2$ | 13.50 | 0.000 |
| $P_5$ | 5.644 | 0.000 | $L_4$ | 8.484 | 0.000 | $D_3$ | 10.45 | 0.000 |
| $P_6$ | 12.44 | 0.000 | $L_5$ | 3.709 | 0.000 | $D_4$ | 13.88 | 0.000 |
| $P_7$ | 11.71 | 0.000 | $L_7$ | 13.79 | 0.000 | $D_7$ | 6.406 | 0.000 |
| $P_8$ | 17.11 | 0.000 | $L_9$ | 18.77 | 0.000 | $D_8$ | 3.258 | 0.000 |
| $P_{10}$ | 11.74 | 0.000 | $L_{11}$ | 12.96 | 0.000 | | | |
| $P_{12}$ | 9.224 | 0.000 | | | | | | |
| $P_{13}$ | 3.879 | 0.000 | | | | | | |

Source: Calculations based on BACH database

**Table 4.13** The mean ratios for clusters of industries in countries

| | Cluster | | | | | | | | | | | | |
|---|---|---|---|---|---|---|---|---|---|---|---|---|---|
| Ratio | 1 | 2 | 3 | 4 | 5 | 6 | 7 | 8 | 9 | 10 | 11 | 12 | 13 |
| $P_2$ | 0,231 | 0,338 | 0,223 | 0,680 | 0,587 | 0,313 | 0,826 | **0,914** | 0,223 | 0,427 | 0,119 | 0,418 | 0,242 |
| $P_4$ | 0,484 | 0,211 | 0,434 | 0,150 | 0,738 | 0,588 | 0,565 | 0,800 | 0,242 | 0,591 | 0,412 | 0,369 | **0,829** |
| $P_5$ | 0,179 | 0,324 | 0,180 | 0,501 | 0,492 | 0,437 | 0,611 | **0,973** | 0,562 | 0,620 | 0,456 | 0,730 | 0,355 |
| $P_6$ | 0,140 | 0,398 | 0,894 | 0,834 | 0,255 | 0,590 | 0,283 | 0,776 | 0,712 | **0,904** | 0,527 | 0,852 | 0,438 |
| $P_7$ | 0,603 | 0,508 | 0,522 | 0,601 | 0,693 | **0,950** | 0,841 | 0,590 | 0,582 | 0,779 | 0,069 | 0,185 | 0,459 |
| $P_8$ | 0,220 | 0,259 | 0,382 | 0,126 | 0,245 | 0,488 | 0,157 | 0,277 | 0,151 | 0,383 | **0,946** | 0,618 | 0,451 |
| $P_{10}$ | 0,568 | 0,512 | 0,441 | 0,561 | 0,608 | **0,928** | 0,852 | 0,601 | 0,460 | 0,530 | 0,073 | 0,191 | 0,395 |
| $P_{12}$ | 0,311 | 0,394 | 0,228 | 0,868 | 0,578 | 0,098 | 0,354 | **0,885** | 0,274 | 0,498 | 0,336 | 0,404 | 0,283 |
| $P_{13}$ | 0,211 | 0,377 | 0,097 | 0,470 | 0,139 | 0,030 | **0,551** | 0,248 | 0,534 | 0,181 | 0,114 | 0,016 | 0,075 |
| $L_1$ | 0,213 | 0,390 | 0,231 | 0,110 | 0,215 | 0,377 | 0,772 | 0,789 | 0,572 | 0,602 | 0,272 | **0,855** | 0,380 |
| $L_3$ | 0,267 | 0,223 | 0,249 | 0,223 | 0,241 | 0,627 | **0,838** | 0,637 | 0,445 | 0,785 | 0,097 | 0,225 | 0,241 |
| $L_4$ | 0,323 | 0,104 | 0,244 | 0,693 | 0,537 | **0,804** | 0,232 | 0,270 | 0,072 | 0,518 | 0,166 | 0,098 | 0,132 |
| $L_5$ | 0,544 | 0,293 | 0,596 | 0,459 | 0,322 | 0,536 | 0,193 | 0,630 | 0,217 | 0,426 | **0,715** | 0,433 | 0,400 |
| $L_7$ | 0,244 | 0,473 | 0,500 | 0,048 | 0,172 | 0,438 | 0,372 | 0,297 | 0,331 | 0,405 | **0,891** | 0,838 | 0,723 |
| $L_9$ | 0,926 | 0,738 | 0,491 | 0,738 | **0,989** | 0,884 | 0,913 | 0,639 | 0,718 | 0,599 | 0,146 | 0,220 | 0,695 |
| $L_{11}$ | 0,202 | 0,267 | 0,896 | 0,664 | 0,056 | 0,370 | 0,232 | 0,578 | 0,634 | 0,806 | 0,592 | **0,926** | 0,394 |
| $D_1$ | 0,122 | 0,232 | 0,107 | 0,209 | 0,515 | 0,712 | 0,372 | **0,996** | 0,125 | 0,398 | 0,263 | 0,465 | 0,406 |
| $D_2$ | 0,128 | 0,480 | 0,302 | 0,362 | 0,445 | 0,703 | 0,590 | 0,840 | 0,862 | 0,636 | **0,887** | 0,867 | 0,821 |
| $D_3$ | 0,195 | 0,504 | 0,418 | 0,459 | 0,748 | 0,828 | 0,758 | **0,981** | 0,891 | 0,470 | 0,826 | 0,664 | 0,888 |
| $D_4$ | 0,155 | 0,351 | 0,154 | 0,519 | 0,594 | 0,570 | 0,770 | **0,981** | 0,861 | 0,555 | 0,173 | 0,520 | 0,383 |
| $D_7$ | 0,346 | 0,614 | 0,508 | 0,249 | 0,465 | 0,735 | 0,180 | 0,550 | 0,569 | **0,847** | 0,795 | 0,560 | 0,803 |
| $D_8$ | 0,869 | 0,699 | 0,820 | 0,475 | 0,498 | 0,871 | 0,481 | 0,678 | 0,628 | 0,763 | **0,877** | 0,678 | 0,873 |

Minimum values are shaded, maximum values – **bolded**

Source: Calculations based on BACH database

no. 8) – the third. A limited ability to cover current liabilities is a characteristic feature of the Dutch-Finnish cluster no. 2), the transport cluster no. 5) and again the first cluster of the Benelux countries.

The best performing clusters in the area of solvency are: the mining cluster no. 8), the education and health cluster no. 6) and the 13th cluster, which links the industries of construction and manufacturing, as well as France and Spain. On average, the Dutch and Belgian cluster no. 1), the energy cluster no. 4) and the cluster dominated by Italy and hotels industry no. 3) are characterised by the highest debt.

To summarise the presented analysis, it can be concluded that all the identified clusters show quite distinctive economic and financial characteristics in at least one of the three analytical areas. These features can be observed both in the clusters of industrial character, as well as in the clusters dominated by countries. The distinct characteristics of certain industries, particularly evident in relation to the mining, trade and construction, which determined the structure of clusters, confirm the prevalence of the industry effect over the country effect. The pattern observed in most clusters is the greater compatibility of their composition with the industrial breakdown of the population than with the national classification. This does not mean, however, that corporate performance is not affected by the country factors, but that on average the importance of the country specificity is slightly smaller in comparison with the significance of the industry specificity. The structure of clusters also confirms that the impact of national and industrial factors is not uniform across all objects, as mentioned in the conclusions from agglomerative cluster analysis.

# Chapter 5
# Factors Affecting Corporate Performance in Countries and Industries

## 5.1 Factors Influencing Corporate Performance in Countries and Industries

First, the procedure of the factor analysis was conducted on the objects treated as industries in countries in order to initially verify the number of factors. Since the use of Kaiser's criterion would lead to retaining too many factors (eight), difficult to interpret and not simplifying the data structure significantly, the Cattell's scree plot test shown in Fig. 5.1. was applied in order to determine the optimal number of factors. According to this test, the first four factors should be retained, as that is where the scree plot shows a separation between the most important components and the less important ones.

After taking into account the readability of the factors, only the first three of them were retained for further analysis. Although the first three factors (from the total of eight, for which the eigenvalues are greater than 1.0) explain only a little more than half of the total variance, as shown in Table 5.1, their contribution in explaining the total variance exceed 10 % in each case, which was also taken into account when selecting the factors.

The values of the factor loadings, shown in Table 5.2, show which variables affect the retained factors. In order to obtain a clear structure of the factor loadings (also referred to as the simple structure), i.e. such factors which are characterised by high loadings with some variables and low with the other, a procedure of factor rotation was employed (Comrey & Lee, 1992). Of the many available rotation strategies, the most commonly used method of *Varimax* normalised was applied.

As shown in the Table 5.2., only few variables are significantly correlated with the factors. The first factor is positively correlated with the return on sales, and negatively with the total assets turnover and fixed assets turnover, as well as the ratio of assets elasticity. The second factor is related to the profitability of assets, current liquidity, interest cover ratio and the relation of long-term debt to equity. The third factor is positively correlated with the ratios of costs of sales to turnover,

J. Koralun-Bereźnicka, *Corporate Performance*, Contributions to Management Science, 
DOI 10.1007/978-3-319-00345-0_5, © Springer International Publishing Switzerland 2013

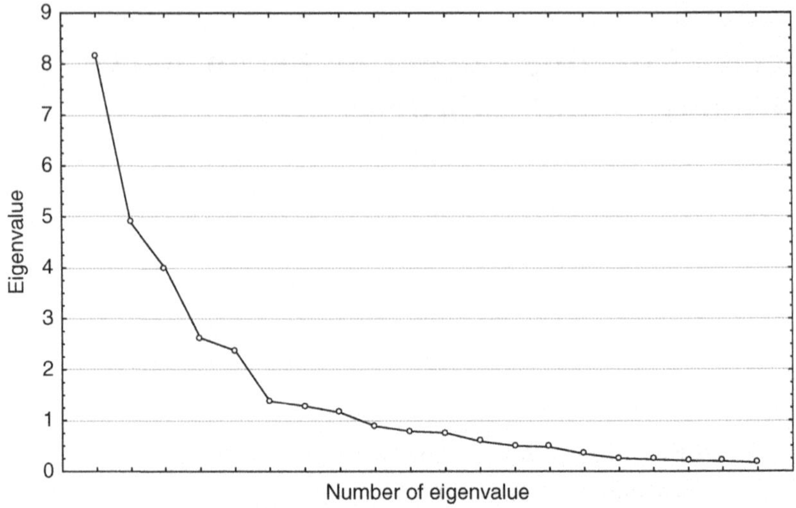


**Fig. 5.1** Scree plot test for industries in countries (Source: Calculations based on BACH database)

**Table 5.1** Eigenvalues of factors for industries in countries

| Factor | Eigenvalue | % of total variance | Cumulative eigenvalue | Cumulative % of total variance |
|---|---|---|---|---|
| 1 | 8.159 | 25.50 | 8.16 | 25.50 |
| 2 | 4.896 | 15.30 | 13.06 | 40.80 |
| 3 | 4.005 | 12.52 | 17.06 | 53.31 |
| 4 | 2.626 | 8.21 | 19.69 | 61.52 |
| 5 | 2.376 | 7.42 | 22.06 | 68.94 |
| 6 | 1.385 | 4.33 | 23.45 | 73.27 |
| 7 | 1.285 | 4.01 | 24.73 | 77.29 |
| 8 | 1.156 | 3.61 | 25.89 | 80.90 |

Source: Calculations based on BACH database

added value to turnover and inventory to working capital, and inversely with the ratio of staff costs to turnover.

Due to the fact that the variables correlated with the factors come from different categories, it is more difficult to formulate a generalised interpretation of the factors. Nevertheless, within the group of ratios which correlate with the first factor, the most common element is the assets. Therefore this factor could be associated with the structure of the business assets. The interpretation of the second factor is even more complicated due to the lack of a characteristic common element of the ratios correlated with the factor. However, since this factor is mainly affected by the debt and liquidity ratio, the most reasonable interpretation seems the solvency. The most frequent item occurring in the construction of the ratios correlated with

**Table 5.2** Factor loadings for industries in countries; rotation *Varimax* normalised (the absolute values > 0.7 are highlighted)

| Variable | Factor 1 | Factor 2 | Factor 3 |
|---|---|---|---|
| $P_1$ | 0.745 | 0.331 | 0.224 |
| $P_2$ | 0.541 | 0.608 | 0.054 |
| $P_3$ | 0.494 | 0.555 | -0.036 |
| $P_4$ | -0.082 | 0.124 | 0.074 |
| $P_5$ | 0.111 | 0.758 | -0.273 |
| $P_6$ | 0.103 | 0.147 | -0.354 |
| $P_7$ | 0.229 | 0.169 | 0.824 |
| $P_8$ | -0.767 | 0.043 | -0.387 |
| $P_9$ | -0.808 | 0.040 | -0.389 |
| $P_{10}$ | 0.230 | 0.185 | 0.871 |
| $P_{11}$ | 0.133 | 0.010 | -0.881 |
| $P_{12}$ | 0.652 | 0.301 | -0.429 |
| $P_{13}$ | 0.545 | 0.057 | 0.076 |
| $L_1$ | -0.104 | 0.638 | 0.074 |
| $L_2$ | 0.057 | 0.706 | 0.438 |
| $L_3$ | 0.070 | 0.597 | 0.510 |
| $L_4$ | 0.140 | 0.044 | 0.341 |
| $L_5$ | -0.213 | -0.060 | -0.321 |
| $L_6$ | -0.694 | 0.166 | 0.319 |
| $L_7$ | -0.850 | 0.072 | -0.220 |
| $L_8$ | -0.813 | 0.240 | 0.085 |
| $L_9$ | 0.405 | 0.016 | 0.719 |
| $L_{10}$ | 0.351 | 0.152 | 0.595 |
| $L_{11}$ | -0.091 | 0.016 | -0.475 |
| $D_1$ | -0.164 | 0.696 | 0.071 |
| $D_2$ | -0.501 | 0.577 | -0.269 |
| $D_3$ | -0.263 | 0.717 | -0.167 |
| $D_4$ | 0.398 | 0.688 | 0.107 |
| $D_5$ | 0.156 | 0.044 | -0.348 |
| $D_6$ | -0.682 | 0.304 | -0.161 |
| $D_7$ | -0.679 | 0.100 | -0.070 |
| $D_8$ | -0.338 | -0.116 | -0.112 |

Source: Calculations based on BACH database

the third factor is the turnover, so this factor may be associated with the broadly defined sales profitability.

It is likely that the factor analysis carried out in two other sections – separately for countries and industries – will allow for a more precise identification of the components that affect corporate performance in these categories.

## 5.2 Factors Influencing Corporate Performance in Countries

When performing the factor analysis for each country, the target number of factors – as in the previously analysed case – was established as three, which was to preserve the greater comparability of the factors in the different sections. The results of the factor analysis for the countries in the form of the list of variables highly correlated ($|r| > 0.7$) with individual factors are presented in Table 5.3, which also shows the percentage of all three factors in explaining the total variance.

**Table 5.3** Variables with factor loadings > 0.7 in the factor analysis for countries

| Country | Factor 1 | Factor 2 | Factor 3 | % of explained variance |
|---|---|---|---|---|
| NL | $P_7, P_{10}, P_{11},$<br>$L_1, L_2, L_3, L_5, L_6,$<br>$D_8$ | $P_1, P_2, P_3, P_4, P_5, P_{12},$<br>$L_4,$<br>$D_1$ | $P_8, P_9,$<br>$L_7, L_8$<br>$D_2, D_6, D_7$ | 72.9 |
| B | $P_2, P_7, P_8, P_9, P_{10},$<br>$L_7, L_9, L_{10},$<br>$D_7$ | $P_2, P_3, P_5,$<br>$L_1, L_2,$<br>$D_2, D_3, D_4$ | $P_6,$<br>$L_5$ | 70.6 |
| FR | $P_5, P_8, P_9,$<br>$L_6, L_7, L_8$<br>$D_1, D_2, D_3, D_6, D_7$ | $P_1, P_2, P_3, P_4,$<br>$L_2,$<br>$D_4$ | $P_7, P_{10}, P_{11},$<br>$L_4, L_{10}$ | 70.5 |
| ES | $P_8, P_{13},$<br>$L_1, L_2,$<br>$D_1$ | $P_5, P_6, P_7, P_{10}, P_{11},$<br>$L_{10},$<br>$D_3$ | $P_1, P_2, P_{12},$<br>$L_7, L_8,$<br>$D_7$ | 66.4 |
| I | $P_2, P_3, P_4, P_5, P_{13},$<br>$L_2, L_3,$<br>$D_1, D_4$ | $P_7, P_{10}, P_{11}$<br>$L_4, L_5, L_9, L_{10}, L_{11}$<br>$D_5, D_8$ | $L_6, L_7, L_8$<br>$D_6, D_7$ | 80.4 |
| A | $P_1, P_5, P_8, P_9, P_{12},$<br>$L_7, L_8$ | $P_6, P_7, P_{10}, P_{11}$<br>$L_9, L_{11}$<br>$D_5$ | $P_3$<br>$L_1, L_2, L_5$ | 71.1 |
| D | $P_1, P_2, P_7, P_8, P_9, P_{10},$ $P_{13},$<br>$L_5, L_7, L_8, L_9, L_{11}$<br>$D_6$ | $L_1, L_2,$<br>$D_1, D_3, D_4, D_8$ | $P_3, P_4, P_5, P_6,$<br>$L_4, L_{10},$<br>$D_7$ | 87.9 |
| P | $P_1,$<br>$L_1, L_2, L_6, L_7, L_8$<br>$D_2$ | $P_7, P_{10}, P_{11},$<br>$L_9$ | $P_3, P_5$ | 61.9 |
| FIN | $P_8, P_9,$<br>$L_7, L_8,$<br>$D_2, D_3, D_5, D_6, D_7$ | $P_2, P_3, P_5,$<br>$L_1,$<br>$D_4$ | $P_7, P_{10}, P_{11},$<br>$L_3, L_6$ | 74.9 |
| PL | $P_8, P_9,$<br>$L_7, L_8, L_9, L_{11}$ | $P_1, P_2, P_{13},$<br>$D_6, D_7, D_8$ | $P_7$<br>$L_1, L_2, L_3, L_6$ | 59.3 |
| All countries | $P_5, P_{10}, P_{11},$<br>$L_1, L_2, L_3, L_6, L_7, L_8,$<br>$D_1, D_4$ | $P_7,$<br>$L_9, L_{10}, L_{11},$<br>$D_2, D_5$ | $P_1, P_2, P_3,$ $P_{13},$<br>$L_5,$<br>$D_6$ | 75.7 |

Source: Calculations based on BACH database

Despite the significant differences between countries in terms of the variables correlated with the individual factors, one can attempt to find some characteristic common features for all countries and to formulate a generalised interpretation. The first factor is correlated with the largest number of variables, the most common of which are the ratios characterising the liquidity and the structure of current assets. At the same time, however, the variables illustrating assets turnover often affect this factor. Therefore, in simple terms, the discussed factor can be interpreted as the elasticity of assets.

The second factor, in turn, could be associated primarily with the operating and sales profitability, as well as the ratio of costs of sales to turnover and the ratios related to working capital. Therefore, the most appropriate generalised interpretation of the factor is the company's ability to generate profits.

The last factor is most often associated with the company's ability to service debt, as well as the profitability of sales, which is why it may be called a solvency factor. It should be emphasised, however, that the structure of factors is different depending on the country, which indicates the impact of country specificity on the corporate performance. At the same time the percentage of variance explained by the three factors is similar across all countries, and also much higher in comparison with the factor analysis performed on the binary objects, i.e. industries in countries.

## 5.3 Factors Influencing Corporate Performance in Industries

A similar factor analysis was also conducted for the cross-industry section, which on the one hand, allows identifying factors for the different industries, and on the other hand – comparing the structure of these factors with the factors identified for countries. The variables which are highly correlated ($|r| > 0.7$) with individual factors relating to the industries, as well as the contribution of the factors in explaining the total variance are shown in Table 5.4.

Due to the dissimilarity between the structures of the factors in each industry, as in the case of the differences between countries, these factors should be in fact interpreted separately for each object. Nevertheless, when analysing the factors in terms of the variables most frequently highly correlated with the factors, it can be concluded that the first of these factors is mainly related to the operational and sales profitability, the ratios of assets flexibility, long-term debt and capital structure. The first factor is therefore affected by the ratios from all categories of analysis. In general, this factor can thus be interpreted as the elasticity of the assets and liabilities.

The situation is similar in the case of other factors. The second one tends to be associated with the ratios of working capital (its profitability, turnover and the relation of long-term debt to working capital), and therefore it seems that this factor is mostly affected by the size of working capital. The third factor is often correlated with liquidity, debtors turnover and the interest cover ratio, so in simple terms the factor can be interpreted as solvency (both long- and short-term).

Comparison of the structure of factors in the cross-industry section with the cross-country section reveals that the corporate performance in industries and in countries is actually affected by quite similar factors. However, it should be borne in mind that when trying to identify the industry- and country-specific factors, it is not possible to fully isolate these two effects, as each industry contains a number of characteristics of the country in which it operates. Similarly, the situation of enterprises in a given country to some extent is also determined by the structure

**Table 5.4** Variables with factor loadings > 0.7 in the factor analysis for industries

| Industry | Factor 1 | Factor 2 | Factor 3 | % of explained variance |
|---|---|---|---|---|
| AGR | $P_1, P_2, P_7, P_{10}, P_{11}, P_{13},$<br>$L_6, L_7, L_8,$<br>$D_2, D_3, D_4, D_6$ | $P_6,$<br>$L_4, L_{11},$<br>$D_5$ | $P_5, P_8,$<br>$L_1, L_2, L_3, L_5,$<br>$D_1$ | 75.1 |
| FSH | $L_4, L_7, L_{10},$<br>$D_3, D_6, D_7$ | $P_1, P_3, P_6, P_{12},$<br>$L_9, L_{11},$<br>$D_5$ | $P_7, P_{10},$<br>$L_2, L_3, L_5, L_6,$<br>$D_1$ | 67.8 |
| MIN | $P_1, P_2, P_7, P_{10}, P_{11}, P_{12}, P_{13},$<br>$L_6, L_7, L_8,$<br>$D_2, D_4, D_6, D_7, D_8$ | $P_5, P_6, P_8,$<br>$L_4, L_{11},$<br>$D_1, D_5$ | $L_1, L_2$ | 78.3 |
| MNF | $P_2, P_3, P_5, P_6, P_8, P_9, P_{13},$<br>$L_7, L_8,$<br>$D_6$ | $P_4, P_7,$<br>$L_5, L_9, L_{10}, L_{11}$ | $L_1, L_3,$<br>$D_4$ | 75.0 |
| ELE | $P_1, P_8, P_9,$<br>$D_2, D_3$ | $P_6, P_{12},$<br>$L_1, L_2, L_9, L_{11},$<br>$D_5$ | $P_3, P_5, P_7, P_{11}$ | 73.7 |
| CST | $P_3, P_5,$<br>$L_2, L_3, L_4, L_{10}, L_{11}$ | $P_7, P_8, P_{10}, P_{11}, P_{13},$<br>$L_5,$<br>$D_6$ | $P_1, P_9,$<br>$L_7,$<br>$D_2, D_3, D_5$ | 67.9 |
| TRD | $P_1, P_2, P_3, P_5, P_9,$<br>$L_7$ | $P_6,$<br>$L_1, L_2, L_6, L_9, L_{11},$<br>$D_5$ | $P_7, P_{11}, P_{13},$<br>$L_{10},$<br>$D_6, D_7$ | 69.1 |
| HOT | $P_7,$<br>$L_4, L_7, L_8, L_{10},$<br>$D_3, D_6, D_7$ | $P_6, P_{13},$<br>$L_8, L_{11},$<br>$D_4, D_5$ | $P_8, P_9,$<br>$L_3, L_5, L_6,$<br>$D_1$ | 73.1 |
| TRS | $P_6,$<br>$L_9, L_{11},$<br>$D_2, D_3, D_4, D_8$ | $L_1, L_2, L_5, L_7, L_8$ | $P_1, P_2, P_{10}$ | 58.3 |
| RLE | $P_1, P_2, P_7, P_{10}, P_{11},$<br>$L_1, L_2, L_3, L_6, L_7, L_8,$<br>$D_2, D_3, D_4$ | $P_3, P_8, P_9, P_{13},$<br>$D_1, D_6, D_8$ | $P_6,$<br>$L_9, L_{10}, L_{11},$<br>$D_5$ | 82.2 |
| EDU | $P_1, P_2, P_3, P_7, P_{10}, P_{11}, P_{13},$<br>$L_1, L_2, L_3, L_4, L_6, L_7, L_8,$<br>$D_2, D_3, D_4, D_6$ | $P_6,$<br>$L_9, L_{10}, L_{11},$<br>$D_5$ | $P_4, P_5, P_8,$<br>$L_5,$<br>$D_1$ | 88.6 |
| HLT | $P_1, P_2, P_7, P_9, P_{10}, P_{11}, P_{13},$<br>$L_6, L_7, L_8, L_{10},$<br>$D_3, D_4, D_6$ | $P_3, P_5, P_{12},$<br>$L_1, L_2, L_3$ | $P_6,$<br>$L_9, L_{11},$<br>$D_5, D_7$ | 81.4 |
| COM | $P_1, P_2, P_7, P_{10}, P_{11}, P_{12}, P_{13},$<br>$L_1, L_2, L_3, L_6, L_7, L_8$<br>$D_2, D_3, D_4, D_6, D_8$ | $P_3, P_4, P_5,$<br>$L_5,$<br>$D_1$ | $P_6,$<br>$L_9, L_{11},$<br>$D_5, D_7$ | 90.0 |

(continued)

**Table 5.4** (continued)

| Industry | Factor 1 | Factor 2 | Factor 3 | % of explained variance |
|---|---|---|---|---|
| All industries | $P_1$, $P_2$, $P_7$, $P_{10}$, $P_{11}$, $P_{13}$, $L_6$, $L_7$, $L_8$, $D_2$, $D_3$, $D_4$, $D_6$ | $P_6$, $L_4$, $L_{11}$, $D_5$ | $P_5$, $P_8$, $L_1$, $L_2$, $L_3$, $L_5$, $D_1$ | 78.0 |

Source: Calculations based on BACH database

of the industries. Therefore it is risky to attempt to precisely determine to what extent the industrial factors are responsible for corporate performance, and to what extent – the domestic factors.

## 5.4 Two-Dimensional Map of Countries and Industries

The purpose of multidimensional scaling algorithm is to reconstruct the ranked order of the distances between the analysed objects. This method allows organising objects in a space of a declared number of dimensions in such a way as to reproduce the observed distances, so that the distances can be explained by the means of hidden dimensions. Multidimensional scaling (MDS) is therefore a way to locate objects in such an efficient manner, that the resulting configuration is the best approximation of the actual distances. The most common measure of assessing the quality of representing the observed matrix of distances by a given configuration is *stress* (*Fi*).[1]

In the MDS procedure, there is the problem of determining the optimal number of dimensions. The bigger it is, the smaller the value of *stress*, indicating a better fit of the reconstituted matrix to the observed one, but also proportionally the more difficult it is to interpret these dimensions. Given the fact that the study aims at reducing the complexity of the observed data, i.e. explaining the distance matrix by using a smaller number of hidden dimensions, a number of options of the final configuration were analysed including different number of dimensions. The criterion for deciding how many dimensions should be interpreted was the transparency of the final two-dimensional configuration.

Similarly to the previous analyses, the multidimensional scaling algorithm, designed to simplify the data structure and visualise the results, was applied in three sections: for the industries – based on average ratios for all countries, for countries – based on average ratios for all industries, and for the industries in countries. In all three situations the time means of ratios were used. The results of the analyses in the form of scatter plots are shown in Figs. 5.2, 5.3, 5.4, and 5.5.

Location of industries in the scatter plot largely confirms the similarity of objects resulting from the earlier performed cluster analysis. It is evidenced for example,

[1] $Fi = \sum [d_{ij} - f(\delta_{ij})]^2$, where: $d_{ij}$ – reproduced distances for a given number of dimensions, $\delta_{ij}$ – input data (distances observed), $f(\delta_{ij})$ – non-metric monotonic transformation of the observed input data (distances).

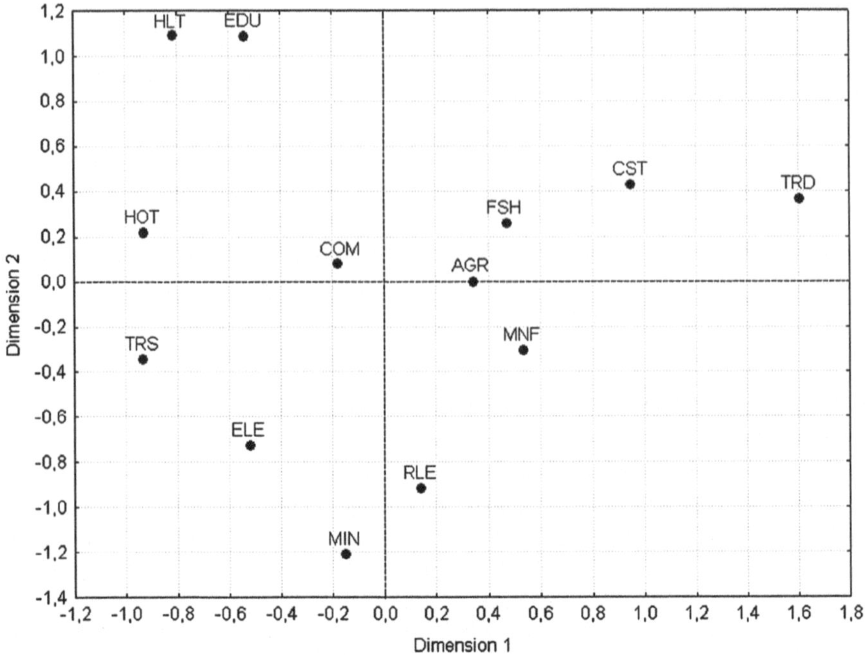


**Fig. 5.2** Two-dimensional scatter plot of industries (Source: Calculations based on BACH database)

by the industries of agriculture, fisheries, construction, manufacturing and trade which were placed in the same cluster and now are located in the same quadrant.

The next and the most challenging stage of the analysis is to assign meaning to the dimensions. The scatter plot of industries for which the stress value is 0.167, allows for a clear interpretation of the two dimensions. Since the industries located in the first and fourth quadrant are characterised by generally higher debt ratios than the objects of the other two quadrants, the first dimension can be broadly interpreted as solvency. The other dimension reflects the profitability and turnover ratios, hence its reasonable interpretation seems to be the effectiveness, but the objects in the first and second quadrant are characterised by generally lower parameters in this area than the industries in the third and fourth quadrant.

The scatter plot shown in Fig. 5.3. is the result of multidimensional scaling performed for countries. The stress value for the configuration is 0.133. The dimensions can be interpreted as follows.

A glance at the values of ratios for different countries indicates that the first dimension can be described as the profitability, because taking into account the average for all industries, Finland definitely stands out positively from the rest of the countries, in contrast to Spain, located at the opposite end of the graph. The analysis of mean values of ratios for the countries situated at the opposite ends of the other axis, suggests that this dimension can be described as solvency,

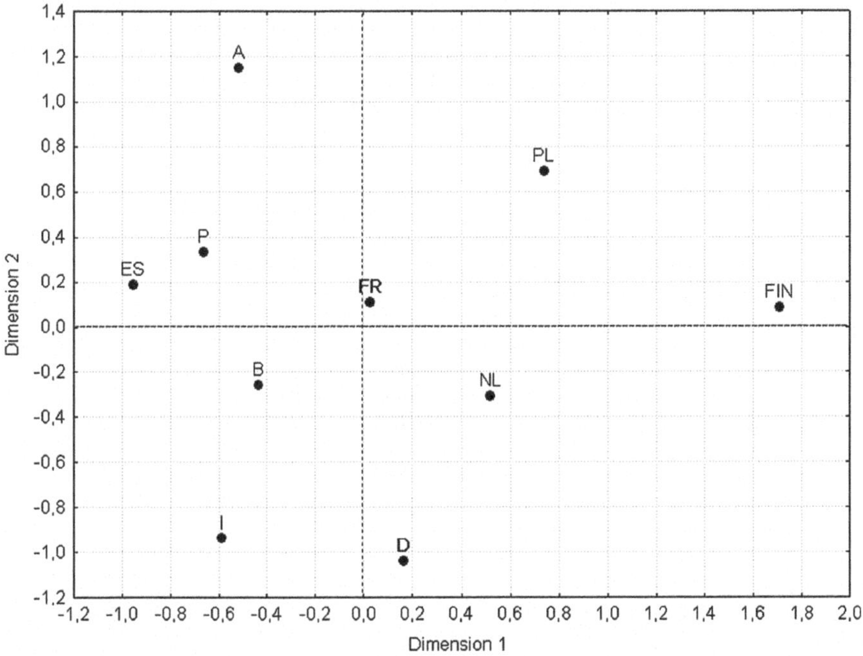


**Fig. 5.3** Two-dimensional scatter plot of countries (Source: Calculations based on BACH database)

both long- and short-term. The objects located in the third and fourth quadrant of the graph are characterised by favourable values of the parameters in this category.

As for the analysis of the binary objects, i.e. the industries in countries, there are 120 such items in the examined population. In the multidimensional scaling procedure, the maximum number of objects that can be included in one graph is limited to 90. Therefore, it is necessary to divide the analysis into two stages – e.g. for five-item groups of countries. Such a division also makes the graphs clearer.

The interpretation of the dimensions of these charts in both cases is quite similar. The first dimension for both groups of countries can be interpreted as solvency, as evidenced e.g. by the extreme position of the Italian mining industry with good solvency and the opposed Italian trade sector with a much poorer performance in terms of debt and liquidity. However, in the first group of countries (Fig. 5.4.) the objects from the first and fourth quadrant are characterised by more favourable parameters in this respect than the objects from the second and third quadrants, whereas in the second group of countries (Fig. 5.5.) – the other way round. The second dimension corresponds to the profitability or – more broadly – effectiveness, since it also reflects the turnover ratios. The objects of the first and second quadrant of both graphs are usually more effective than the objects of the third and fourth quadrant.

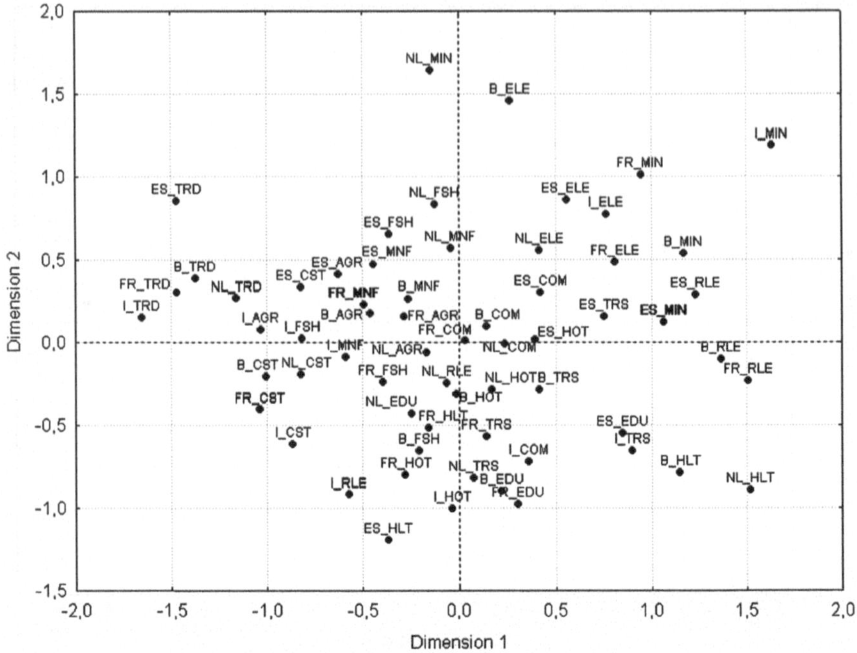


**Fig. 5.4** Two-dimensional scatter plot of industries in countries for the 1st group of countries: NL, B, FR, ES, I (Source: Calculations based on BACH database)

The location of objects treated as industries in countries on the scatter plots can also provide valuable information on the country and industry effects, which are the main subject of the study. Proximity of the same of industries from different countries in the graphs, particularly visible in the case of the trade, construction, mining and energy industry, proves a generally greater similarity between the industries than countries. However there are also some regularities revealing the impact of the country effect, such as for example the close location of different industries from Finland and the Netherlands.

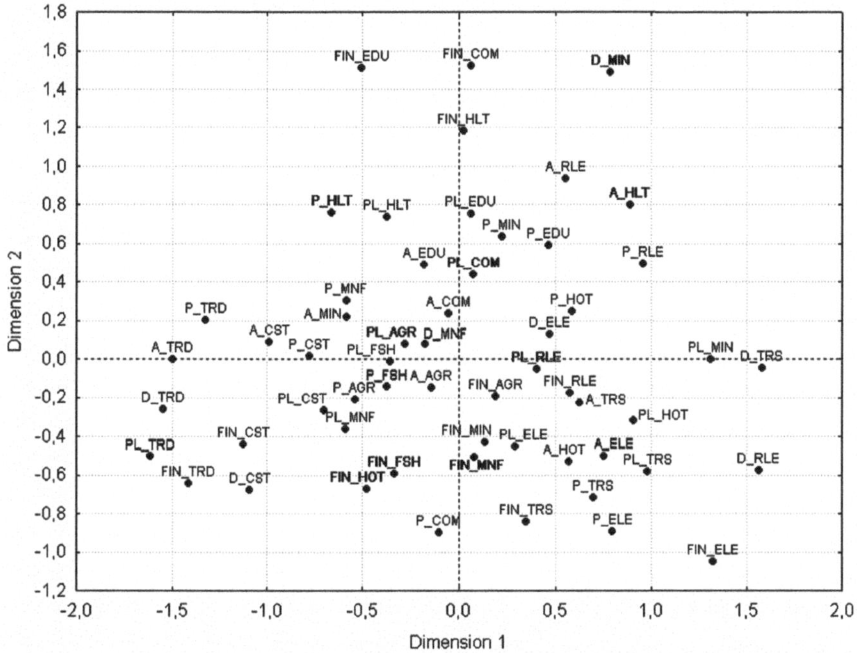


**Fig. 5.5** Two-dimensional scatter plot of industries in countries for the 2nd group of countries: A, D, P, FIN, PL (Source: Calculations based on BACH database)

# Ending

One of the most important economic changes taking place on the European continent is the economic integration, initiated in the middle of the previous century and still progressing, both in terms of quality of this process and its territorial expansion. One of the main effects of these changes, and also the motives behind the efforts to integrate, is to reduce the economic disparities dividing the countries unified in the European structures, i.e. to decrease the differences in various economic, social, financial or political areas. The disappearance of these differences may occur at various levels. On the one hand it concerns the economic convergence among the countries. On the other hand, it may relate to the harmonisation of the various sectors of the economies in one or several countries. Everything is related to the influence of the factors specific to individual countries, as well as the industrial factors that are typical for certain types of sector or sectors. The occurrence of these factors and their impact on businesses operating in different countries and industries is referred to as the country and industry effect, respectively.

The evaluation of the relative importance of the two effects is the subject of many studies, which aim at formulating possible recommendations concerning adequate investment strategies – based on the international diversification in the event of the dominance of the country effect, or on the industrial diversification in the case of the advantage of the industry effect. Lack of consensus in the literature on the relative importance of these two effects was the main reason for the attempt to resettle the issue in the European perspective. In addition, most of the hitherto research in this area has been limited to the analysis of the impact of the national and industrial factors on corporate performance reflected mainly in the stock returns. Studies on the impact of these two effects on the broadly defined corporate performance of enterprises, characterised by a carefully chosen set of financial parameters of fundamental nature, are much less frequent. The study presented and discussed in this publication is an attempt to at least partly fill this gap, as well as to update the state of knowledge in the area of interest.

To measure the corporate performance, which is a term of a large semantic meaning, a set of several financial ratios was used. Despite many imperfections of these tools, it was assumed that their ability to synthesise and relativise the studied

J. Koralun-Bereźnicka, *Corporate Performance*, Contributions to Management Science, DOI 10.1007/978-3-319-00345-0, © Springer International Publishing Switzerland 2013

phenomena predispose them to quantify corporate financial condition. Moreover, the selection of appropriate financial ratios from their numerous collection enables to incorporate the complexity of the concept of corporate performance, understood as an economic and financial state of a company during a given period, characterised among others by its ability to generate revenues and profits, as well as by its solvency, both long- and short-term. An additional advantage of the use of financial ratios is the versatility of their application, both in the theory and business practice, which makes the analyses comparable with other studies in the area of corporate finance.

The selection of ratios included in the study was primarily determined by aiming at a comprehensive characteristic of the corporate performance, while eliminating the duplication of information by the use of ratios of similar informative content, or the use of variables directly interdependent. Therefore the ratios highly correlated with other variables were excluded from the study, so that the target set of variables contained orthogonal ratios. The selected ratios reflect two fundamental decision-making criteria applied by the investors, i.e. the efficiency and risk. The diagnostic variables also illustrate corporate solvency, both in the short and long term. The presented study is therefore based on the ratios of the three analytical categories: performance (profitability and turnover ratios), short-term solvency (liquidity ratios and working capital) and long-term solvency (debt ratios and the ratios describing the ability to service debt). The choice of ratios was also based on their variability. Thus, the variables not showing sufficient diversity in the population were removed.

The results of most of the previous research designed to determine the priority of the country or industry effect generally confirm the greater importance of the first of them, which is why they suggest higher effectiveness of the international diversification of investments. At the same time, however, the insightful study of literature leads to the conclusion that the later the period of analysis, the greater the tendency of researchers to recognise the industry effect as equivalent to the country effect, and sometimes even superior to it, which in turn suggests industrial investment diversification as more reasonable. The shift is sometimes explained as a consequence of the progress of the integration processes taking place primarily in Europe, but also as a result of the broadly defined globalisation involving other continents. This trend is also reflected in practice. In the face of the globalisation, investors often are willing to recognise the primacy of the industrial diversification over the international one.

Referring to the main purpose of the study, which was to determine and verify which of the two effects prevails in affecting corporate performance, it can be concluded that in the light of the comprehensive analysis of the problem, the industry effect should be considered as the one of a slightly greater impact. At the same time it must be emphasised that this does not mean that country factors are irrelevant in determining the performance of businesses. Mostly, however, the country specific factors are dominated by the industrial specificity of enterprises.

The most natural justification for the conclusions of the study seems to be the progress of economic integration, leading to greater convergence between the economies of countries rather than between industries. However, the presented reasoning is not confirmed by the analysis of the impact of integration on the diversity of corporate performance. In the analytical period there was no significant reduction in the diversity of economic and financial performance of companies, either in the international section, let alone across industries.

The lack of identifiable impact of the integration process on the cross-country and cross-industry differentiation of financial ratios could indicate that the feasible level of unification in terms of corporate performance has already been reached as a result of the adjustment process, conducted at an earlier stage of integration. The present state may have reached the target level of harmonisation, the further increase of which would be unrealistic. The lack of significant effect of the integration on the effects of business activities, evidenced by the analysis, may also result from a relatively short time horizon of the study, limited to seven years' period, which might not be sufficient to identify a clear trend towards the disappearance of the discussed differences. Thus, one can state that the considered country and industry effects occurring during the research period interact in a manner independent of the integration, and that their intensity is stable over time. It is evidenced by the analysis of variance of financial ratios over time, which does not indicate significant diversity of most means of ratios between the annual sub-periods.

One can not deny, however, the significance of diversification of corporate financial ratios between countries or between industries, as evidenced by the results of analysis of variance performed in these two sections. The mean values of most variables included in the analysis are significantly different across countries and industries, treated both as separate objects, as well as aggregated. The combined effect of the country and the industry is also significant for all financial ratios, as shown by the two-way analysis of variance. The analysis also reveals the dominance of the industrial factors over the national ones in the case of most financial ratios. This means that the corporate performance in most analytical aspects is under stronger influence of the industry in which an entity operates, rather than the country of origin.

Further confirmation of these conclusions can be found in the results of the classification procedures of objects, treated as countries, industries or industries in countries. There are considerably more similarities in the grouping results for the classification of industries in different countries than in the grouping results obtained for countries between industries. Moreover, the classification of binominal objects treated as industries in countries with the use of agglomerative cluster analysis reveals that most of the identified groups show greater similarity with the industrial breakdown of the population than the international one.

However, despite a marked tendency of the objects to group mostly according to their industrial specificity, there are also clusters of a definitely national character, albeit in a smaller number. This draws the attention to the still present domestic factors, whose significance should not be ignored. The most prominent example of the occurrence of such effect in the study population is Austria, where most of the industries are characterised by mutual similarity far greater than the similarity to the respective industries in other countries.

As for the specificity of Poland, as the only country in the examined population from outside the euro area, taking into account the average economic and financial performance across all industries, the country is characterised by the greatest cross-industry diversity of ratios. Poland has very often very good liquidity characteristics, especially in the education sector, and also large variation in the profitability and debt, depending on the industry. The industries with high profitability, even in comparison with other European countries, include for example, mining and education. The low profitability, in turn, can be observed in the sectors of trade, agriculture and fisheries. Similar disparities exist in the area of debt, where a high level of indebtedness is typical for the Polish mining industry, whereas a relatively low financial leverage is observed in the sectors of manufacturing, energy and construction.

When evaluating the relative importance of the country and industry factors in the studied analytical and territorial area, it should be emphasised that the intensity of the impact of those factors is not the same for all objects, as one can identify both countries and industries with low sensitivity to the impact of country and industry effects, respectively. Countries, whose economic industries do not show significant industrial specificity, are the Netherlands and Finland. The industries most resistant to the influence of common domestic factors include the trade and construction. This also means that these objects (countries and industries), demonstrate their national and industrial characteristics in the most pronounced way, and thus determine the occurrence of certain effects.

The differences between the drivers of the financial condition of enterprises in the countries and industries are also evidenced by the factor analysis carried out in these two sections. Comparing the structure of factors in the international section with the structure of factors identified for the industries reveals that the corporate performance in countries and industries is affected by quite similar factors. However, the differences exist between the factors identified separately for individual countries and industries. Significant similarity between factors influencing the financial situation of companies in countries and industries may be associated with the difficulty to completely isolate the industrial and national factors, which results from the confluence of these two kinds of factors. This makes it hardly possible to accurately quantify the influence of the industrial and national specificity on corporate performance.

To summarise the above reasoning, it should be emphasised that the main conclusion from the analysis of the occurrence of the country and industry effects and the strength of their impact on corporate performance in the EU countries is that both types of factors are present. Comparison of the intensity of their impact on the results of the economic activity of enterprises during the analytical period confirms the prevalence of the industry effect over the country effect. These observations may help formulate some implications concerning the optimisation of investment diversification strategies. The relatively greater importance of the industrial factors in comparison with the national ones suggests that the role of cross-industry diversification of investments should also increase compared to the traditional method of international diversification.

It should however be borne in mind that this recommendation is limited to the analysed territory of the ten countries with a high degree of economic integration, most of which belong to the common currency area. Extrapolating these suggestions on other areas of the world or even Europe is not at all obvious. Including in the study a larger number of countries or performing the analyses on other continents could in fact lead to an inverse verification of the hypotheses and strengthen the role of the regional factors. Moreover, it is worth mentioning that the above conclusions stem from the research based on the book values of non-public companies, which does not mean that they have the same use for listed companies. In the case of the latter, the effects of portfolio diversification, after all, are obtained by the correlation of market returns and not by measuring corporate performance with the use of ratios based on financial statements.

Thus, despite the observed regularities concerning industries, the importance of the geographic diversification should not be underestimated. However, it can be expected that, according to the trend initiated in the nineties of the previous century, the importance of the country effect, and consequently the international diversification will gradually decrease. The probability of this kind of changes seems to be the greater, the more advanced the integration processes.

# References


Accountancy. (1991). *Study text*. London: BPP Publishing Limited.

Aczel, A. D. (2000). *Statystyka w zarządzaniu*. Warszawa, Poland: Wydawnictwo Naukowe PWN.

Adjaouté, K., & Danthine, J. P. (2003). *European financial integration and equity returns: a theory-based assessment*. FAME Working Paper No. 84, http://ssrn.com/abstract=423160. Accessed 27 April 2013.

Adler, M., & Dumas, B. (1984). Exposure to currency risk: Definition and measurement. *Financial Management, 13*(2), 41–50.

Adner, R., & Helfat, C. E. (2003). Corporate effects and dynamic managerial capabilities. *Strategic Management Journal, 24*, 1011–1025. doi:10.1002/smj.331.

Afifi, A. A., & Clark, V. (1990). *Computer-aided multivariate analysis* (2nd ed.). New York: Van Nostrand Reinhold.

Altman, E. (1968). Financial ratios, discriminant analysis and the prediction of corporate bankruptcy. *Journal of Finance, 23*(4), 589–609.

Altman, E. (1993). *Corporate financial distress and bankruptcy*. New York: John Wiley & Sons.

Altman, E. (2001). *Predicting financial distress of companies: Revisiting the Z-score and Zeta® models*. New York: New York University.

Altman, E., Haldeman, R., & Narayanan, P. (1977). ZETA analysis: A new model to identify bankruptcy risk of corporations. *Journal of Banking and Finance, 1*(1), 29–54.

Arabie, P., & Boorman, S. A. (1973). Multidimensional scaling of measures of distance between partitions. *Journal of Mathematical Psychology, 10*(2), 148–203.

Archer, S. H., & Faerber, L. G. (1966). Firm size and cost of equity. *Journal of Finance, 21*(2), 69–84.

Arena, R., Benzoli, L., de Bandt, J., & Romani, P. M. (Eds.). (1991). *Traité d'Economie Industrielle*. Paris: Economica.

Baca, S., Garbe, B., & Weiss, R. (2000). The rise of sector effects in major equity markets. *Financial Analysts Journal, 56*(5), 34–40.

Bain, J. S. (1951). Relation of profit rate to industry concentration: American manufacturing, 1936-1940. *Quarterly Journal of Economics, 65*(3), 293–324.

Bain, J. S. (1968). *Industrial organization*. New York: JohnWiley & Sons.

Ball, R., & Brown, P. (1968). An empirical evaluation of accounting income numbers. *Journal of Accounting Research, 6*(2), 159–178.

Bank for the Accounts of Companies Harmonised. http://ec.europa.eu/economy_finance/bach. Accessed 1 July 2010.

Beaver, W. H. (1966). Financial ratios as predictors of failure. *Journal of Accounting Research, 4*(Empirical Research in Accounting: Selected Studies), 71–111.



J. Koralun-Bereźnicka, *Corporate Performance*, Contributions to Management Science, DOI 10.1007/978-3-319-00345-0,
 

Beaver, W.H., McNichols, M. F., & Rhie, J. (2004). *Have financial statements become less informative? Evidence from the ability of financial ratios to predict bankruptcy*. http://ssrn.com/abstract=634921. Accessed 18 June 2010.

Beckers, S., Connor, G., & Curds, R. (1996). National versus global influences on equity returns. *Financial Analysts Journal, 52*(2), 31–39.

Beckers, S., Grinold, S., Rudd, A., & Stefek, D. (1992). The relative importance of common factors across the European equity markets. *Journal of Banking and Finance, 16*(1), 75–95.

Bednarski, L. (1999). *Analiza finansowa w przedsiębiorstwie*. Warszawa, Poland: PWE.

Bednarski, L., Borowiecki, R., Duraj, J., Kurtys, E., Waśniewski, T., & Wersty, B. (2001). *Analiza ekonomiczna przedsiębiorstwa*. Wrocław, Poland: Wydawnictwo Akademii Ekonomicznej im. Oskara Langego.

Bednarski, L., & Kurtys, E. (Eds.). (2001). *Analiza ekonomiczna w przedsiębiorstwie*. Wrocław, Poland: Wydawnictwo Akademii Ekonomicznej im. Oskara Langego.

Benninga, S., & Sarig, O. (1993). *Corporate finance. A valuation approach*. Warsaw–London: McGraw-Hill, International Edition.

Bieliński, J. (2006). *Rozwój sektorów we współczesnej gospodarce*. Gdańsk, Poland: Wydawnictwo Uniwersytetu Gdańskiego.

Bień, W. (2000). *Zarządzanie finansami przedsiębiorstwa*. Warszawa, Poland: Difin.

Bień, W. (2002). *Ocena efektywności finansowej spółek kapitałowych*. Warszawa, Poland: Finans-Servis.

Biliński, L. (1987). Mierzenie efektywności gospodarowania w skali gospodarki narodowej. In: Społeczno- -gospodarcze warunki wzrostu efektywności (Referaty). Warszawa: Instytut Funkcjonowania Gospodarki Narodowej, SGPiS.

Blajer-Gołębiewska, A., & Zielenkiewicz, M. (2005). Teoria gier jako narzędzie ekonomii XX i XXI wieku. In D. Kopycińska (Ed.), *Teoretyczne aspekty gospodarowania* (pp. 77–86). Szczecin, Poland: Uniwersytet Szczeciński.

Bodnar, G., & Gentry, W. (1993). Exchange rate exposure and industry characteristics: Evidence from Canada, Japan, and the US. *Journal of International Money and Finance, 12*(1), 29–45.

Boillat, P., de Skowronsky, N., & Tuchschmid, N. (2002). Cluster analysis: Application to sector indices and empirical validation. *Financial Markets and Portfolio Management, 16*(4), 467–486.

Bolch, B. W., & Huang, C. J. (1974). *Multivariate statistical methods for business and economics*. Englewood Cliffs, NJ: Prentice-Hall.

Bolliger, G. (2004). The characteristics of individual analysts' forecasts in Europe. *Journal of Banking and Finance, 28*(9), 2283–2309.

Bolshakova, A., & Azuaje, F. (2003). Cluster validation techniques for genome expression data. *Signal Porcessing, 83*(4), 825–833.

Borkowski, B., Dudek, H., & Szczęsny, W. (2004). *Ekonometria. Wybrane zagadnienia*. Warszawa: Wydawnictwo Naukowe PWN.

Borys, T. (1978). Metody normowania cech w statystycznych badaniach porównawczych. *Przegląd Statystyczny, 3*(2), 371–382.

Borys, T. (1984). Kategoria jakości w statystycznej analizie porównawczej. Prace Naukowe AE we Wrocławiu, 284, Seria: Monografie i Opracowania, 23, AE, Wrocław.

Bougen, P. D., & Drury, J. C. (1980). U.K. statistical distributions of financial ratios. *Journal of Business Finance and Accounting, 7*(1), 39–47.

Brabazon, A., & Keenan, P. B. (2004). A hybrid genetic model for the prediction of corporate failure. *Computational Management Science, 1*, 293–310. doi:10.1007/s10287-004-0017-6.

Brennan, M. J. (1987). Capital asset pricing model. In J. Eatwell, M. Milgate, & P. Newman (Eds.), *The new Palgrave, finance* (pp. 91–102). New York: W.W. Norton.

Brooks, R., & Del Negro, M. (2004). The rise in comovement across national stock markets: Market integration or IT bubble? *Journal of Empirical Finance, 11*(5), 649–680.

Burgstahler, D., & Dichev, I. (1997). Earnings management to avoid earnings decreases and losses. *Journal of Accounting and Economics, 24*(1), 99–126.

Buzzel, R. D., & Gale, B. T. (1987). *The PIMS principles: Linking strategy to performance*. New York: Free Press.

Cabral, L. M. B. (2000). *Introduction to industrial organization*. Cambridge: MIT.

Calof, J. L. (1994). The relationship between firm size and export behavior revisited. *Journal of International Business Studies, 25*(2), 367–388.

Caloghirou, Y., Protogerou, A., Spanos, Y., & Papagiannakis, L. (2004). Industry- versus firm-specific effects on performance: Contrasting SMEs and large-sized firms. *European Management Journal, 22*(2), 231–243.

Campbell, J., & Shiller, R. (1988). The dividend-price ratio and expectations of future dividends and discount factors. *Review of Financial Studies, 1*(3), 195–228.

Cattell, R. B. (1966). The scree test for the number of factors. *Multivariate Behavioral Research, 1*(2), 629–637.

Cavaglia, S., Brightman, C., & Aked, M. (2000). The increasing importance of industry factors. *Financial Analysts Journal, 56*(5), 41–54.

Cavaglia, S., Cho, D., & Singer, B. (2001). Risks of sector rotation strategies. *Journal of Portfolio Management, 27*(4), 35–44.

Chang, H. J., & Singh, A. (2000). Corporate and industry effects on business unit competitive position. *Strategic Management Journal, 21*(7), 739–752.

Charoenwong, C., & Pornsit, J. (2009). Earnings management to exceed thresholds: Evidence from Singapore and Thailand. *Journal of Multinational Financial Management, 19*(3), 221–236.

Chung, F. H. (1993). Asset characteristics and corporate debt policy: An empirical test. *Journal of Business Finance and Accounting, 20*(1), 83–98.

Cinca, C. S., Molinero, C. M., & Larraz, J. L. (2005). Country and size effects in financial ratios: A European perspective. *Global Finance Journal, 16*(1), 26–47.

Clarke, R. (1985). *Industrial economics*. Oxford: Blackwell.

Claver, E., Molina, J., & Tari, J. (2002). Firm and industry effects on firm profitability: A Spanish empirical analysis. *European Management Journal, 20*(3), 321–328.

Comrey, A. L., & Lee, H. B. (1992). *A first course in factor analysis*. Hillsdale, NJ: Lawrence Erlbaum Associates.

Cooke, T. E. (1992). The impact of size, stock market listing and industry type on disclosure in the annual reports of Japanese listed corporations. *Accounting and Business Research, 22*(1), 229–237.

Coval, J., & Moskowitz, T. (2001). The geography of investment: Informed trading and asset prices. *Journal of Political Economy, 109*(4), 811–841.

Czechowski, L. (1997). *Wielowymiarowa ocean efektywności ekonomicznej przedsiębiorstwa przemysłowego*. Gdańsk, Poland: Wydawnictwo Uniwersytetu Gdańskiego.

Czekanowski, J. (1913). *Zarys metod statystycznych w zastosowaniach do antropologii*. Warszawa, Poland: Wydawnictwo Towarzystwo Naukowe Warszawskie.

De Moor, L., & Sercu, P. (2005). *Country and sector effects in international stock returns revisited* (SSRN Working Paper). http://papers.ssrn.com/sol3/papers.cfm?abstract_id=676394, 1–32. Accessed 20 June 2009.

Deakin, E. B. (1976). Distributions of financial accounting ratios: Some empirical evidence. *The Accounting Review, 51*(1), 90–96.

Dębski, W. (2005). *Teoretyczne i praktyczne aspekty zarządzania finansami przedsiębiorstwa*. Warszawa, Poland: PWN.

Dechow, P., Sloan, R., & Sweeney, A. (1995). Detecting earnings management. *The Accounting Review, 70*(2), 193–225.

DeJong, D., & Whiteman, C. (1991). The temporal stability of dividends and stock prices: Evidence from the likelihood function. *American Economic Review, 81*(3), 600–617.

Delbreil, M., Estaban, A., Friderichs, H., Paranque, B., Partych, F., Varetto, F., et al. (1997). *Corporate finance in Europe from 1986 to 1996*. European Committee of Central Balance Sheet Offices, Own Funds Working Group. www.ssrn.com. Accessed 15 June 2010.

Dempsey, S. J., Laber, G., & Rozeff, M. S. (1993). Dividend policies in practice: Is there an industry effect? *Quaterly Journal of Business and Economics, 32*(4), 3–13.

Demsetz, H. (1973). Industry structure, market rivalry, and public policy. *Journal of Law and Economics, 16*(1), 1–9.

Dobosz, M. (2001). *Wspomagana komputerowo statystyczna analiza wyników badań.* Warszawa, Poland: EXIT.

Domański, C. (1990). *Testy statystyczne*. Warszawa, Poland: PWE.

Domański, C., Pruska, K., & Wagner, W. (1998). *Wnioskowanie statystyczne przy nieklasycznych założeniach*. Łódź, Poland: Wydawnictwo Uniwersytetu Łódzkiego.

Dornbusch, R. (1973). Devaluation, money and nontraded goods. *American Economic Review, 63*(5), 871–880.

Dornbusch, R. (1987). Exchange rates and prices. *American Economic Review, 77*(1), 93–106.

Drummen, M., & Zimmermann, H. (1992). The structure of European stock returns. *Financial Analysts Journal, 48*(4), 15–26.

Dudycz, T., & Wrzosek, S. (2000). *Analiza finansowa. Problemy metodyczne w ujęciu praktycznym*. Wrocław, Poland: Wydawnictwo Akademii Ekonomicznej im. Oskara Langego we Wrocławiu.

Edwards, J., Kay, J., & Mayer, C. (1987). *The economic analysis of accounting profitability*. Oxford: Oxford University Press.

Eiling, E., Gerard, B., & de Roon, F. (2005). *International diversification in the euro-zone: The increasing riskiness of industry portfolios*. http://ssrn.com/abstract=796764. Accessed 20 July 2009.

Eisenbeis, R. A. (1977). Pitfalls in the application of discriminant analysis in business, finance and economics. *Journal of Finance, 32*(3), 875–900.

Falk, H., & Heintz, J. A. (1975). Assessing industry risk by ratio analysis. *The Accounting Review, 50*(4), 758–779.

Fama, E., & French, K. (1988). Dividend yields and expected stock returns. *Journal of Financial Economics, 22*(1), 3–25.

Fama, E., & Schwert, G. (1977). Asset returns and inflation. *Journal of Financial Economics, 5*(2), 115–146.

Fan, J. P. H., Twite, G. J., & Titman, S. (2012). An international comparison of capital structure and debt maturity choices. *Journal of Financial and Quantitative Analysis, 47*(1), 23–56.

Faulkner, D., & Bowman, C. (1996). *Strategie konkurencji*. Warszawa, Poland: Gebethner i S-ka.

Fedorowicz, Z. (1990). *System gospodarczy i efektywność ekonomiczna*. Warszawa, Poland: Wydawnictwo Naukowe PWN.

Feildstein, S., Longford, N., & McLeay, S. (1987). Industry effects and the proportionality assumption in ratio analysis: A variance component analysis. *Journal of Business, Finance and Accounting, 14*(4), 497–517.

Felbur, S., & Ważniewski, P. (1994). Efektywność gospodarowania w okresie transformacji systemowej (1989–93). *Ekonomista, 4*, 461–479.

Ferguson, G. A., & Takane, Y. (2003). *Analiza statystyczna w psychologii i pedagogice*. Warszawa, Poland: PWN.

Ferson, W. E., & Harvey, C. R. (1993). The risk and predictability of international equity returns. *Review of Financial Studies, 6*(3), 527–566.

Fess, P. E., & Warren, C. S. (1984). *Accounting principles*. Cincinnati, OH: South Western Publishing.

Fieldsend, S., Longford, N., & McLeay, S. (1987). Industry effects and proportionality assumption in ratio analysis: A variance component analysis. *Journal of Business Finance and Accounting, 14*(4), 497–517.

Fisher, R. A. (1954). *Statistical methods for research workers*. Edinburgh: Oliver and Boyd.

Fisher, T., & Martel, J. (2000). A *comparison of business bankruptcies across industries in Canada, 1981–2000*. http://papers.ssrn.com/paper.taf?abstract_id=256132. Accessed 7 July 2009.

Fisher, F. M., & McGowan, J. J. (1983). On the misuse of accounting rates of return to infer monopoly profits. *American Economic Review, 73*(1), 82–97.

Fiszel, H. (1973). *Teoria gospodarowania*. Warszawa, Poland: PWN.

Fitzpatrick, P. (1932). *A comparison of the ratios of successful industrial enterprises with those of failed companies*. Washington, DC: The Accountants' Publishing Company.

Flavin, T. J. (2004). The effect of the euro on country versus industry portfolio diversification. *Journal of International Money and Finance, 23*(7–8), 1137–1158.

Foster, G. (1986). *Financial statement analysis*. New York: Prentice Hall.

Fowkles, E. B., & Mallows, C. L. (1983). A method for comparing two hierarchical clusterings. *Journal of the American Statistical Association, 78*(383), 553–569.

Freimann, E. (1998). Economic integration and country allocation in Europe. *Financial Analysts Journal, 54*(5), 32–41.

Frost, C. A. (1994). Discussion of the effects of accounting diversity: Evidence from the European Union. *Journal of Accounting Research, 32*(Supplement: Studies on Accounting, Financial Disclosures, and the Law), 169–175.

Fudenberg, D., & Tirole, J. (1987). Understanding rent dissipation: On the use of game theory in industrial organization. *American Economic Review, 77*(2), 176–183.

Fudenberg, D., & Tirole, J. (2001). *Dynamic models of oligopoly*. Chur, Switzerland: Harwood Academic Publishers.

Furman, J. L. (2000). *Does industry matter differently in different places? A comparison of industry, corporate parent, and business segment effects in four OECD countries*. Boston: MIT Sloan School of Management Working Paper.

Gabrusewicz, W. (2002). *Podstawy analizy finansowej*. Warszawa, Poland: PWE.

Gajdka, J. (2002). *Teorie struktury kapitału i ich aplikacja w warunkach polskich*. Łódź, Poland: Wydawnictwo Uniwersytetu Łódzkiego.

Galati, G., & Tsatsaronis, K. (2003). The impact of the euro on Europe's financial markets. *Financial Markets, Institutions and Instruments, 12*(3), 165–221.

Gallizo, J. L., & Salvador, M. (2002). What factors drive and which act as a brake on the convergence of financial statements in EMU member countries? *Review of Accounting and Finance, 1*(4), 49–68.

Gatward, P., & Sharpe, I. G. (1996). Capital structure dynamics with interrelated adjustment: Australian evidence. *Australian Journal of Management, 21*(2), 89–112.

Geroski, P. A., & Mata, J. (2001). The evolution of markets. *International Journal of Industrial Organization, 19*(7), 999–1002.

Gierszewska, G., & Romanowska, M. (1994). *Analiza strategiczna przedsiębiorstwa*. Warszawa, Poland: PWE.

Goetzmann, W., & Jorion, P. (1993). Testing the predictive power of dividend yields. *Journal of Finance, 48*(2), 663–679.

Goetzmann, W., Li, L., & Rouwenhorst, G. (2005). Long-term global market correlations. *Journal of Business, 78*(1), 1–38.

Goodman, L. A., & Kruskal, W. H. (1979). *Measures of association for cross classifications*. Heidelberg/New York: Springer-Veralg.

Gordon, A. D. (1987). A review of hierarchical classification. *Journal of the Royal Statistical Society. Series A, 150*(2), 119–137.

Grabiński, T. (1992). *Metody aksonometrii*. Kraków, Poland: Wydawnictwo AE.

Grabiński, T., Wydymus, S., & Zeliaś, A. (1989). *Metody taksonomii numerycznej w modelowaniu zjawisk społeczno-gospodarczych*. Warszawa, Poland: Wydawnictwo Naukowe PWN.

Griffin, J. M., & Karolyi, G. A. (1998). Another look at the role of the industrial structure of markets for international diversification strategies. *Journal of Financial Economics, 50*(3), 351–373.

Grinblatt, M., & Keloharju, M. (2001). How distance, language, and culture influence stockholdings and trades. *Journal of Finance, 56*(3), 1053–1073.

Grinold, R., Rudd, A., & Stefek, D. (1989). Global factors: Fact or fiction? *Journal of Portfolio Management, 16*(1), 79–88.

Grubel, H. (1968). Internationally diversified portfolios: Welfare gains and capital flows. *American Economic Review, 58*(5), 1299–1314.

Gupta, M. C. (1969). The effect of size, growth, and industry on the financial structure of manufacturing companies. *Journal of Finance, 24*(3), 517–529.

Gupta, M. C., & Huefner, R. J. (1972). A cluster analysis study of financial ratios and industry characteristics. *Journal of Accounting Research, 10*(1), 77–95.

Hall, B. H. (1987). The relationship between firm size and firm growth in the U.S. Manufacturing sector. *The Journal of Industrial Economics, 35*(4), 583–605.

Harman, H. H. (1967). *Modern factor analysis*. Chicago: University of Chicago Press.

Hartigan, J. A. (1975). *Clustering algorithms*. New York: John Wiley & Sons.

Haskins, M. E. (2001). *Ratios tell a story, Darden Case No.: UVA-C-2162-SSRN*. http://ssrn.com/abstract=333383. Accessed 25 May 2009.

Hawawini, G., Subramanian, V., & Verdin, P. (2003). Is performance driven by industry or firm-specific factors? A new look on the evidence. *Strategic Management Journal, 24*(1), 1–16.

Hawawini, G., Subramanian, V., & Verdin, P. (2004). The home country in the age of globalization; how much does it matter for firm performance? *Journal of World Business, 39*(2), 121–135.

Helg, R., Manasse, P., Monacelli, T., & Rovelli, R. (1995). How much (a)symmetry in Europe? Evidence from industrial sectors. *European Economic Review, 39*(5), 1017–1041.

Hellwig, Z. (1968). Zastosowanie metody taksonomicznej do typologicznego podziału krajów ze względu na poziom ich rozwoju i strukturę wykwalifikowanych kadr. *Przegląd Statystyczny, 4*, 307–324.

Hellwig, Z. (1981). *Wielowymiarowa analiza porównawcza i jej zastosowanie w badaniach wielocechowych obiektów gospodarczych*. Warszawa, Poland: PWE.

Hellwig, Z. (1988). Nieuzgodnione problemy WAP. Prace Naukowe Akademii Ekonomicznej im. Oskara Langego we Wrocławiu 449, Wrocław.

Heston, S. L., & Rouwenhorst, K. G. (1994). Does industrial structure explain the benefits of international diversification. *Journal of Financial Economics, 36*(1), 3–27.

Heston, S. L., & Rouwenhorst, K. G. (1995). Industry and country effects in international stock returns. *Journal of Portfolio Management, 21*(3), 53–58.

Hodrick, R. (1992). Dividend yields and expected stock returns: Alternative procedures for inference and measurement. *Review of Financial Studies, 5*(3), 357–386.

Hopwood, W., & McKeown, J. (1998). *An examination of the underlying usefulness of financial ratios* (Working Paper Series). http://papers.ssrn.com/sol3/papers.cfm?abstract_id=104683. Accessed 17 June 2009.

Horrigan, J. (1965). Some empirical bases of financial ratio analysis. *The Accounting Review, 40* (3), 558–568.

Huberman, G. (1987). Arbitrage pricing theory. In J. Eatwell, M. Milgate, & P. Newman (Eds.), *The new Palgrave, finance* (pp. 72–80). New York: W.W. Norton.

Hubert, L. J., & Arabie, P. (1985). Comparing partitions. *Journal of Classification, 2*(1), 193–218.

Hunt, S. D. (1983). *Marketing theory: The philosophy of marketing science*. Homewood, IL: Irwin.

Jacobson, R. (1987). The validity of ROI as a measure of business performance. *American Economic Review, 77*(3), 470–478.

Jacquemin, A. (1985). *Pouvoir et selection dans la Nouvelle Economie Industrielle*. Economica-Cabay: Paris–Louvain-la-Neuve.

Jajuga, K. (1993). *Statystyczna analiza wielowymiarowa*. Warszawa, Poland: Wydawnictwo Naukowe PWN.

Jerzemowska, M. (2004). *Analiza ekonomiczna w przedsiębiorstwie*. Warszawa, Poland: PWE.

Jog, V., & Suszyński, C. (2000). *Zarządzanie finansami przedsiębiorstwa*. Warszawa, Poland: Centrum Informacji Menedżera CIM.

Julien, P. A., Joyal, A., Deshaies, L., & Ramangalahy, C. (1997). A typology of strategic behaviour among small and medium-sized exporting businesses. *International Small Business Journal, 15*(20), 33–50.

Kaiser, H. F. (1960). The application of electronic computers to factor analysis. *Educational and Psychological Measurement, 20*(1), 141–151.

Kaminski, K. A., Wetzel, T. S., & Guan, L. (2004). Can financial ratios detect fraudulent financial reporting? *Managerial Auditing Journal, 19*(1), 15–28.

Kang, J. K., & Stulz, R. M. (1997). Why is there a home bias? an analysis of foreign portfolio equity ownership in Japan. *Journal of Financial Economics, 46*(1), 3–28.

Karels, G. V., & Prakash, A. J. (1987). Multivariate normality and forecasting of business bankruptcy. *Journal of Business Finance and Accounting, 14*(4), 573–593.

Kauffman, L., & Rousseeuw, P. J. (1990). *Finding groups in data: An introduction to cluster analysis*. New York: Wiley-Interscience.

Kessides, I. N. (1990). Internal versus external conditions and firm profitability: An exploratory model. *The Economic Journal, 100*(402), 773–792.

Ketz, J. E., Doogar, R. K., & David, E. (1990). *A cross-industry analysis of financial ratios: Comparabilities and corporate performance*. New York: Quorum Books.

King, B. F. (1966). Market and industry factors in stock price behavior. *Journal of Business, 39*(1), 139–190.

Koralun-Bereźnicka, J. (2006). Ocena możliwości wykorzystania wybranych funkcji dyskryminacji w analizie polskich spółek giełdowych. *Studia i Prace Kolegium Zarządzania i Finansów, 69*, 18–28.

Koralun-Bereźnicka, J. (2008a). Efekt sektorowy wskaźników finansowych przedsiębiorstw w krajach Unii Europejskiej. Prace naukowe Akademii Ekonomicznej im. Oskara Langego we Wrocławiu. Zarządzanie finansami firm – teoria i praktyka 1200, 296–304.

Koralun-Bereźnicka, J. (2008b). Wpływ procesu integracji europejskiej na międzysektorowe zróżnicowanie wskaźników finansowych przedsiębiorstw. *Zeszyty Naukowe Politechniki Rzeszowskiej. Zarządzanie i marketing, 14*, 135–142.

Koralun-Bereźnicka, J. (2009a). Efekt sektorowy w wynikach finansowych przedsiębiorstw w wybranych krajach Unii Europejskiej na podstawie analizy skupień. Prace Naukowe Uniwersytetu Ekonomicznego we Wrocławiu. Inwestycje finansowe i ubezpieczenia – tendencje światowe a polski rynek 60, 174–185.

Koralun-Bereźnicka, J. (2009b). Kraj i sektor jako czynniki kształtujące rynkowe stopy zwrotu w świetle przeglądu badań. Prace Naukowe Uniwersytetu Ekonomicznego we Wrocławiu. Zarządzanie finansami firm – teoria i praktyka 48, 466–473.

Koralun-Bereźnicka, J. (2009c). Międzynarodowe i międzysektorowe zróżnicowanie struktury kapitału przedsiębiorstw w wybranych krajach Unii Europejskiej. In J. Ostaszewski (Ed.), *Dylematy kształtowania struktury kapitału w przedsiębiorstwie* (pp. 199–209). Warszawa, Poland: Oficyna Wydawnicza SGH.

Koralun-Bereźnicka, J. (2010). *Krajowe i sektorowe czynniki różnicujące kondycję finansową przedsiębiorstw w krajach Unii Europejskiej*. Gdańsk, Poland: Uniwersytet Gdański.

Kornai, J. (1986). *Wzrost, niedobór, efektywność*. Warszawa, Poland: PWN.

Kotarbiński, T. (1973). *Traktat o dobrej robocie*. Wrocław, Poland: Ossolineum.

Kothari, S. P., & Shanken, J. (1997). Book-to-market, dividend yield, and expected market returns: A time-series analysis. *Journal of Financial Economics, 44*(2), 169–203.

Kotler, P. (1994). *Marketing, analiza, planowanie, wdrażanie i kontrola*. Warszawa, Poland: Gebethner i S-ka.

Kowalak, R. (2003). *Ocena kondycji finansowej przedsiębiorstwa*. Gdańsk, Poland: ODDK.

Kuo, W., & Satchell, S. E. (2001). Global equity styles and industry effects: The pre-eminence of value relative to size. *Journal of International Financial Markets, Institutions and Money, 11*(1), 1–28.

Kutlaca, D., & Radosevic, S. (2002). *Industries, costs and macroeconomic regimes in central and eastern European countries: Towards stylised facts* (Economics Working Papers 27). London, UK: Centre for the Study of Economic and Social Change in Europe, SSEES, UCL.

L'Her, J. F., Sy, O., & Tnani, Y. (2002). Country, industry and risk factor loadings in portfolio management. *Journal of Portfolio Management, 28*(4), 70–79.

Lamont, O. (1998). Earnings and expected returns. *Journal of Finance, 53*(5), 1563–1587.

Lanez, J. A., & Callao, S. (2001). The effect of accounting diversity on international financial analysis: Empirical evidence. *The International Journal of Accounting, 35*(3), 65–83.

Lang, M. H., & Lundholm, R. J. (1993). Cross-sectional determinants of analysts ratings of corporate disclosures. *Journal of Accounting Research, 31*(2), 246–271.

Leal, R. P., & Powers, T. L. (1997). A taxonomy of countries based on inventive activity. *International Marketing Review, 14*(6), 445–460.

Leary, M. T., & Graham, J. R. (2011). A review of empirical capital structure research and directions for the future. *Annual Review of Financial Economics, 3*(2011). doi.org/10.2139/ssrn.1729388.

Leibenstein, H. (1978). *General X – efficiency theory and economic development*. Oxford: University Press.

Lessard, D. R. (1974). World, national and industry factors in equity returns. *Journal of Finance, 29*(2), 379–391.

Lessard, D. R. (1976). World, country, and industry relationships in equity returns: Implications for risk reduction through international diversification. *Financial Analysts Journal, 32*(1), 32–38.

Lev, B. (1969). Industry averages as targets for financial ratios. *Journal of Accounting Research Autumn, 7*(2), 290–299.

Lev, B. (1974). On the association between operating leverage and risk. *Journal of Financial and Quantitative Analysis, 9*(4), 627–641.

Lev, B., & Sunder, S. (1979). Methodological issues in the use of financial ratios. *Journal of Accounting and Economics, 1*(3), 187–210.

Levi, M. (1994). Exchange rates and the valuation of firms. In Y. Amihud & R. Levich (Eds.), *Exchange rates and corporate performance* (pp. 67–84). New York: Irwin Publishing.

Levy, H., & Sarnat, A. (1970). International diversification of investment portfolios. *American Economic Review, 60*(4), 668–675.

Lewellen, J. (2004). Predicting returns with financial ratios. *Journal of Financial Economics, 74*(2), 209–235.

Libby, R., Libby, P. A., & Short, D. G. (2009). *Financial accounting*. New York: IMcGraw-Hill/Irwin Publishing.

Lintner, J. (1965). The valuation of risk assets and the selection of risky investments in stock portfolios and capital budgets. *The Review of Economics and Statistics, 47*(1), 13–37.

Lipczynski, J., Wilson, J., & Goddard, J. (2005). *Industrial organization. Competition, strategy, policy*. London: Financial Times/Prentice Hall.

Lipiec-Zajchowska, M. (Ed.). (2003). *Wspomaganie procesów decyzyjnych. Ekonometria*. Warszawa, Poland: C.H. Beck.

Łubieński, T., Makowski, K., & Rybak, M. (1988). *Efektywność i jakość pracy*. Warszawa, Poland: SGPiS.

Lucey, B. M. (2003). *Distributional aspects of Irish financial accounting ratios* (Working Paper Series). doi.org/10.2139/ssrn.377220.

Łyszkiewicz, W. (2003). *Industrial organization. Organizacja rynku i konkurencja*. Warszawa, Poland: Wyższa Szkoła Handlu i Finansów Międzynarodowych.

Mączyńska, E., & Zawadzki, M. (1997). Czynniki kształtujące poziom rentowności przedsiębiorstw. *Bank i Kredyt, 3*, 21–31.

Mauri, A., & Michaels, M. P. (1998). Firm and industry effects within strategic management: An empirical examination. *Strategic Management Journal, 19*(3), 211–219.

McDonald, B., & Morris, M. H. (1984). The statistical validity of the ratio method in financial analysis: An empirical examination. *Journal of Business Finance and Accounting, 11*(1), 89–97.

McDonald, B., & Morris, M. H. (1985). The functional specification of financial ratios: An empirical examination. *Accounting and Business Research, 15*(59), 223–228.

McGahan, A. M. (1999a). The performance of US Corporations: 1981–1994. *The Journal of Industrial Economics, 47*(4), 373–398.

McGahan, A. M. (1999b). Competition, strategy and business performance. *California Management Review, 41*(3), 74–101.

McGahan, A. M., & Porter, M. E. (1997). How much does industry matter really? *Strategic Management Journal, 18*(Summer Special Issue), 15–30.

McGahan, A. M., & Porter, M. E. (2002). What do we know about the variance in accounting profitability? *Management Science, 48*(7), 834–851.

McGahan, A. M., & Porter, M. E. (2003). The emergence and sustainability of abnormal profits. *Strategic Organization, 1*(1), 79–108.

McGurr, P. T., & DeVaney, S. A. (1998). Predicting business failure of retail firms. An analysis using mixed industry models. *Journal of Business Research, 43*(3), 169–176.

McLeay, S. (1986). The ratio of means, the means of ratio and other benchmarks: An examination of characteristic financial ratios in the French corporate sector. *The Journal of the French Finance Association, 7*(1), 75–93.

McLeay, S., & Fieldsend, S. (1987). Sector and size effects in ratio analysis: An indirect test of ratio proportionality. *Accounting and Business Research, 17*(66), 133–140.

McLeay, S., & Stevenson, M. (2006). Modelling the longitudinal properties of financial ratios of European firms, IIIS Discussion Paper No. 184. http://ssrn.com/abstract=945336. Accessed 28 July 2009.

McLeay, S., & Trigueiros, D. (2002). Proportionate growth and the theoretical foundations of financial ratios. *Abacus, 38*(3), 297–316.

Melich, A. (1980). *Efektywność gospodarowania*. PWE: Istota – metody – warunki. Warszawa.

Melich, A. (1985). *Podstawy teorii gospodarowania*. Warszawa, Poland: PWE.

Melnyk, Z. L., & Mathur, I. (1972). Business risk homogeneity: A multivariate application and evaluation. *Proceedings of the 1972 Midwest AIDS conference*.

Meyers, S. L. (1973). A re-examination of market and industry factors in stock price behaviour. *Journal of Finance, 28*(3), 695–705.

Migdał-Najman, K., & Najman, K. (2005). Analityczne metody ustalania liczby skupień. Prace Naukowe Akademii Ekonomicznej im. Oskara Langego we Wrocławiu, 1076, 265–273

Migdał-Najman, K., & Najman, K. (2006). Wykorzystanie indeksu silhouette do ustalania optymalnej liczby skupień. *Wiadomości Statystyczne, 6*, 1–10.

Milligan, G. W. (1996). Clustering validation: Results and implications for applied analyses. In P. Arabie, L. Hubert, & G. De Soete (Eds.), *Clustering and classification* (pp. 341–375). River Edge, NJ: World Scientific Press.

Modares, A., Abedi, S., & Mirshama, M. (2008). *Testing linear relationship between excess rate of return and financial ratios* (Working paper). doi.org/10.2139/ssrn.1264912.

Moreira, J., & Pope, P. (2007). *Earnings management to avoid losses: A cost of debt explanation* (CEF.UP Working Papers, 0704). Universidade do Porto, Faculdade de Economia do Porto.

Morgan, Y. (1990). *Fondements d'Economie Industrielle*. Paris: Economica.

Morrison, D. F. (1990). *Wielowymiarowa analiza statystyczna*. Warszawa, Poland: Wydawnictwo Naukowe PWN.

Mramor, D., & Marmor-Kosta, N. (1997). Accounting ratios as factors of rate of return on equity. In *New operational approaches for financial modeling* (pp. 335–348). Heidelberg: Physica-Verlag.

Muresan, E., & Wolitzer, P. (2004). *Organize your financial ratios analysis with PALMS* (EMuresan Working Paper No. 02–01). doi.org/10.2139/ssrn.375880.

Nahotko, S. (1992). *Rachunek ekonomiczny w modelowaniu efektywności procesów innowacyjnych w przedsiębiorstwie*. Wrocław, Poland: Wydawnictwo Politechniki Wrocławskiej.

Najman, K. (2007). Charakterystyka mierników oceny podobieństwa wyników podziałów. Prace i Materiały Wydziału Zarządzania Uniwersytetu Gdańskiego. Finanse i informatyka w zarządzaniu, wybrane aspekty, *3*, 191–201.

Nowak, E. (1990). *Metody taksonomiczne w klasyfikacji obiektów społeczno-gospodarczych*. Warszawa, Poland: PWE.

Ohlson, J. (1980). Financial ratios and the probabilistic prediction of bankruptcy. *Journal of Accounting Research, 18*(1), 109–131.

Orłowski, K. (2001). *Zastosowanie pakietu Statistica w analizie wyników badań społecznych*. Poznań: Wydawnictwo Naukowe Stowarzyszenia Psychologia i Architektura.

Ostasiewicz, W. (1999). *Statystyczne metody analizy danych*. Wrocław, Poland: Wydawnictwo Akademii Ekonomicznej im. Oskara Langego we Wrocławiu.

Ostaszewski, J. (1991). *Ocena efektywności przedsiębiorstwa według standardów EWG*. Warszawa, Poland: Centrum Informacji Menedżera CIM.

Pahor, M., & Mramor, D. (2001). *Testing nonlinear relationships between excess rate of return on equity and financial ratios* (Working Papers Series). doi:10.2139/ssrn.266928.

Peel, M. J., Peel, D. A., & Pope, P. F. (1986). Predicting corporate failure – some results for the UK corporate sector. *Omega International Journal of Management Science, 14*(1), 5–12.

Peltzman, S. (1977). The gains and losses from industrial concentration. *Journal of Law and Economics, 20*(2), 229–264.

Perttunen, J., & Martikainen, T. (1989). On the proportionality assumption of financial ratios. *Finnish Journal of Business Economics, 38*(4), 343–359.

Phillips, A. (1976). A critique of empirical studies of relations between market structure and profitability. *The Journal of Industrial Economics, 24*(4), 241–249.

Phylaktis, K., & Xia, L. (2006). Sources of firms' industry and country effects in emerging markets. *Journal of International Money and Finance, 25*(3), 459–475.

Pierścionek, Z. (1992). *Przemysł w gospodarce rynkowej*. Warszawa, Poland: Szkoła Główna Handlowa w Warszawie.

Pluta, W. (1977). *Wielowymiarowa analiza porównawcza w badaniach ekonomicznych*. Warszawa, Poland: PWE.

Pontiff, J., & Schall, L. (1998). Book-to-market ratios as predictors of market returns. *Journal of Financial Economics, 49*(2), 141–160.

Porter, M. E. (1992). *Strategia konkurencji, metody analizy sektorów i konkurencji*. Warszawa, Poland: PWE.

Porter, M. E. (1998). *Competitive advantage, creating and sustaining superior performance*. New York: The Free Press.

Powell, T. C. (1996). How much does industry matter? An alternative test. *Strategic Management Journal, 17*(4), 323–334.

Rainelli, M. (1996). *Ekonomia przemysłowa*. Warszawa, Poland: Wydawnictwo Naukowe PWN.

Rand, W. M. (1971). Objective criteria for the evaluation of clustering methods. *Journal of the American Statistical Association, 66*(336), 846–850.

Rees, B. (1995). *Financial analysis*. Hertfordshire: Prentice Hall.

Rivaud-Danset, D., Salais, R., & Dubocage, E. (2001). *Comparison between the financial structure of SMES and that of large enterprises (LES) using the BACH database* (Economic Paper 155). Brussels: European Commission, Directoate-General for Ecomomic and Financial Affairs. doi.org/10.2139/ssrn.141478.

Rohlf, F. J. (1974). Method of comparing classifications. *Annual Review of Ecology and Systematics, 5*, 101–113.

Roll, R. (1992). Industrial structure and the comparative behavior of international stock market indices. *Journal of Finance, 47*(1), 3–41.

Roquebert, J. A., Phillips, R. L., & Westfall, P. A. (1996). Markets versus management: What derives profitability? *Strategic Management Journal, 17*(8), 653–664.

Rószkiewicz, M. (2002). *Metody ilościowe w badaniach marketingowych*. Warszawa, Poland: Wydawnictwo Naukowe PWN.

Rousseeuw, P. J. (1987). Silhouettes: A graphical aid to the interpretation and validation of cluster analysis. *Journal of Computational Applications in Math, 20*, 53–65.

Rouwenhorst, K. G. (1999). European equity markets and the EMU. *Financial Analysts Journal, 55*(3), 57–64.
Ruefli, T. W., & Wiggins, R. R. (2003). Industry, corporate, and segment effects and business performance: A non-parametric approach. *Strategic Management Journal, 24*(9), 861–879.
Rumelt, R. P. (1991). How much does industry matter? *Strategic Management Journal, 12*(3), 167–185.
Sagan, A. (2009). Przykłady zaawansowanych technik analitycznych w badaniach marketingowych. http://www.statsoft.pl/czytelnia/marketing/przykladyzaawans.html. Accessed 12 August 2009.
Scherer, F. M., & Ross, D. (1990). *Industrial market structure and economic performance*. Boston: Houghton-Mifflin Company.
Schmalensee, R. C. (1985). Do markets differ much? *American Economic Review, 75*(3), 341–351.
Schmalensee, R. C., & Williga, R. (1989). *Handbook of industrial economics*. Amsterdam: North Holland.
Sell, C. W. (2005). The importance of country versus sector characteristics. *Managerial Finance, 31*(1), 78–95.
Serra, A. P. (2000). Country and industry factors in returns: Evidence from emerging markets' stocks. *Emerging Markets Review, 1*(2), 127–151.
Serrano-Cinca, C. (1998). From financial information to strategic groups – a self organizing neural network approach. *Journal of Forecasting, 17*(5–6), 415–428.
Serrano-Cinca, C., Mar-Molinero, C., & Gallizo, J. L. (2001). Change and invariance in EU aggregate financial statement data, Discussion papers in Accounting and Finance, AF01-1, School of Management, UK University of Southampton. http://eprints.soton.ac.uk/35732/. Accessed 19 September 2009.
Serrano-Cinca, C., Mar-Molinero, C., & Gallizo, J. L. (2002). A multivariate study of the EU economy via financial statements analysis. *Journal of the Royal Statistical Society: Series D, 51*(3), 335–354.
Sharpe, W. F. (1964). Capital asset prices: A theory of market equilibrium under conditions of risk. *Journal of Finance, 19*(3), 425–442.
Siemińska, E. (2002). *Metody pomiaru i oceny kondycji finansowej przedsiębiorstwa*. Toruń: Tonik.
Sierpińska, M., & Jachna, T. (2004). *Ocena przedsiębiorstwa według standardów światowych*. Warszawa, Poland: Wydawnictwo Naukowe PWN.
Siudek, T. (2006). Badanie regionalnego zróżnicowania sytuacji ekonomiczno-finansowej banków spółdzielczych w Polsce z wykorzystaniem metod taksonomicznych. Zeszyty Naukowe SGGW – Ekonomika i Organizacja Gospodarki Żywnościowej, 58, 41–53.
Slade, M. E. (2004). Competing models of firm profitability. *International Journal of Industrial Organization, 22*(3), 289–308.
Smith, J. K., & Skousen, K. F. (1984). *Intermediate accounting* (9th ed.). Cincinnati, OH: South Western Publishing.
Smith, R., & Winakor, A. (1935). Changes in the financial structure of unsuccessful industrial corporations. Bulletin (University of Illinois). Bureau of Business Research, 51. University of Illinois Bulletin, 32(46).
Solnik, B. (1974). The international pricing of risk: An empirical investigation of the world capital market structure. *Journal of Finance, 29*(2), 365–378.
Sonney, F. (2007). Country versus sector influences and financial analysts' specialization. Université de Neuchâtel. http://www2.unine.ch/webdav/site/iaf/shared/documents/TheseFredericSonney.pdf. Accessed 9 August 2009.
Sori, M.Z., Hamid, A., Ali, M., Annuar, N., & Shamsher, M. (2006). Some basic properties of financial ratios: Evidence from an emerging capital market. *International Research Journal of Finance and Economics*, doi.org/10.2139/ssrn.923736.
Spanos, Y., Zaralis, G., & Lioukas, S. (2004). Strategy and industry effects on profitability: Evidence from Greece. *Strategic Management Journal, 25*(2), 139–165.

Stanisz, A. (2000). *Przystępny kurs statystyki z wykorzystaniem programu Statistica pl. na przykładach z medycyny* (Modele liniowe i nieliniowe, Vol. 2). Kraków, Poland: StatSoft Polska.

Steinhaus, H. (1956). Sur la division des cors materiel en partie. *Bulletin Academie Polonaise des Sciences, 4*, 801–804.

Stonehouse, G., Hamill, J., Campbell, D., & Purdie, T. (2001). *Globalizacja, strategia i zarządzanie*. Warszawa, Poland: Felberg.

Storey, D., Keasey, K., Watson, R., & Wynarczyk, P. (1987). *The performance of small firms*. London: Croom-Helm.

Subramanyam, K. R., & Wild, J. J. (2009). *Financial statement analysis*. Boston: McGraw-Hill International Edition.

Sudarsanam, P. S., & Taffler, R. J. (1985). Industrial classification in UK capital markets: A test of economic homogeneity. *Applied Economics, 17*(2), 291–308.

Tadeusiewicz, R. (1993). *Biometria*. Kraków, Poland: Wydawnictwo Akademii Górniczo-Hutniczej.

Tarczyński, W. (2002). *Fundamentalny portfel papierów wartościowych*. Warszawa, Poland: PWE.

Tay, J., & Parker, R. (1990). Measuring international harmonization and standardization. *Abacus, 26*(1), 71–88.

Tirole, J. (1988). *The theory of industrial organization*. Cambridge: MIT Press.

Trimbath, S. (2001). *Lemmings to the sea: The inappropriate use of financial ratios in empirical analysis* (Milken Institute Working Paper No. 2001–01). doi.org/10.2139/ssrn.270342.

Tyran, M. (1992). *Business and financial ratios*. Hemel Hempstead, Hertfordshire: Woodhead-Faulkner.

United States International Trade Commission. (1985). *Analysis of the international competitiveness of U.S. commercial shipbuilding and repair industries*. Washington, DC: Author.

Varadarajan, P. R. (1986). Horizontal cooperative sales promotion: A framework for classification and additional perspectives. *Journal of Marketing, 50*(2), 61–73.

Wach, K. (2006). *Systemy podatkowe w Unii Europejskiej*. Kraków, Poland: Oficyna Ekonomiczna.

Wallace, D. L. (1983). A method for comparing two hierarchical clusterings: Comment. *Journal of the American Statistical Association, 78*(383), 569–576.

Walton, P. J. (1993). Introduction: The true and fair view in British accounting. *The European Accounting Review, 2*(1), 49–58.

Walton, P. J. (1997). The true and fair view and the drafting of the Fourth Directive. *The European Accounting Review, 6*(4), 721–730.

Ward, J. H. (1963). Hierarchical grouping to optimize an objective function. *Journal of the American Statistical Association, 58*(301), 236–244.

Waśniewski, T. (1997). *Analiza finansowa w przedsiębiorstwie*. Warszawa, Poland: Fundacja Rozwoju Rachunkowości w Polsce.

Waśniewski, T., & Skoczylas, W. (2002). *Teoria i praktyka analizy finansowej w przedsiębiorstwie*. Warszawa, Poland: Fundacja Rozwoju Rachunkowości w Polsce.

Wędzki, D. (2006). *Analiza wskaźnikowa sprawozdania finansowego*. Kraków, Poland: Wolters Kluwer.

Weiss, L. W. (1974). The concentration profits relationship and antitrust. In H. J. Goldschmidt, H. M. Mann, & J. F. Weston (Eds.), *Industrial concentration: The new learning* (pp. 184–233). Boston: Little Brown.

Weiss, R. A. (1998). Global sector rotation: New look at an old idea. *Financial Analysts Journal, 54*(3), 6–8.

Welch, I. (2011). Two common problems in capital structure research: The financial-debt-to-asset ratio and issuing activity versus leverage changes. *International Review of Finance, 11*(1), 1–17.

Wernerfelt, B., & Montgomery, C. A. (1988). Tobin's q and the importance of focus in firm performance. *American Economic Review, 78*(1), 246–250.

Westwick, C. A. (1988). *How to use management ratios* (2nd ed.). Aldershot: Gower Publishing Company Limited.

White, G. I., Sondhi, A. C., & Fried, D. (1994). *The analysis and use of financial statements*. New York: John Wiley & Sons.

Whittington, G. (1980). Some basic properties of accounting ratios. *Journal of Business Finance and Accounting, 7*(2), 219–232.

Wieczorkowska, G., Kochański, P., & Eljaszuk, M. (2003). *Statystyka. Wprowadzenie do analizy danych sondażowych i eksperymentalnych*. Warszawa, Poland: Scholar.

Wilcox, J. (1970). A simple theory of financial ratios as predictors of failure. *Journal of Accounting Research, 9*(2), 389–395.

Yu, Q., Du, B., & Sun, Q. (2006). Earnings management at rights issues thresholds – Evidence from China. *Journal of Banking and Finance, 30*(12), 3453–3468.

Zaleska, M. (2002). *Identyfikacja ryzyka upadłości przedsiębiorstwa i banku. Systemy wczesnego ostrzegania*. Warszawa, Poland: Difin.

Zarzecki, D. (1997). *Wykorzystanie wskaźników finansowych w ocenie przedsiębiorstwa*. Szczecin, Poland: Interbook.

Zarzecki, D. (2007). Wykorzystanie wskaźników finansowych w zarządzaniu. Prace naukowe Akademii Ekonomicznej im. Oskara Langego we Wrocławiu. Inwestycje finansowe i ubezpieczenia – tendencje światowe a polski rynek 1176, 564–573.

Żółkiewski, S. (1993). *Techniczna efektywność produkcji w przemyśle i budownictwie na przykładzie wybranych branż. Z prac Zakładu Badań Statystyczno-Ekonomicznych 213*. Warszawa, Poland: GUS-PAN.

Żurek, J. (Ed.). (2007). *Przedsiębiorstwo. Zasady działania, funkcjonowanie, rozwój*. Gdańsk, Poland: Fundacja Rozwoju Uniwersytetu Gdańskiego.

# Appendices

# Appendix 1. Normalisation Procedure of Variables

The method of normalising diagnostic variables depends on their nature. Stimulants, therefore, are normalised according to the following formula:

$$z_{ij} = \frac{x_{ij} - \min\limits_i x_{ij}}{\max\limits_i x_{ij} - \min\limits_i x_{ij}},$$

where:

$z_{ij} \in [0,1]$,

$\max\limits_i x_{ij} \neq \min\limits_i x_{ij}$.

Anti-stimulants are normalised according to the formula:

$$z_{ij} = \frac{\max\limits_i x_{ij} - x_{ij}}{\max\limits_i x_{ij} - \min\limits_i x_{ij}},$$

where:

$z_{ij} \in [0,1]$,

$\max\limits_i x_{ij} \neq \min\limits_i x_{ij}$,

and variables whose desired level is $c_{oj}$ – according to the formulas:

$$z_{ij} = \frac{x_{ij} - \min\limits_i x_{ij}}{c_{oj} - \min\limits_i x_{ij}},$$

for $x_{ij} < c_{oj}$,

J. Koralun-Bereźnicka, *Corporate Performance*, Contributions to Management Science, DOI 10.1007/978-3-319-00345-0, © Springer International Publishing Switzerland 2013

$$z_{ij} = \frac{x_{ij} - \max\limits_i x_{ij}}{c_{oj} - \max\limits_i x_{ij}},$$

for $x_{ij} > c_{oj}$,
where:

$c_{oj}$ – nominal value of variable $x_j$, $z_{ij} \in [0,1]$.

Since the diagnostic variables characterising the corporate performance (financial ratios) were either stimulants or anti-stimulants, only the first two formulas were applied in the normalisation procedure.

# Appendix 2. Correlation Matrix of Diagnostic Variables

| | $P_1$ | $P_2$ | $P_3$ | $P_4$ | $P_5$ | $P_6$ | $P_7$ | $P_8$ | $P_9$ | $P_{10}$ | $P_{11}$ | $P_{12}$ | $P_{13}$ | $L_1$ | $L_2$ | $L_3$ | $L_4$ | $L_5$ | $L_6$ | $L_7$ | $L_8$ | $L_9$ | $L_{10}$ | $L_{11}$ | $D_1$ | $D_2$ | $D_3$ | $D_4$ | $D_5$ | $D_6$ | $D_7$ | $D_8$ |
|---|---|---|---|---|---|---|---|---|---|---|---|---|---|---|---|---|---|---|---|---|---|---|---|---|---|---|---|---|---|---|---|---|
| $P_1$ | 1.00 | | | | | | | | | | | | | | | | | | | | | | | | | | | | | | | |
| $P_2$ | 0.83 | 1.00 | | | | | | | | | | | | | | | | | | | | | | | | | | | | | | |
| $P_3$ | 0.48 | 0.49 | 1.00 | | | | | | | | | | | | | | | | | | | | | | | | | | | | | |
| $P_4$ | −0.13 | −0.01 | −0.21 | 1.00 | | | | | | | | | | | | | | | | | | | | | | | | | | | | |
| $P_5$ | 0.49 | 0.61 | 0.81 | −0.21 | 1.00 | | | | | | | | | | | | | | | | | | | | | | | | | | | |
| $P_6$ | 0.08 | 0.00 | 0.06 | −0.14 | −0.03 | 1.00 | | | | | | | | | | | | | | | | | | | | | | | | | | |
| $P_7$ | 0.27 | 0.33 | 0.50 | 0.24 | 0.50 | 0.09 | 1.00 | | | | | | | | | | | | | | | | | | | | | | | | | |
| $P_8$ | −0.28 | −0.15 | −0.27 | 0.15 | −0.09 | −0.14 | −0.30 | 1.00 | | | | | | | | | | | | | | | | | | | | | | | | |
| $P_9$ | −0.32 | −0.28 | −0.35 | 0.12 | −0.18 | −0.10 | −0.26 | 0.91 | 1.00 | | | | | | | | | | | | | | | | | | | | | | | |
| $P_{10}$ | 0.51 | 0.56 | 0.42 | −0.01 | 0.42 | −0.18 | 0.23 | −0.23 | −0.39 | 1.00 | | | | | | | | | | | | | | | | | | | | | | |
| $P_{11}$ | −0.11 | −0.14 | −0.22 | 0.09 | −0.23 | 0.23 | −0.08 | 0.26 | 0.39 | −0.82 | 1.00 | | | | | | | | | | | | | | | | | | | | | |
| $P_{12}$ | 0.41 | 0.43 | 0.42 | 0.12 | 0.46 | 0.20 | 0.65 | −0.20 | −0.17 | −0.21 | 0.50 | 1.00 | | | | | | | | | | | | | | | | | | | | |
| $P_{13}$ | 0.32 | 0.26 | 0.52 | 0.00 | 0.39 | −0.09 | 0.48 | −0.51 | −0.60 | 0.56 | −0.52 | 0.14 | 1.00 | | | | | | | | | | | | | | | | | | | |
| $L_1$ | 0.28 | 0.26 | −0.15 | 0.01 | 0.05 | 0.09 | −0.01 | 0.09 | 0.18 | 0.15 | 0.00 | −0.01 | −0.29 | 1.00 | | | | | | | | | | | | | | | | | | |
| $L_2$ | 0.27 | 0.28 | −0.12 | 0.22 | 0.04 | 0.12 | 0.12 | 0.02 | 0.07 | 0.30 | −0.10 | −0.02 | −0.16 | 0.86 | 1.00 | | | | | | | | | | | | | | | | | |
| $L_3$ | 0.30 | 0.32 | 0.22 | −0.07 | 0.11 | 0.16 | 0.29 | −0.37 | −0.41 | 0.38 | −0.38 | 0.00 | 0.38 | 0.26 | 0.34 | 1.00 | | | | | | | | | | | | | | | | |
| $L_4$ | 0.38 | 0.32 | 0.36 | 0.01 | 0.35 | 0.00 | 0.22 | 0.03 | −0.17 | 0.40 | −0.21 | 0.18 | 0.42 | −0.31 | −0.10 | 0.13 | 1.00 | | | | | | | | | | | | | | | |
| $L_5$ | 0.12 | 0.25 | 0.12 | 0.04 | 0.22 | 0.20 | 0.05 | 0.08 | −0.03 | −0.22 | 0.25 | 0.31 | −0.03 | −0.31 | −0.37 | −0.08 | 0.22 | 1.00 | | | | | | | | | | | | | | |
| $L_6$ | 0.07 | 0.09 | 0.05 | −0.04 | −0.03 | −0.04 | −0.05 | −0.36 | −0.42 | 0.35 | −0.53 | −0.30 | 0.21 | 0.01 | 0.14 | 0.73 | 0.11 | −0.05 | 1.00 | | | | | | | | | | | | | |
| $L_7$ | −0.31 | −0.40 | −0.45 | −0.05 | −0.43 | −0.18 | −0.59 | 0.25 | 0.41 | −0.03 | −0.10 | −0.66 | −0.36 | 0.18 | 0.18 | −0.24 | −0.31 | −0.57 | 0.02 | 1.00 | | | | | | | | | | | | |
| $L_8$ | −0.31 | −0.36 | −0.38 | 0.00 | −0.36 | −0.19 | −0.52 | 0.39 | 0.50 | 0.06 | −0.16 | −0.67 | −0.27 | 0.11 | 0.15 | −0.18 | −0.19 | −0.55 | 0.03 | 0.95 | 1.00 | | | | | | | | | | | |
| $L_9$ | 0.10 | 0.09 | 0.03 | 0.01 | −0.01 | 0.58 | −0.07 | −0.11 | −0.11 | −0.09 | 0.00 | 0.04 | −0.12 | 0.07 | 0.10 | 0.31 | −0.04 | 0.26 | 0.30 | −0.14 | −0.12 | 1.00 | | | | | | | | | | |
| $L_{10}$ | −0.57 | −0.51 | −0.31 | −0.03 | −0.34 | 0.09 | −0.20 | 0.23 | 0.34 | −0.59 | 0.35 | −0.13 | −0.40 | 0.04 | −0.16 | −0.20 | −0.74 | 0.07 | −0.24 | 0.09 | 0.03 | −0.01 | 1.00 | | | | | | | | | |
| $L_{11}$ | 0.06 | 0.02 | −0.04 | −0.09 | −0.05 | 0.66 | 0.02 | −0.10 | −0.08 | −0.09 | 0.11 | 0.06 | −0.08 | 0.20 | 0.28 | 0.22 | −0.05 | −0.03 | 0.01 | −0.01 | −0.03 | 0.62 | −0.05 | 1.00 | | | | | | | | |
| $D_1$ | 0.33 | 0.38 | 0.05 | −0.04 | 0.36 | 0.03 | 0.19 | 0.39 | 0.38 | 0.11 | 0.05 | 0.22 | −0.32 | 0.46 | 0.39 | −0.07 | 0.08 | 0.09 | −0.16 | −0.11 | −0.08 | 0.03 | −0.13 | 0.12 | 1.00 | | | | | | | |
| $D_2$ | −0.35 | −0.37 | −0.04 | −0.09 | 0.03 | −0.18 | 0.26 | 0.30 | 0.35 | −0.22 | 0.02 | 0.08 | −0.01 | −0.17 | −0.23 | −0.26 | 0.05 | −0.21 | −0.26 | −0.02 | 0.07 | −0.29 | 0.11 | −0.07 | 0.25 | 1.00 | | | | | | |
| $D_3$ | 0.39 | 0.26 | 0.17 | −0.20 | 0.29 | −0.26 | 0.05 | 0.28 | 0.19 | 0.38 | −0.29 | −0.04 | 0.08 | 0.19 | 0.17 | −0.01 | 0.44 | −0.21 | −0.03 | 0.01 | 0.10 | −0.19 | −0.46 | −0.04 | 0.54 | 0.49 | 1.00 | | | | | |
| $D_4$ | 0.21 | 0.15 | 0.17 | 0.06 | 0.30 | 0.16 | 0.62 | 0.01 | 0.07 | −0.11 | 0.17 | 0.52 | 0.04 | 0.22 | 0.24 | 0.09 | 0.13 | 0.12 | −0.15 | −0.46 | −0.43 | 0.00 | −0.05 | 0.20 | 0.56 | 0.56 | 0.45 | 1.00 | | | | |
| $D_5$ | 0.09 | 0.10 | −0.02 | 0.15 | −0.06 | 0.59 | 0.08 | −0.18 | −0.15 | −0.02 | 0.11 | 0.09 | −0.13 | 0.33 | 0.45 | 0.19 | −0.21 | −0.12 | 0.01 | 0.01 | −0.04 | 0.55 | 0.01 | 0.83 | 0.09 | −0.27 | −0.22 | 0.10 | 1.00 | | | |
| $D_6$ | −0.21 | −0.09 | −0.22 | 0.18 | −0.03 | −0.10 | −0.09 | 0.83 | 0.81 | −0.45 | 0.50 | 0.13 | −0.57 | 0.02 | −0.08 | −0.40 | 0.01 | 0.19 | −0.38 | 0.03 | 0.15 | −0.10 | 0.20 | −0.13 | 0.52 | 0.45 | 0.27 | 0.31 | −0.20 | 1.00 | | |
| $D_7$ | −0.26 | −0.23 | −0.28 | −0.19 | −0.11 | −0.17 | −0.24 | 0.41 | 0.38 | −0.15 | −0.09 | −0.31 | −0.34 | −0.06 | −0.16 | −0.20 | −0.12 | −0.04 | −0.02 | 0.21 | 0.27 | −0.01 | 0.19 | 0.01 | 0.42 | 0.55 | 0.43 | 0.27 | −0.19 | 0.48 | 1.00 | |
| $D_8$ | −0.32 | −0.40 | 0.13 | 0.09 | −0.15 | 0.06 | 0.04 | −0.33 | −0.22 | −0.37 | 0.30 | 0.17 | 0.15 | −0.36 | −0.31 | −0.16 | −0.26 | −0.13 | −0.20 | 0.01 | −0.06 | −0.08 | 0.32 | −0.01 | −0.61 | −0.13 | −0.60 | −0.30 | 0.11 | −0.27 | −0.45 | 1.00 |

Source: Authors own calculations based on BACH database.

J. Koralun-Bereźnicka, *Corporate Performance*, Contributions to Management Science,
DOI 10.1007/978-3-319-00345-0, © Springer International Publishing Switzerland 2013

# Appendix 3. Silhouette Index Algorithm

First, for each object from cluster $X_j (j = 1, \ldots, c)$ a measure $s(i)$ $(i = 1, \ldots, m)$ is determined, which is a measure of membership of the $i$-th object to cluster $X_j$:

$$s(i) = \frac{b(i) - a(i)}{\max\{a(i);b(i)\}}$$

The expression $a(i)$ in the above definition is the average dissimilarity of the $i$-th object to all other objects in the same cluster $X_j$. It is calculated as the average distance between the $i$-th object in cluster $X_j$, and all other objects in cluster $X_j$:

$$a(i) = \frac{\sum\limits_{j \in X_j, j \neq i} d(i,j)}{m_j - 1}$$

It is therefore called the internal distance. Then the $b(i)$ is calculated, which is the minimum average distance between the $i$-th object in cluster $X_j$ and all the objects in cluster $X_k$ $(k = 1, \ldots, c;\ k \neq j)$.

$$b(i) = \min_{X_k \neq X_j} d(i, X_k),$$

where $d(i,X_k)$ is the external distance, i.e. the average dissimilarity of the $i$-th object to all other objects in cluster $X_k$:

$$d(i, X_k) = \frac{\sum\limits_{j \in X_k} d(i,j)}{m_k}$$

The cluster $X_l$ $(l = 1, \ldots, c;\ l \neq k \neq j)$, which achieves the minimum $(d(i,X_k) = b(i))$ is the second closest cluster for the $i$-th object, where this object could be placed and it is called the neighbour of the $i$-th object (Migdał-Najman & Najman, 2006). Since the distance measure between objects applied previously in

J. Koralun-Bereźnicka, *Corporate Performance*, Contributions to Management Science,
DOI 10.1007/978-3-319-00345-0, © Springer International Publishing Switzerland 2013

the study was the squared Euclidean distance, it is consistently assumed that it will also be an adequate distance measure for the silhouette index. The measures of membership of the objects to clusters ($s(i)$) are then used to construct a synthetic indicator evaluating the quality of clustering, which is called *global silhouette index*, defined as:

$$SI = \frac{\sum_{j=1}^{c} S_j}{c},$$

where:

$$S_j = \frac{\sum_{i=1}^{m} s(i)}{m},$$

$m$ – number of objects in $X_j$.

# Appendix 4. The Method of Calculating the Adjusted Rand's Measure ($R_{AD}$)

The adjusted Rand's measure is defined by the formula (Hubert & Arabie, 1985, pp. 286–288):

$$R_{AD} = \frac{2(ad - cb)}{2ad + (a + d)(b + c) + b^2 + c^2},$$

where:

$a$ – number of cases where the objects forming a pair belong to the same group in either grouping;
$b$ – number of cases where the objects forming a pair belong to the same group in one grouping, but to different groups in the other grouping;
$c$ – number of cases where the objects forming a pair belong to different groups in one grouping, but to the same group in the other grouping;
$d$ – number of cases where the objects forming a pair belong to different groups in one grouping and to different groups in the other grouping.

These relationships can be presented in the table of associations, where the symbols S and D denote the assignment to the same or different cluster in the compared groupings.

Table of associations 2 × 2

| | S | D | Sum |
|---|---|---|---|
| **S** | $a$ | $b$ | $a + b$ |
| **D** | $c$ | $d$ | $c + d$ |
| Sum | $a + c$ | $b + d$ | $M$ |

Source: Najman, 2007, p. 192.

Letters $a$, $b$, $c$ and $d$ represent respectively the number of cases of combinations SS, SD, DS and DD. $M$ is the maximum number of all pairs of objects in the population, which is calculated as:


DOI 10.1007/978-3-319-00345-0, © Springer International Publishing Switzerland 2013

$$M = \frac{n(n-1)}{2} = a + b + c + d,$$

where $n$ is the number of objects in the population.

# Appendix 5. Descriptive Statistics of Industry Ratios: Means for All Countries from the Period 1999 to 2005

| Ratio | AGR | FSH | MIN | MNF | ELE | CST | TRD | HOT | TRS | AGR | FSH | MIN | MNF |
|---|---|---|---|---|---|---|---|---|---|---|---|---|---|
| $P_1$ | 0.383 | 0.360 | 0.985 | 0.318 | 1.000 | 0.139 | 0.000 | 0.530 | 0.849 | 0.614 | 0.495 | 0.573 | 0.764 |
| $P_2$ | 0.199 | 0.000 | 1.000 | 0.274 | 0.688 | 0.172 | 0.083 | 0.351 | 0.475 | 0.456 | 0.347 | 0.510 | 0.386 |
| $P_3$ | 0.101 | 0.014 | 1.000 | 0.289 | 0.530 | 0.073 | 0.000 | 0.100 | 0.000 | 0.935 | 0.312 | 0.376 | 0.326 |
| $P_4$ | 0.782 | 0.000 | 0.806 | 0.902 | 0.782 | 0.796 | 0.780 | 0.820 | 0.838 | 0.814 | 0.906 | 0.830 | 1.000 |
| $P_5$ | 0.253 | 0.000 | 1.000 | 0.560 | 0.365 | 0.401 | 0.578 | 0.274 | 0.001 | 0.196 | 0.880 | 0.906 | 0.723 |
| $P_6$ | 0.630 | 1.000 | 0.528 | 0.707 | 0.945 | 0.615 | 0.750 | 0.276 | 0.389 | 0.619 | 0.521 | 0.000 | 0.835 |
| $P_7$ | 0.401 | 0.477 | 0.622 | 0.323 | 0.433 | 0.409 | 0.000 | 0.783 | 0.656 | 0.687 | 0.979 | 1.000 | 0.749 |
| $P_8$ | 0.244 | 0.243 | 0.186 | 0.376 | 0.061 | 0.441 | 1.000 | 0.285 | 0.092 | 0.000 | 0.415 | 0.410 | 0.251 |
| $P_9$ | 0.155 | 0.146 | 0.098 | 0.262 | 0.000 | 0.634 | 1.000 | 0.108 | 0.021 | 0.029 | 0.272 | 0.246 | 0.129 |
| $P_{10}$ | 0.371 | 0.441 | 0.647 | 0.253 | 0.433 | 0.357 | 0.000 | 0.675 | 0.622 | 0.656 | 1.000 | 0.933 | 0.606 |
| $P_{11}$ | 0.712 | 0.618 | 0.670 | 0.827 | 0.896 | 0.627 | 1.000 | 0.406 | 0.604 | 0.465 | 0.000 | 0.113 | 0.587 |
| $P_{12}$ | 0.393 | 0.114 | 0.688 | 0.461 | 1.000 | 0.196 | 0.470 | 0.213 | 0.556 | 0.362 | 0.000 | 0.034 | 0.463 |
| $P_{13}$ | 0.009 | 0.079 | 0.361 | 0.109 | 0.117 | 0.022 | 0.002 | 0.033 | 0.065 | 1.000 | 0.000 | 0.001 | 0.066 |
| $L_1$ | 0.808 | 0.836 | 1.000 | 0.558 | 0.258 | 0.592 | 0.480 | 0.000 | 0.102 | 0.760 | 0.653 | 0.965 | 0.687 |
| $L_2$ | 0.199 | 0.246 | 0.697 | 0.174 | 0.219 | 0.129 | 0.000 | 0.008 | 0.175 | 0.657 | 0.711 | 1.000 | 0.569 |
| $L_3$ | 0.353 | 0.469 | 0.309 | 0.000 | 0.171 | 0.087 | 0.005 | 0.327 | 0.189 | 0.515 | 0.994 | 1.000 | 0.666 |
| $L_4$ | 0.000 | 0.119 | 0.360 | 0.062 | 0.699 | 0.014 | 0.178 | 0.511 | 0.914 | 0.076 | 1.000 | 0.666 | 0.316 |
| $L_5$ | 0.481 | 0.662 | 0.431 | 0.326 | 0.481 | 0.252 | 0.802 | 1.000 | 0.332 | 0.000 | 0.666 | 0.657 | 0.615 |
| $L_6$ | 0.378 | 0.431 | 0.128 | 0.166 | 0.000 | 0.547 | 0.384 | 0.358 | 0.157 | 0.282 | 1.000 | 0.834 | 0.460 |
| $L_7$ | 0.457 | 0.419 | 0.322 | 0.562 | 0.000 | 1.000 | 0.880 | 0.126 | 0.107 | 0.290 | 0.462 | 0.490 | 0.346 |
| $L_8$ | 0.319 | 0.303 | 0.356 | 0.544 | 0.000 | 1.000 | 0.815 | 0.188 | 0.200 | 0.412 | 0.746 | 0.781 | 0.481 |
| $L_9$ | 0.696 | 0.758 | 0.845 | 0.624 | 0.864 | 0.664 | 0.000 | 1.000 | 0.929 | 0.900 | 0.928 | 0.972 | 0.878 |
| $L_{10}$ | 0.000 | 0.134 | 0.533 | 0.238 | 0.819 | 0.137 | 0.044 | 0.831 | 1.000 | 0.750 | 0.989 | 0.960 | 0.763 |
| $L_{11}$ | 0.660 | 0.669 | 0.556 | 0.718 | 0.688 | 0.628 | 1.000 | 0.000 | 0.314 | 0.542 | 0.498 | 0.281 | 0.604 |
| $D_1$ | 0.319 | 0.164 | 0.851 | 0.338 | 0.258 | 0.253 | 0.254 | 0.178 | 0.151 | 0.000 | 0.711 | 1.000 | 0.619 |
| $D_2$ | 0.594 | 0.430 | 0.840 | 0.871 | 0.346 | 0.897 | 1.000 | 0.000 | 0.156 | 0.382 | 0.615 | 0.489 | 0.570 |
| $D_3$ | 0.639 | 0.321 | 0.978 | 1.000 | 0.593 | 0.716 | 0.974 | 0.325 | 0.000 | 0.510 | 0.882 | 0.136 | 0.536 |
| $D_4$ | 0.625 | 0.509 | 1.000 | 0.626 | 0.885 | 0.000 | 0.163 | 0.163 | 0.453 | 0.674 | 0.518 | 0.501 | 0.520 |
| $D_5$ | 0.839 | 0.989 | 0.844 | 0.810 | 0.817 | 0.757 | 0.789 | 0.000 | 0.531 | 0.815 | 0.676 | 0.279 | 1.000 |
| $D_6$ | 0.868 | 0.786 | 0.692 | 0.869 | 0.641 | 0.932 | 1.000 | 0.780 | 0.586 | 0.000 | 0.907 | 0.939 | 0.793 |
| $D_7$ | 0.637 | 0.306 | 0.000 | 0.255 | 0.164 | 1.000 | 0.751 | 0.301 | 0.044 | 0.270 | 0.638 | 0.730 | 0.444 |
| $D_8$ | 0.826 | 1.000 | 0.000 | 0.595 | 0.212 | 0.745 | 0.792 | 0.954 | 0.481 | 0.853 | 0.845 | 0.699 | 0.643 |

Source: Calculations based on BACH database.

J. Koralun-Bereźnicka, *Corporate Performance*, Contributions to Management Science,
DOI 10.1007/978-3-319-00345-0, 

# Appendix 6. Descriptive Statistics of Industry Ratios: Standard Deviations for All Countries from the Period 1999 to 2005

| Ratio | AGR | FSH | MIN | MNF | ELE | CST | TRD | HOT | TRS | AGR | FSH | MIN | MNF |
|---|---|---|---|---|---|---|---|---|---|---|---|---|---|
| $P_1$ | 0.223 | 0.228 | 0.331 | 0.094 | 0.193 | 0.064 | 0.025 | 0.157 | 0.232 | 0.229 | 0.138 | 0.350 | 0.243 |
| $P_2$ | 0.206 | 0.142 | 0.263 | 0.166 | 0.225 | 0.193 | 0.191 | 0.213 | 0.222 | 0.285 | 0.175 | 0.387 | 0.308 |
| $P_3$ | 0.133 | 0.283 | 0.349 | 0.255 | 0.234 | 0.162 | 0.174 | 0.187 | 0.299 | 0.356 | 0.280 | 0.272 | 0.349 |
| $P_4$ | 0.320 | 0.333 | 0.406 | 0.398 | 0.435 | 0.359 | 0.339 | 0.315 | 0.369 | 0.396 | 0.311 | 0.381 | 0.349 |
| $P_5$ | 0.165 | 0.331 | 0.327 | 0.318 | 0.382 | 0.229 | 0.270 | 0.176 | 0.318 | 0.226 | 0.275 | 0.320 | 0.352 |
| $P_6$ | 0.321 | 0.371 | 0.333 | 0.277 | 0.362 | 0.297 | 0.343 | 0.428 | 0.430 | 0.349 | 0.288 | 0.392 | 0.281 |
| $P_7$ | 0.257 | 0.186 | 0.258 | 0.145 | 0.163 | 0.133 | 0.000 | 0.117 | 0.172 | 0.137 | 0.108 | 0.146 | 0.235 |
| $P_8$ | 0.162 | 0.122 | 0.238 | 0.181 | 0.086 | 0.178 | 0.000 | 0.194 | 0.100 | 0.162 | 0.139 | 0.162 | 0.135 |
| $P_9$ | 0.154 | 0.088 | 0.163 | 0.150 | 0.041 | 0.218 | 0.029 | 0.115 | 0.052 | 0.162 | 0.151 | 0.092 | 0.084 |
| $P_{10}$ | 0.206 | 0.132 | 0.271 | 0.101 | 0.217 | 0.145 | 0.000 | 0.106 | 0.182 | 0.164 | 0.121 | 0.198 | 0.214 |
| $P_{11}$ | 0.204 | 0.175 | 0.309 | 0.127 | 0.127 | 0.212 | 0.047 | 0.160 | 0.191 | 0.218 | 0.059 | 0.184 | 0.191 |
| $P_{12}$ | 0.183 | 0.181 | 0.273 | 0.154 | 0.101 | 0.140 | 0.146 | 0.188 | 0.218 | 0.284 | 0.152 | 0.199 | 0.185 |
| $P_{13}$ | 0.169 | 0.206 | 0.404 | 0.392 | 0.305 | 0.139 | 0.143 | 0.180 | 0.328 | 0.349 | 0.164 | 0.203 | 0.196 |
| $L_1$ | 0.227 | 0.302 | 0.379 | 0.197 | 0.224 | 0.274 | 0.224 | 0.130 | 0.152 | 0.326 | 0.143 | 0.373 | 0.368 |
| $L_2$ | 0.160 | 0.141 | 0.375 | 0.148 | 0.172 | 0.208 | 0.172 | 0.143 | 0.213 | 0.356 | 0.280 | 0.372 | 0.332 |
| $L_3$ | 0.077 | 0.208 | 0.390 | 0.195 | 0.293 | 0.118 | 0.137 | 0.118 | 0.205 | 0.270 | 0.266 | 0.343 | 0.303 |
| $L_4$ | 0.051 | 0.202 | 0.295 | 0.038 | 0.316 | 0.075 | 0.098 | 0.249 | 0.248 | 0.138 | 0.316 | 0.306 | 0.285 |
| $L_5$ | 0.227 | 0.143 | 0.314 | 0.177 | 0.296 | 0.102 | 0.259 | 0.251 | 0.274 | 0.116 | 0.134 | 0.296 | 0.217 |
| $L_6$ | 0.156 | 0.251 | 0.242 | 0.210 | 0.052 | 0.262 | 0.189 | 0.160 | 0.084 | 0.267 | 0.145 | 0.247 | 0.225 |
| $L_7$ | 0.155 | 0.212 | 0.203 | 0.148 | 0.065 | 0.023 | 0.115 | 0.120 | 0.115 | 0.279 | 0.209 | 0.250 | 0.092 |
| $L_8$ | 0.117 | 0.110 | 0.258 | 0.132 | 0.121 | 0.176 | 0.196 | 0.161 | 0.164 | 0.340 | 0.272 | 0.251 | 0.125 |
| $L_9$ | 0.251 | 0.325 | 0.254 | 0.211 | 0.221 | 0.271 | 0.183 | 0.248 | 0.192 | 0.187 | 0.148 | 0.155 | 0.171 |
| $L_{10}$ | 0.147 | 0.298 | 0.276 | 0.201 | 0.177 | 0.246 | 0.207 | 0.078 | 0.045 | 0.196 | 0.048 | 0.056 | 0.126 |
| $L_{11}$ | 0.366 | 0.398 | 0.383 | 0.330 | 0.388 | 0.324 | 0.333 | 0.440 | 0.341 | 0.391 | 0.265 | 0.302 | 0.322 |
| $D_1$ | 0.190 | 0.149 | 0.450 | 0.302 | 0.296 | 0.286 | 0.305 | 0.151 | 0.211 | 0.105 | 0.302 | 0.289 | 0.363 |
| $D_2$ | 0.269 | 0.368 | 0.192 | 0.089 | 0.261 | 0.263 | 0.107 | 0.146 | 0.258 | 0.358 | 0.137 | 0.318 | 0.284 |
| $D_3$ | 0.296 | 0.352 | 0.248 | 0.094 | 0.292 | 0.321 | 0.163 | 0.316 | 0.351 | 0.374 | 0.179 | 0.382 | 0.319 |
| $D_4$ | 0.354 | 0.297 | 0.368 | 0.143 | 0.227 | 0.144 | 0.177 | 0.275 | 0.244 | 0.328 | 0.304 | 0.278 | 0.312 |
| $D_5$ | 0.357 | 0.396 | 0.365 | 0.356 | 0.340 | 0.384 | 0.369 | 0.409 | 0.357 | 0.355 | 0.358 | 0.385 | 0.380 |
| $D_6$ | 0.118 | 0.205 | 0.283 | 0.137 | 0.349 | 0.234 | 0.013 | 0.201 | 0.395 | 0.370 | 0.071 | 0.061 | 0.190 |
| $D_7$ | 0.190 | 0.316 | 0.339 | 0.152 | 0.343 | 0.200 | 0.118 | 0.255 | 0.306 | 0.363 | 0.317 | 0.318 | 0.115 |
| $D_8$ | 0.327 | 0.342 | 0.340 | 0.186 | 0.299 | 0.135 | 0.144 | 0.099 | 0.389 | 0.135 | 0.216 | 0.320 | 0.254 |

Source: Calculations based on BACH database.

J. Koralun-Bereźnicka, *Corporate Performance*, Contributions to Management Science, DOI 10.1007/978-3-319-00345-0, 

# Appendix 7. Descriptive Statistics of Country Ratios: Means for All Industries from the Period 1999 to 2005

| Ratio | NL | B | FR | ES | I | A | D | P | FIN | PL |
|---|---|---|---|---|---|---|---|---|---|---|
| $P_1$ | 0.563 | 0.189 | 0.273 | 0.319 | 0.439 | 0.304 | 0.000 | 0.278 | 1.000 | 0.427 |
| $P_2$ | 0.659 | 0.282 | 0.274 | 0.665 | 0.398 | 0.360 | 0.291 | 0.000 | 1.000 | 0.627 |
| $P_3$ | 0.816 | 0.645 | 0.323 | 0.523 | 0.395 | 0.440 | 0.030 | 0.299 | 1.000 | 0.000 |
| $P_4$ | 0.808 | 0.686 | 0.610 | 0.000 | 0.677 | 0.536 | 0.665 | 0.679 | 0.659 | 1.000 |
| $P_5$ | 0.673 | 0.166 | 0.275 | 0.187 | 0.108 | 0.322 | 0.043 | 0.000 | 1.000 | 0.101 |
| $P_6$ | 0.700 | 1.000 | 0.609 | 0.647 | 0.438 | 0.000 | 0.550 | 0.416 | 0.707 | 0.438 |
| $P_7$ | 0.338 | 0.114 | 0.362 | 0.266 | 0.000 | 1.000 | 0.443 | 0.215 | 0.867 | 0.995 |
| $P_8$ | 0.534 | 0.372 | 0.763 | 0.162 | 0.365 | 0.645 | 1.000 | 0.000 | 0.976 | 0.905 |
| $P_9$ | 0.156 | 0.109 | 0.625 | 0.000 | 0.331 | 0.194 | 1.000 | 0.029 | 0.422 | 0.264 |
| $P_{10}$ | 0.658 | 0.216 | 0.912 | 0.949 | 0.000 | 1.000 | 0.187 | 0.709 | 0.769 | 0.758 |
| $P_{11}$ | 0.415 | 0.709 | 0.073 | 0.055 | 1.000 | 0.000 | 0.672 | 0.269 | 0.460 | 0.365 |
| $P_{12}$ | 0.949 | 0.196 | 0.000 | 0.039 | 1.000 | 0.831 | 0.877 | 0.126 | 0.265 | 0.183 |
| $P_{13}$ | 0.033 | 0.854 | 0.390 | 1.000 | 0.212 | – | 0.252 | 0.841 | 0.000 | 0.168 |
| $L_1$ | 0.525 | 0.168 | 0.567 | 0.288 | 0.200 | 0.000 | 0.556 | 0.134 | 1.000 | 0.463 |
| $L_2$ | 0.781 | 0.311 | 0.647 | 0.367 | 0.243 | 0.000 | 0.526 | 0.141 | 1.000 | 0.522 |
| $L_3$ | 0.585 | 0.537 | 0.405 | 0.177 | 0.000 | 0.173 | 0.191 | 0.106 | 1.000 | 0.677 |
| $L_4$ | 1.000 | 0.713 | 0.346 | 0.345 | 0.418 | 0.000 | 0.283 | 0.290 | 0.212 | 0.198 |
| $L_5$ | 0.178 | 0.392 | 0.205 | 0.062 | 0.000 | 0.445 | 0.292 | 0.216 | 0.932 | 1.000 |
| $L_6$ | 1.000 | 0.310 | 0.265 | 0.000 | 0.133 | 0.327 | 0.213 | 0.204 | 0.780 | 0.602 |
| $L_7$ | 0.541 | 0.335 | 0.867 | 0.445 | 1.000 | 0.141 | 0.781 | 0.332 | 0.423 | 0.000 |
| $L_8$ | 0.834 | 0.474 | 0.954 | 0.531 | 1.000 | 0.101 | 0.498 | 0.305 | 0.367 | 0.000 |
| $L_9$ | 0.586 | 0.400 | 0.604 | 0.000 | 0.416 | 1.000 | 0.265 | 0.900 | 0.634 | 0.089 |
| $L_{10}$ | 1.000 | 0.778 | 0.530 | 0.572 | 0.473 | 0.356 | 0.000 | 0.398 | 0.252 | 0.385 |
| $L_{11}$ | 0.934 | 1.000 | 0.863 | 0.979 | 0.593 | 0.000 | 0.712 | 0.282 | 0.811 | 0.479 |
| $D_1$ | 0.263 | 0.000 | 0.373 | 0.188 | 0.172 | – | 0.239 | 0.080 | 1.000 | 0.565 |
| $D_2$ | 0.368 | 0.394 | 0.223 | 0.541 | 0.938 | 0.000 | 1.000 | 0.609 | 0.353 | 0.923 |
| $D_3$ | 0.342 | 0.170 | 0.000 | 0.374 | 0.730 | 0.391 | 0.999 | 0.558 | 0.574 | 1.000 |
| $D_4$ | 0.468 | 0.335 | 0.204 | 0.464 | 0.230 | 0.000 | 0.764 | 0.523 | 0.851 | 1.000 |
| $D_5$ | 1.000 | 0.799 | 0.840 | 0.823 | 0.628 | 0.000 | 0.598 | 0.343 | 0.787 | 0.439 |
| $D_6$ | 0.644 | 0.014 | 0.677 | 0.116 | 0.738 | – | 0.780 | 0.000 | 0.914 | 1.000 |
| $D_7$ | 0.124 | 0.101 | 0.868 | 1.000 | 0.743 | – | 0.318 | 0.809 | 0.648 | 0.000 |
| $D_8$ | 0.671 | 0.983 | 0.797 | 0.911 | 0.785 | 0.579 | 0.000 | 1.000 | 0.888 | 0.988 |

Source: Calculations based on BACH database.

J. Koralun-Bereźnicka, *Corporate Performance*, Contributions to Management Science,
DOI 10.1007/978-3-319-00345-0, © Springer International Publishing Switzerland 2013

# Appendix 8. Descriptive Statistics of Country Ratios: Standard Deviations for All Industries from the Period 1999 to 2005

| Ratio | NL | B | FR | ES | I | A | D | P | FIN | PL |
|---|---|---|---|---|---|---|---|---|---|---|
| $P_1$ | 0.287 | 0.278 | 0.312 | 0.342 | 0.337 | 0.291 | 0.429 | 0.314 | 0.293 | 0.298 |
| $P_2$ | 0.289 | 0.264 | 0.224 | 0.314 | 0.301 | 0.326 | 0.388 | 0.247 | 0.268 | 0.265 |
| $P_3$ | 0.274 | 0.274 | 0.296 | 0.272 | 0.292 | 0.291 | 0.330 | 0.234 | 0.259 | 0.227 |
| $P_4$ | 0.227 | 0.240 | 0.265 | 0.275 | 0.227 | 0.262 | 0.394 | 0.266 | 0.242 | 0.317 |
| $P_5$ | 0.230 | 0.273 | 0.251 | 0.254 | 0.280 | 0.340 | 0.391 | 0.311 | 0.291 | 0.230 |
| $P_6$ | 0.247 | 0.244 | 0.303 | 0.238 | 0.258 | 0.294 | 0.301 | 0.271 | 0.280 | 0.253 |
| $P_7$ | 0.260 | 0.280 | 0.265 | 0.352 | 0.382 | 0.321 | 0.359 | 0.271 | 0.279 | 0.261 |
| $P_8$ | 0.340 | 0.244 | 0.259 | 0.271 | 0.268 | 0.294 | 0.348 | 0.250 | 0.308 | 0.261 |
| $P_9$ | 0.334 | 0.281 | 0.320 | 0.298 | 0.283 | 0.304 | 0.368 | 0.277 | 0.306 | 0.275 |
| $P_{10}$ | 0.260 | 0.283 | 0.274 | 0.309 | 0.363 | 0.279 | 0.351 | 0.244 | 0.256 | 0.264 |
| $P_{11}$ | 0.314 | 0.292 | 0.294 | 0.331 | 0.368 | 0.301 | 0.366 | 0.264 | 0.308 | 0.308 |
| $P_{12}$ | 0.283 | 0.310 | 0.325 | 0.267 | 0.327 | 0.297 | 0.344 | 0.272 | 0.281 | 0.290 |
| $P_{13}$ | 0.213 | 0.274 | 0.267 | 0.308 | 0.287 | – | 0.376 | 0.272 | 0.326 | 0.296 |
| $L_1$ | 0.244 | 0.296 | 0.346 | 0.249 | 0.288 | 0.325 | 0.322 | 0.313 | 0.306 | 0.287 |
| $L_2$ | 0.252 | 0.328 | 0.275 | 0.305 | 0.281 | 0.250 | 0.345 | 0.304 | 0.342 | 0.279 |
| $L_3$ | 0.245 | 0.330 | 0.289 | 0.267 | 0.262 | 0.337 | 0.332 | 0.298 | 0.317 | 0.271 |
| $L_4$ | 0.286 | 0.358 | 0.293 | 0.292 | 0.398 | 0.281 | 0.414 | 0.341 | 0.307 | 0.364 |
| $L_5$ | 0.258 | 0.247 | 0.315 | 0.293 | 0.291 | 0.273 | 0.306 | 0.255 | 0.323 | 0.328 |
| $L_6$ | 0.289 | 0.284 | 0.273 | 0.338 | 0.301 | 0.310 | 0.335 | 0.255 | 0.288 | 0.292 |
| $L_7$ | 0.327 | 0.287 | 0.296 | 0.272 | 0.377 | 0.345 | 0.384 | 0.333 | 0.278 | 0.338 |
| $L_8$ | 0.302 | 0.316 | 0.271 | 0.261 | 0.295 | 0.353 | 0.386 | 0.311 | 0.268 | 0.310 |
| $L_9$ | 0.261 | 0.299 | 0.263 | 0.271 | 0.303 | 0.262 | 0.368 | 0.275 | 0.344 | 0.232 |
| $L_{10}$ | 0.321 | 0.397 | 0.372 | 0.393 | 0.410 | 0.391 | 0.370 | 0.288 | 0.298 | 0.358 |
| $L_{11}$ | 0.236 | 0.230 | 0.277 | 0.253 | 0.280 | 0.286 | 0.327 | 0.267 | 0.262 | 0.234 |
| $D_1$ | 0.271 | 0.299 | 0.254 | 0.308 | 0.278 | – | 0.357 | 0.281 | 0.384 | 0.252 |
| $D_2$ | 0.289 | 0.298 | 0.329 | 0.337 | 0.317 | 0.299 | 0.373 | 0.353 | 0.347 | 0.281 |
| $D_3$ | 0.260 | 0.289 | 0.295 | 0.268 | 0.303 | 0.288 | 0.347 | 0.273 | 0.373 | 0.258 |
| $D_4$ | 0.316 | 0.321 | 0.319 | 0.265 | 0.281 | 0.284 | 0.348 | 0.315 | 0.283 | 0.299 |
| $D_5$ | 0.231 | 0.242 | 0.284 | 0.228 | 0.304 | 0.281 | 0.327 | 0.235 | 0.285 | 0.268 |
| $D_6$ | 0.295 | 0.270 | 0.277 | 0.269 | 0.314 | – | 0.421 | 0.261 | 0.266 | 0.311 |
| $D_7$ | 0.300 | 0.264 | 0.273 | 0.330 | 0.296 | – | 0.300 | 0.296 | 0.276 | 0.255 |
| $D_8$ | 0.270 | 0.276 | 0.265 | 0.274 | 0.272 | 0.303 | 0.339 | 0.364 | 0.328 | 0.255 |

Source: Calculations based on BACH database.

J. Koralun-Bereźnicka, *Corporate Performance*, Contributions to Management Science, DOI 10.1007/978-3-319-00345-0, 

# Appendix 9. Taxonomic Measure of Development for Industries in Countries. A Separate Standard Object for Each Year

| | | Industry | | | | | | | | | | | | |
|---|---|---|---|---|---|---|---|---|---|---|---|---|---|---|
| Country | Year | AGR | FSH | MIN | MNF | ELE | CST | TRD | HOT | TRS | RLE | EDU | HLT | COM |
| NL | 1999 | 0.113 | 0.163 | 0.150 | 0.168 | 0.033 | 0.190 | 0.139 | 0.096 | 0.107 | 0.249 | 0.242 | 0.350 | 0.115 |
| | 2000 | 0.177 | 0.120 | 0.216 | 0.189 | 0.048 | 0.264 | 0.116 | 0.173 | 0.019 | 0.212 | 0.232 | 0.354 | 0.170 |
| | 2001 | 0.218 | 0.170 | 0.292 | 0.168 | 0.093 | 0.305 | 0.180 | 0.180 | 0.006 | 0.252 | 0.328 | 0.434 | 0.199 |
| | 2002 | 0.208 | 0.194 | 0.234 | 0.143 | 0.104 | 0.263 | 0.187 | 0.128 | 0.016 | 0.214 | 0.286 | 0.391 | 0.190 |
| | 2003 | 0.145 | 0.166 | 0.228 | 0.149 | 0.006 | 0.192 | 0.119 | 0.136 | 0.138 | 0.186 | 0.170 | 0.395 | 0.203 |
| | 2004 | 0.085 | 0.199 | 0.238 | 0.143 | 0.092 | 0.165 | 0.082 | 0.078 | 0.088 | 0.219 | 0.115 | 0.328 | 0.145 |
| | 2005 | 0.096 | 0.135 | 0.216 | 0.110 | 0.089 | 0.130 | 0.069 | 0.069 | 0.025 | 0.199 | 0.175 | 0.240 | 0.102 |
| B | 1999 | 0.096 | 0.023 | 0.205 | 0.179 | 0.328 | 0.175 | 0.138 | 0.052 | 0.180 | 0.246 | 0.262 | 0.304 | 0.284 |
| | 2000 | 0.169 | 0.029 | 0.206 | 0.156 | 0.270 | 0.178 | 0.136 | 0.107 | 0.085 | 0.169 | 0.199 | 0.286 | 0.255 |
| | 2001 | 0.187 | 0.030 | 0.300 | 0.128 | 0.283 | 0.189 | 0.133 | 0.104 | 0.069 | 0.178 | 0.270 | 0.325 | 0.283 |
| | 2002 | 0.213 | 0.016 | 0.236 | 0.105 | 0.313 | 0.209 | 0.156 | 0.070 | 0.106 | 0.200 | 0.255 | 0.313 | 0.303 |
| | 2003 | 0.202 | 0.003 | 0.242 | 0.182 | 0.320 | 0.205 | 0.142 | 0.054 | 0.108 | 0.239 | 0.237 | 0.341 | 0.235 |
| | 2004 | 0.199 | 0.000 | 0.242 | 0.153 | 0.333 | 0.269 | 0.201 | 0.097 | 0.104 | 0.292 | 0.283 | 0.400 | 0.303 |
| | 2005 | 0.209 | 0.032 | 0.265 | 0.192 | 0.334 | 0.251 | 0.176 | 0.073 | 0.217 | 0.248 | 0.310 | 0.413 | 0.282 |
| FR | 1999 | 0.193 | 0.101 | 0.300 | 0.189 | 0.131 | 0.160 | 0.106 | 0.190 | 0.021 | 0.104 | 0.241 | 0.232 | 0.239 |
| | 2000 | 0.192 | 0.065 | 0.338 | 0.207 | 0.105 | 0.221 | 0.138 | 0.196 | 0.014 | 0.095 | 0.232 | 0.239 | 0.235 |
| | 2001 | 0.198 | 0.098 | 0.350 | 0.171 | 0.114 | 0.225 | 0.144 | 0.186 | 0.005 | 0.100 | 0.234 | 0.236 | 0.224 |
| | 2002 | 0.192 | 0.125 | 0.326 | 0.191 | 0.123 | 0.232 | 0.134 | 0.153 | 0.030 | 0.025 | 0.233 | 0.250 | 0.219 |
| | 2003 | 0.194 | 0.148 | 0.352 | 0.169 | 0.118 | 0.223 | 0.139 | 0.149 | 0.010 | 0.135 | 0.000 | 0.242 | 0.198 |
| | 2004 | 0.144 | 0.041 | 0.352 | 0.165 | 0.115 | 0.208 | 0.105 | 0.099 | 0.091 | 0.129 | 0.214 | 0.235 | 0.211 |
| | 2005 | 0.127 | 0.103 | 0.405 | 0.147 | 0.126 | 0.198 | 0.092 | 0.144 | 0.091 | 0.133 | 0.208 | 0.241 | 0.185 |
| ES | 1999 | 0.208 | 0.508 | 0.044 | 0.293 | 0.094 | 0.287 | 0.207 | 0.324 | 0.172 | 0.207 | 0.265 | 0.157 | 0.361 |
| | 2000 | 0.215 | 0.311 | 0.121 | 0.231 | 0.086 | 0.260 | 0.165 | 0.148 | 0.096 | 0.156 | 0.110 | 0.025 | 0.280 |
| | 2001 | 0.205 | 0.247 | 0.153 | 0.189 | 0.147 | 0.243 | 0.173 | 0.102 | 0.097 | 0.090 | 0.160 | 0.031 | 0.236 |
| | 2002 | 0.167 | 0.140 | 0.131 | 0.190 | 0.177 | 0.268 | 0.175 | 0.082 | 0.097 | 0.031 | 0.218 | 0.017 | 0.161 |
| | 2003 | 0.158 | 0.072 | 0.089 | 0.220 | 0.123 | 0.318 | 0.172 | 0.051 | 0.125 | 0.107 | 0.149 | 0.104 | 0.117 |
| | 2004 | 0.191 | 0.234 | 0.016 | 0.250 | 0.061 | 0.268 | 0.196 | 0.075 | 0.237 | 0.101 | 0.303 | 0.214 | 0.292 |
| | 2005 | 0.147 | 0.105 | 0.037 | 0.206 | 0.178 | 0.206 | 0.202 | 0.044 | 0.170 | 0.104 | 0.228 | 0.119 | 0.330 |
| I | 1999 | 0.166 | 0.085 | 0.426 | 0.224 | 0.150 | 0.084 | 0.197 | 0.173 | 0.122 | 0.254 | – | – | 0.223 |
| | 2000 | 0.173 | 0.105 | 0.436 | 0.213 | 0.135 | 0.094 | 0.196 | 0.227 | 0.112 | 0.245 | – | – | 0.170 |
| | 2001 | 0.154 | 0.090 | 0.402 | 0.216 | 0.206 | 0.095 | 0.245 | 0.111 | 0.144 | 0.263 | – | – | 0.125 |
| | 2002 | 0.158 | 0.049 | 0.354 | 0.329 | 0.144 | 0.170 | 0.317 | 0.118 | 0.175 | 0.361 | – | – | 0.176 |
| | 2003 | 0.153 | 0.083 | 0.341 | 0.294 | 0.108 | 0.230 | 0.295 | 0.076 | 0.178 | 0.385 | – | – | 0.183 |
| | 2004 | 0.131 | 0.151 | 0.398 | 0.251 | 0.122 | 0.175 | 0.203 | 0.037 | 0.159 | 0.280 | – | – | 0.175 |
| | 2005 | 0.078 | 0.182 | 0.313 | 0.177 | 0.175 | 0.051 | 0.120 | 0.084 | 0.093 | 0.211 | – | – | 0.205 |

(continued)

J. Koralun-Bereźnicka, *Corporate Performance*, Contributions to Management Science,
DOI 10.1007/978-3-319-00345-0, 

| | | Industry | | | | | | | | | | | | |
|---|---|---|---|---|---|---|---|---|---|---|---|---|---|---|
| Country | Year | AGR | FSH | MIN | MNF | ELE | CST | TRD | HOT | TRS | RLE | EDU | HLT | COM |
| A | 1999 | 0.095 | – | 0.302 | – | 0.039 | 0.236 | 0.227 | 0.122 | 0.063 | 0.296 | 0.230 | 0.269 | 0.287 |
| | 2000 | 0.024 | – | 0.320 | – | 0.127 | 0.238 | 0.225 | 0.122 | 0.103 | 0.345 | 0.286 | 0.246 | 0.348 |
| | 2001 | 0.117 | – | 0.220 | – | 0.076 | 0.168 | 0.133 | 0.128 | 0.018 | 0.310 | 0.163 | 0.235 | 0.184 |
| | 2002 | 0.150 | – | 0.240 | – | 0.089 | 0.164 | 0.152 | 0.052 | 0.067 | 0.274 | 0.294 | 0.239 | 0.121 |
| | 2003 | 0.138 | – | 0.236 | – | 0.020 | 0.163 | 0.132 | 0.057 | 0.200 | 0.287 | 0.148 | 0.211 | 0.111 |
| | 2004 | 0.159 | – | 0.187 | – | 0.092 | 0.071 | 0.104 | 0.082 | 0.047 | 0.248 | 0.108 | 0.208 | 0.231 |
| | 2005 | 0.063 | – | 0.169 | – | 0.115 | 0.105 | 0.084 | 0.036 | 0.215 | 0.211 | 0.115 | 0.131 | 0.251 |
| D | 1999 | – | – | 0.212 | 0.216 | 0.175 | 0.042 | 0.114 | – | 0.150 | 0.061 | – | – | – |
| | 2000 | – | – | 0.314 | 0.278 | 0.284 | 0.157 | 0.175 | – | 0.048 | 0.121 | – | – | – |
| | 2001 | – | – | 0.330 | 0.246 | 0.242 | 0.117 | 0.172 | – | 0.049 | 0.151 | – | – | – |
| | 2002 | – | – | 0.330 | 0.273 | 0.294 | 0.155 | 0.179 | – | 0.034 | 0.161 | – | – | – |
| | 2003 | – | – | 0.291 | 0.235 | 0.194 | 0.122 | 0.171 | – | 0.149 | 0.025 | – | – | – |
| | 2004 | – | – | 0.231 | 0.208 | 0.195 | 0.095 | 0.147 | – | 0.054 | 0.068 | – | – | – |
| | 2005 | – | – | 0.167 | 0.237 | 0.193 | 0.062 | 0.150 | – | 0.040 | 0.128 | – | – | – |
| P | 1999 | 0.195 | 0.142 | 0.220 | 0.365 | 0.081 | 0.208 | 0.314 | 0.308 | 0.060 | 0.000 | 0.000 | 0.000 | 0.000 |
| | 2000 | 0.206 | 0.161 | 0.247 | 0.356 | 0.106 | 0.271 | 0.295 | 0.201 | 0.011 | 0.000 | 0.000 | 0.000 | 0.269 |
| | 2001 | 0.230 | 0.230 | 0.242 | 0.358 | 0.087 | 0.304 | 0.329 | 0.279 | 0.172 | 0.204 | 0.230 | 0.360 | 0.055 |
| | 2002 | 0.193 | 0.209 | 0.294 | 0.355 | 0.124 | 0.302 | 0.335 | 0.173 | 0.167 | 0.183 | 0.261 | 0.366 | 0.042 |
| | 2003 | 0.167 | 0.130 | 0.368 | 0.370 | 0.124 | 0.287 | 0.318 | 0.263 | 0.075 | 0.238 | 0.173 | 0.367 | 0.052 |
| | 2004 | 0.129 | 0.047 | 0.252 | 0.265 | 0.147 | 0.179 | 0.232 | 0.112 | 0.026 | 0.140 | 0.147 | 0.283 | 0.120 |
| | 2005 | 0.132 | 0.084 | 0.241 | 0.253 | 0.072 | 0.155 | 0.244 | 0.066 | 0.028 | 0.242 | 0.175 | 0.272 | 0.208 |
| FIN | 1999 | 0.184 | 0.120 | 0.191 | 0.178 | 0.077 | 0.172 | 0.125 | 0.144 | 0.174 | 0.155 | 0.261 | 0.371 | 0.424 |
| | 2000 | 0.337 | 0.331 | 0.210 | 0.244 | 0.055 | 0.211 | 0.160 | 0.184 | 0.131 | 0.215 | 0.390 | 0.444 | 0.516 |
| | 2001 | 0.296 | 0.333 | 0.211 | 0.263 | 0.063 | 0.228 | 0.194 | 0.237 | 0.120 | 0.215 | 0.420 | 0.514 | 0.527 |
| | 2002 | 0.299 | 0.245 | 0.186 | 0.197 | 0.036 | 0.167 | 0.139 | 0.234 | 0.100 | 0.193 | 0.353 | 0.369 | 0.442 |
| | 2003 | 0.257 | 0.146 | 0.224 | 0.205 | 0.084 | 0.187 | 0.168 | 0.254 | 0.208 | 0.172 | 0.353 | 0.465 | 0.515 |
| | 2004 | 0.181 | 0.205 | 0.226 | 0.208 | 0.127 | 0.214 | 0.183 | 0.270 | 0.223 | 0.135 | 0.368 | 0.497 | 0.540 |
| | 2005 | 0.151 | 0.192 | 0.149 | 0.142 | 0.177 | 0.172 | 0.145 | 0.220 | 0.145 | 0.159 | 0.322 | 0.439 | 0.446 |
| PL | 1999 | 0.216 | 0.233 | 0.140 | 0.216 | 0.117 | 0.219 | 0.240 | 0.039 | 0.059 | 0.196 | 0.433 | 0.231 | 0.285 |
| | 2000 | 0.294 | 0.225 | 0.114 | 0.281 | 0.116 | 0.304 | 0.391 | 0.168 | 0.002 | 0.196 | 0.411 | 0.221 | 0.256 |
| | 2001 | 0.259 | 0.324 | 0.022 | 0.227 | 0.205 | 0.251 | 0.352 | 0.165 | 0.041 | 0.171 | 0.419 | 0.212 | 0.236 |
| | 2002 | 0.180 | 0.087 | 0.096 | 0.262 | 0.190 | 0.202 | 0.252 | 0.125 | 0.068 | 0.130 | 0.350 | 0.198 | 0.379 |
| | 2003 | 0.135 | 0.285 | 0.092 | 0.207 | 0.175 | 0.156 | 0.203 | 0.062 | 0.015 | 0.140 | 0.201 | 0.113 | 0.286 |
| | 2004 | 0.192 | 0.179 | 0.304 | 0.281 | 0.130 | 0.163 | 0.195 | 0.012 | 0.121 | 0.067 | 0.207 | 0.101 | 0.275 |
| | 2005 | 0.149 | 0.242 | 0.279 | 0.215 | 0.129 | 0.153 | 0.161 | 0.021 | 0.076 | 0.090 | 0.223 | 0.206 | 0.166 |

Source: Calculations based on BACH database.

# Appendix 10. The Economic Potential of Industries in Countries Based on the Taxonomic Measure of Development (1st Group of Industries)


DOI 10.1007/978-3-319-00345-0, 

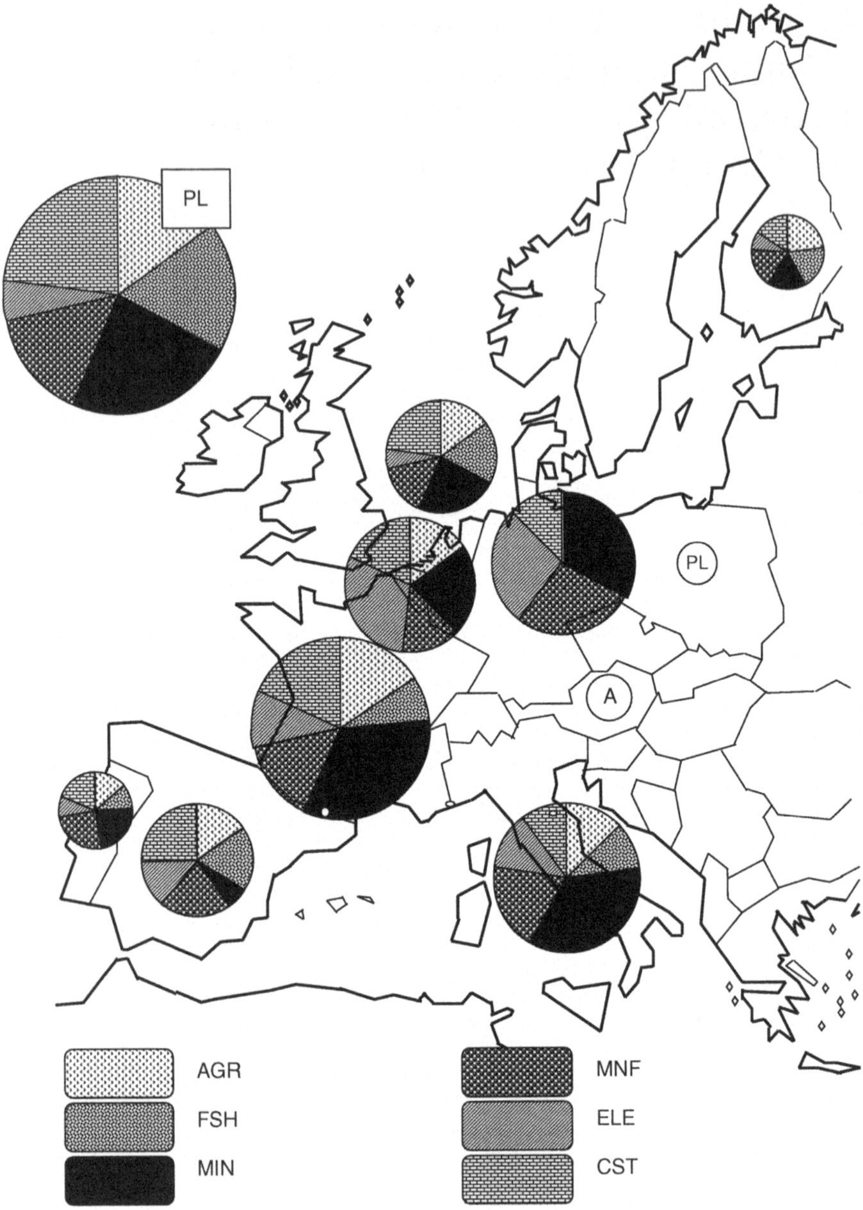


Source: Calculations based on BACH database.

# Appendix 11. The Economic Potential of Industries in Countries Based on the Taxonomic Measure of Development (2nd Group of Industries)

J. Koralun-Bereźnicka, *Corporate Performance*, Contributions to Management Science,
DOI 10.1007/978-3-319-00345-0, 

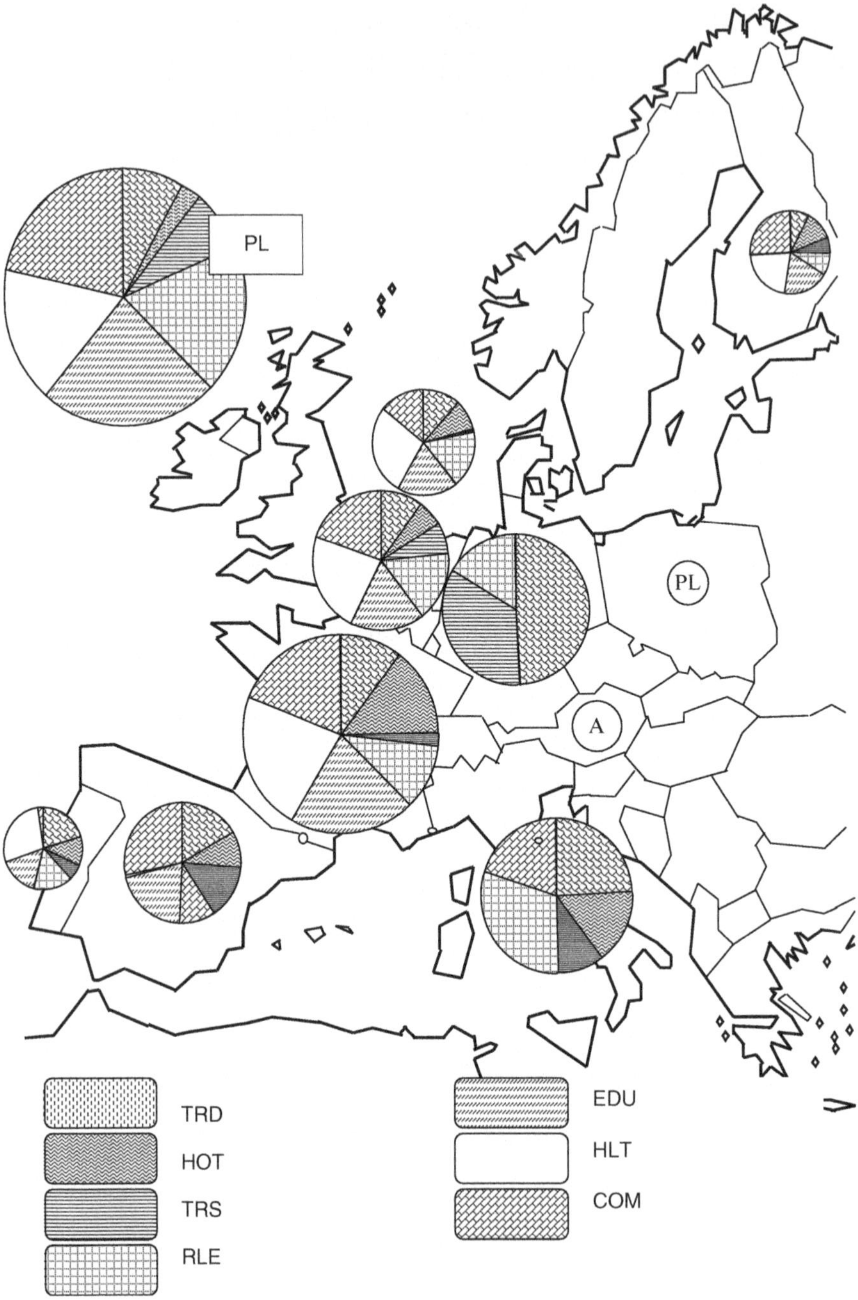


Source: Calculations based on BACH database.

# Appendix 12. One-Way Analysis of Variance Across Industries: Values of F-Statistics and p; p = 0.05 (Deficiencies of Significance Were Highlighted)

J. Koralun-Bereźnicka, *Corporate Performance*, Contributions to Management Science,
DOI 10.1007/978-3-319-00345-0, 

| Ratio | NL | B | FR | ES | I | A | D | P | FIN | PL | All |
|---|---|---|---|---|---|---|---|---|---|---|---|
| $P_1$ | 23.040 (0.000) | 51.917 (0.000) | 48.250 (0.000) | 34.300 (0.000) | 16.976 (0.000) | 12.498 (0.000) | 105.285 (0.000) | 12.384 (0.000) | 34.422 (0.000) | 9.534 (0.000) | **48.83 (0.000)** |
| $P_2$ | 24.109 (0.000) | 56.365 (0.000) | 16.183 (0.000) | 7.112 (0.000) | 10.309 (0.000) | 7.111 (0.000) | 29.579 (0.000) | 6.519 (0.000) | 26.847 (0.000) | 4.716 (0.000) | **20.92 (0.000)** |
| $P_3$ | 4.494 (0.000) | 7.997 (0.000) | 3.997 (0.000) | 1.256 (0.262) | 9.957 (0.000) | 6.442 (0.000) | 7.013 (0.000) | 1.794 (0.066) | 11.329 (0.000) | 2.393 0.012 | **8.530 (0.000)** |
| $P_4$ | 11.448 (0.000) | 4.220 (0.000) | 5.836 (0.000) | 0.034 (1.000) | 2.223 0.027 | 0.505 (0.909) | 5.316 (0.000) | 2.299 (0.016) | 1.801 (0.062) | 0.833 (0.617) | **1.201 (0.277)** |
| $P_5$ | 6.055 (0.000) | 5.884 (0.000) | 6.283 (0.000) | 6.811 (0.000) | 11.524 (0.000) | 5.193 (0.000) | 6.733 (0.000) | 6.245 (0.000) | 36.799 (0.000) | 3.765 (0.000) | **3.536 (0.000)** |
| $P_6$ | 1.700 (0.083) | 1.170 (0.319) | 11.519 (0.000) | 0.931 (0.521) | 0.712 (0.710) | 0.974 (0.476) | 0.655 (0.686) | 1.429 (0.174) | 1.384 (0.192) | 1.557 (0.125) | **1.535 (0.106)** |
| $P_7$ | 47.880 (0.000) | 95.864 (0.000) | 143.404 (0.000) | 63.912 (0.000) | 18.696 (0.000) | 44.669 (0.000) | 206.754 (0.000) | 67.746 (0.000) | 96.754 (0.000) | 3.613 (0.000) | **42.49 (0.000)** |
| $P_8$ | 56.933 (0.000) | 112.486 (0.000) | 586.590 (0.000) | 181.977 (0.000) | 47.244 (0.000) | 35.960 (0.000) | 1194.790 (0.000) | 118.199 (0.000) | 218.718 (0.000) | 83.03 (0.000) | **114.9 (0.000)** |
| $P_9$ | 93.56 (0.000) | 238.2 (0.000) | 1004.8 (0.000) | 125.8 (0.000) | 52.77 (0.000) | 67.43 (0.000) | 1765.6 (0.000) | 283.7 (0.000) | 290.4 (0.000) | 56.45 (0.000) | **137.4 (0.000)** |
| $P_{10}$ | 47.863 (0.000) | 98.110 (0.000) | 101.368 (0.000) | 72.973 (0.000) | 20.027 (0.000) | 23.276 (0.000) | 145.554 (0.000) | 19.901 (0.000) | 68.534 (0.000) | 41.07 (0.000) | **35.38 (0.000)** |
| $P_{11}$ | 807.6 (0.000) | 134.4 (0.000) | 204.0 (0.000) | 165.7 (0.000) | 107.0 (0.000) | 22.38 (0.000) | 111.0 (0.000) | 16.03 (0.000) | 196.7 (0.000) | 143.6 (0.000) | **118.6 (0.000)** |
| $P_{12}$ | 244. 3 (0.000) | 112.0 (0.000) | 79.53 (0.000) | 17.80 (0.000) | 85.80 (0.000) | 13.56 (0.000) | 124.6 (0.000) | 17.32 (0.000) | 102.3 (0.000) | 16.24 (0.000) | **20.15 (0.000)** |
| $P_{13}$ | 3.314 (0.001) | 667.602 (0.000) | 378.071 (0.000) | 49.287 (0.000) | 6.324 (0.000) | . | 41.833 (0.000) | 14.130 (0.000) | 16.730 (0.000) | 6.926 (0.000) | **14.68 (0.000)** |
| $L_1$ | 77.478 (0.000) | 47.121 (0.000) | 60.128 (0.000) | 7.227 (0.000) | 10.924 (0.000) | 8.864 (0.000) | 56.169 (0.000) | 41.076 (0.000) | 31.791 (0.000) | 1.853 (0.055) | **8.000 (0.000)** |
| $L_2$ | 98.258 (0.000) | 66.742 (0.000) | 46.210 (0.000) | 7.302 (0.000) | 15.554 (0.000) | 7.605 (0.000) | 103.672 (0.000) | 9.900 (0.000) | 44.818 (0.000) | 1.821 (0.060) | **9.565 (0.000)** |
| $L_3$ | 65.342 (0.000) | 49.646 (0.000) | 33.471 (0.000) | 8.141 (0.000) | 4.172 (0.000) | 9.130 (0.000) | 3.300 (0.010) | 6.940 (0.000) | 78.188 (0.000) | 2.910 (0.002) | **14.14 (0.000)** |
| $L_4$ | 22.449 (0.000) | 19.219 (0.000) | 59.062 (0.000) | 23.749 (0.000) | 43.455 (0.000) | 13.516 (0.000) | 467.617 (0.000) | 58.979 (0.000) | 106.101 (0.000) | 3.605 (0.000) | **27.88 (0.000)** |
| $L_5$ | 18.564 (0.000) | 17.963 (0.000) | 101.606 (0.000) | 67.375 (0.000) | 20.079 (0.000) | 10.580 (0.000) | 89.702 (0.000) | 8.874 (0.000) | 17.166 (0.000) | 0.414 (0.954) | **4.269 (0.000)** |
| $L_6$ | 64.226 (0.000) | 167.025 (0.000) | 65.775 (0.000) | 21.887 (0.000) | 19.219 (0.000) | 14.821 (0.000) | 21.101 (0.000) | 6.926 (0.000) | 85.177 (0.000) | 26.99 (0.000) | **36.90 (0.000)** |
| $L_7$ | 70.316 (0.000) | 170.477 (0.000) | 284.095 (0.000) | 76.389 (0.000) | 55.844 (0.000) | 40.657 (0.000) | 220.909 (0.000) | 228.084 (0.000) | 158.068 (0.000) | 131.7 (0.000) | **127.1 (0.000)** |
| $L_8$ | 64.623 (0.000) | 173.016 (0.000) | 157.589 (0.000) | 63.531 (0.000) | 51.256 (0.000) | 26.965 (0.000) | 48.526 (0.000) | 110.834 (0.000) | 59.689 (0.000) | 74.83 (0.000) | **58.60 (0.000)** |
| $L_9$ | 5.101 (0.000) | 7.536 (0.000) | 542.620 (0.000) | 60.793 (0.000) | 17.870 (0.000) | 13.053 (0.000) | 16.134 (0.000) | 1.204 (0.298) | 36.468 (0.000) | 7.448 (0.000) | **17.89 (0.000)** |
| $L_{10}$ | 165.523 (0.000) | 213.550 (0.000) | 389.498 (0.000) | 92.042 (0.000) | 158.413 (0.000) | 39.885 (0.000) | 303.633 (0.000) | 78.027 (0.000) | 101.391 (0.000) | 48.06 (0.000) | **115.0 (0.000)** |
| $L_{11}$ | 1.736 (0.075) | 1.568 (0.119) | 121.533 (0.000) | 4.067 (0.000) | 0.844 (0.589) | 2.118 (0.019) | 1.631 (0.165) | 0.847 (0.603) | 5.499 (0.000) | 2.179 (0.021) | **2.238 (0.009)** |
| $D_1$ | 40.369 (0.000) | 36.289 (0.000) | 16.507 (0.000) | 8.614 (0.000) | 12.015 (0.000) | 1.431 (0.157) | 97.548 (0.000) | 9.489 (0.000) | 17.487 (0.000) | 1.338 (0.242) | **9.093 (0.000)** |
| $D_2$ | 20.274 (0.000) | 119.826 (0.000) | 111.223 (0.000) | 57.319 (0.000) | 15.540 (0.000) | 15.596 (0.000) | 414.613 (0.000) | 21.226 (0.000) | 39.956 (0.000) | 15.82 (0.000) | **2.952 (0.000)** |
| $D_3$ | 10.338 (0.000) | 95.179 (0.000) | 80.444 (0.000) | 27.621 (0.000) | 17.537 (0.000) | 2.026 (0.026) | 395.496 (0.000) | 9.896 (0.000) | 24.419 (0.000) | 6.190 (0.000) | **1.352 (0.184)** |
| $D_4$ | 1.415 (0.177) | 2.055 (0.030) | 116.330 (0.000) | 0.573 (0.857) | 0.200 (0.996) | 1.199 (0.289) | 2.680 (0.028) | 0.511 (0.901) | 5.070 (0.000) | 9.499 (0.000) | **20.89 (0.000)** |
| $D_5$ | 1.415 (0.177) | 2.054 (0.030) | 3.258 (0.001) | 0.471 (0.926) | 1.853 (0.068) | 2.922 (0.001) | 1.626 (0.164) | 1.243 (0.273) | 7.846 (0.000) | 2.735 (0.004) | **1.640 (0.076)** |
| $D_6$ | 19.313 (0.000) | 194.542 (0.000) | 134.028 (0.000) | 54.941 (0.000) | 12.390 (0.000) | . | 575.966 (0.000) | 13.017 (0.000) | 49.448 (0.000) | 14.533 (0.000) | **11.84 (0.000)** |
| $D_7$ | 7.653 (0.000) | 39.809 (0.000) | 41.281 (0.000) | 29.874 (0.000) | 8.858 (0.000) | . | 96.765 (0.000) | 13.169 (0.000) | 5.337 (0.000) | 2.251 (0.017) | **6.935 (0.000)** |
| $D_8$ | 168.414 (0.000) | 56.877 (0.000) | 510.486 (0.000) | 41.249 (0.000) | 135.507 (0.000) | 4.199 (0.000) | 271.068 (0.000) | 30.017 (0.000) | 84.393 (0.000) | 4.171 (0.000) | **14.14 (0.000)** |

Source: Calculations based on BACH database.

# Appendix 13. Tukey's test

Tukey's test is a statistical test used mainly as a complementary tool to the analysis of variance. This is a multiple comparisons procedure, designed to detect which means are significantly different from one another. The test is based on the so-called studentised range distribution, which is similar to the distribution of t from the t-test. The test compares all possible pairs of means and detects which differences between the two means $\mu_i - \mu_j$ are greater than resulting from the standard error. The confidence coefficient with equal sample sizes is $1 - \alpha$. The test assumptions are the same as in the analysis of variance. The formula of test is as follows: $q_s = \frac{Y_A - Y_B}{s}$, where $Y_A$ is the larger, and $Y_B$ the smaller of two means being compared, $s$ is the standard error of the data in question. The $q_s$ value is compared with the critical value $q$ from the studentised range distribution. If the $q_s$ value is larger than the critical value, the compared means are significantly different (Stanisz, 2000, p. 416; Ferguson & Takane, 2003; Wieczorkowska, Kochański, & Eljaszuk, 2003, p. 211).

J. Koralun-Bereźnicka, *Corporate Performance*, Contributions to Management Science,
DOI 10.1007/978-3-319-00345-0, 

# Appendix 14. Selected Results of the Post-Hoc Analysis of Cross-Industry Variance for Profitability and Turnover Ratios (Disjoint Homogeneous Groups Are Bolded)

J. Koralun-Bereźnicka, *Corporate Performance*, Contributions to Management Science,
DOI 10.1007/978-3-319-00345-0, © Springer International Publishing Switzerland 2013

| Ratio | Content | All | NL | B | FR | ES | I | A | D | P | FIN | PL |
|---|---|---|---|---|---|---|---|---|---|---|---|---|
| $P_1$ | groups | **9** | 7 | 7 | 5 | 5 | 3 | 5 | **4** | 5 | 8 | 4 |
| | + | **ELE** | MIN | HLT | ELE<br>MIN | TRS<br>ELE | MIN<br>TRS<br>ELE | ELE | RLE<br>MIN<br>TRS | MIN | COM | MIN |
| | – | **TRD** | TRD<br>CST | TRD | TRD | HLT<br>AGR<br>TRD<br>CST<br>MIN<br>FSH | TRD<br>AGR<br>CST<br>FSH<br>MNF<br>RLE | TRD | TRD<br>CST | FSH<br>TRD | TRD | TRD |
| $P_2$ | Groups | **7** | 3 | 7 | 4 | 4 | 3 | 5 | 3 | 3 | 5 | 2 |
| | + | **MIN** | MIN<br>HLT | MIN<br>HLT | MIN | RLE | MIN<br>ELE | HLT | MIN | ELE<br>MIN | COM | MIN |
| | – | **FSH** | TRD<br>CST<br>EDU | FSH | FSH | HLT | COM<br>AGR | TRD | CST<br>TRD<br>MNF | FSH | TRD | All other |
| $P_3$ | Groups | **4** | 3 | 4 | 2 | | 3 | **2** | 3 | | 3 | 2 |
| | + | **MIN** | HLT | MIN | MIN<br>RLE | | MIN | RLE | TRS | | COM | EDU<br>COM |
| | – | **TRS<br>TRD** | TRS<br>TRD | FSH<br>HOT | TRS<br>TRD<br>MNF<br>HOT<br>FSH<br>HLT<br>COM<br>CST | | FSH | All other | TRD<br>CST | | TRD<br>HOT<br>CST | FSH |
| $P_4$ | Groups | | 2 | 2 | 2 | | 2 | | 3 | 2 | | |
| | + | | MIN | ELE | All other | | MIN | | RLE | FSH | | GOR |
| | – | | All other | All other | MIN | | ELE | | ELE | ELE<br>MNF | | All other |
| $P_5$ | Groups | **2** | 3 | 4 | 3 | 4 | 3 | 5 | 3 | 4 | 4 | 3 |
| | + | **EDU** | MIN | ELE | MIN | FSH | MIN | HLT | MNF | TRD<br>ELE<br>MNF | COM<br>HLT | EDU |
| | – | **All other** | TRS | FSH | TRS | HLT | FSH<br>COM | TRS<br>ELE | CST<br>RLE | FSH | ELE | FSH |
| $P_6$ | Groups | | | | 4 | | | | | | | |
| | + | | | | HOT | | | | | | | |
| | – | | | | FSH<br>TRS<br>AGR<br>ELE<br>MNF<br>RLE<br>CST<br>TRD | | | | | | | |
| $P_7$ | Groups | **6** | 7 | 7 | 6 | 5 | 4 | 5 | 5 | 9 | 7 | 2 |
| | + | **TRD** | HLT | HLT<br>EDU | HLT<br>EDU | HLT<br>HOT<br>COM<br>EDU<br>TRS | COM<br>TRS<br>HOT<br>RLE | EDU<br>HLT<br>COM<br>HOT | MIN | EDU | HLT<br>EDU | TRD |
| | – | **HLT** | TRD | TRD | TRD | TRD<br>AGR | TRD<br>AGR<br>FSH | TRD | TRD | TRD | TRD | All other |
| $P_8$ | Groups | **8** | 6 | 6 | 8 | 9 | 5 | 8 | 6 | 8 | 8 | 7 |
| | + | **TRD** | TRD | TRD | TRD | TRD | TRD | TRD | TRD | TRD | TRD | TRD |
| | – | **RLE<br>ELE** | TRS<br>FSH<br>ELE | RLE<br>MIN | RLE | RLE | TRS | RLE | RLE | RLE | ELE | RLE |
| $P_9$ | Groups | **8** | 6 | 7 | **6** | 7 | 4 | 6 | 5 | 8 | 9 | 7 |
| | + | **TRD** | CST<br>TRD | TRD | TRD<br>CST | TRD | TRD | TRD | TRD | TRD | TRD | TRD |
| | – | **ELE** | ELE<br>FSH<br>TRS | RLE<br>MIN | RLE | RLE | TRS<br>ELE<br>MIN<br>COM | RLE<br>ELE | RLE | RLE | ELE | AGR<br>TRS |
| $P_{10}$ | Groups | **6** | 7 | 6 | 6 | 7 | 3 | 7 | **5** | 6 | 9 | 7 |
| | + | **EDU** | HLT | HLT | EDU<br>HLT | EDU | TRS<br>COM<br>HOT<br>RLE<br>MIN | HLT | MIN | EDU | HLT | MIN |
| | – | **TRD** | TRD | TRD | TRD | TRD<br>AGR | TRD<br>AGR<br>FSH | TRD | TRD | TRD | TRD | TRD |
| $P_{11}$ | Groups | **8** | **9** | 8 | 9 | 6 | 6 | 4 | **4** | 5 | 7 | 7 |
| | + | **EDU** | MIN | TRD | TRD | ELE<br>TRD | TRD | TRD | TRD<br>ELE | TRD<br>ELE | TRD<br>ELE | HLT<br>MIN<br>EDU |
| | – | **TRD** | HLT | EDU | EDU<br>HLT | EDU<br>HLT | HOT | HLT | MIN | EDU | EDU<br>HLT | TRD |
| $P_{12}$ | Groups | **6** | 8 | 8 | 7 | 6 | 6 | 5 | **5** | 7 | 8 | 7 |
| | + | **HLT<br>FSH** | MIN | ELE | MIN<br>ELE | ELE | MIN<br>ELE | ELE | ELE | ELE | ELE | HLT |
| | – | **ELE** | EDU<br>RLE<br>CST | CST | HLT | HLT | RLE<br>HOT | CST | CST | FSH | EDU<br>HOT | ELE |
| $P_{13}$ | Groups | **4** | 2 | 4 | 6 | **3** | 2 | | 4 | **2** | 5 | 3 |
| | + | **RLE** | MNF | RLE | RLE | RLE | MIN | | TRS<br>MIN | RLE | MNF | MIN |
| | – | **TRD** | TRS<br>MIN<br>CST<br>ELE<br>TRD<br>AGR<br>EDU<br>HOT | CST<br>HLT<br>AGR<br>HOT | HLT | HLT<br>AGR<br>TRD<br>EDU<br>MNF<br>CST<br>HOT<br>TRS<br>COM<br>ELE<br>FSH | FSH<br>AGR<br>TRD<br>MNF<br>HOT<br>RLE<br>CST<br>TRS | | TRD | All other | HOT<br>EDU | HLT<br>TRD<br>CST<br>EDU<br>MNF<br>ELE<br>AGR |

Source: Calculations based on BACH database.

# Appendix 15. Selected Results of the Post-Hoc Analysis of Cross-Industry Variance for Liquidity Ratios (Disjoint Homogeneous Groups Are Bolded)

J. Koralun-Bereźnicka, *Corporate Performance*, Contributions to Management Science,
DOI 10.1007/978-3-319-00345-0, © Springer International Publishing Switzerland 2013

| Ratio | Content | All | NL | B | FR | ES | I | A | D | P | FIN | PL |
|---|---|---|---|---|---|---|---|---|---|---|---|---|
| L1 | groups | 5 | 5 | 6 | 6 | 4 | 3 | 5 | 4 | 4 | 8 | |
| | + | MIN | HLT | HLT<br>RLE | FSH<br>RLE<br>MIN | MIN<br>RLE | MIN | MIN | MIN | CST | COM | |
| | – | HOT | MIN | HOT<br>FSH | HOT | HOT | HOT<br>ELE<br>COM | HOT | TRS | TRS<br>ELE | TRS | |
| L2 | Groups | 5 | 6 | 7 | 5 | 4 | 4 | 4 | 5 | 6 | 5 | |
| | + | HLT<br>MIN | HLT | HLT<br>RLE | RLE | EDU | MIN | RLE | MIN | HLT | EDU<br>COM<br>HLT | |
| | – | HOT<br>TRD<br>CST<br>TRS | MIN | HOT<br>FSH | TRD | TRD | AGR<br>CST<br>FSH | HOT | CST | AGR | CST | |
| L3 | Groups | 5 | 7 | 7 | 7 | 4 | 2 | 4 | 2 | 4 | 5 | 2 |
| | + | EDU<br>HLT | HLT | HLT<br>MIN | RLE | EDU | MIN | RLE | ELE<br>MIN<br>RLE | EDU | EDU<br>HLT | COM |
| | – | TRD | MIN | MNF | TRD | ELE<br>MNF<br>HLT<br>TRD | FSH<br>ELE<br>CST<br>MNF | ELE<br>CST<br>TRD | TRD | ELE | MNF<br>CST<br>TRD<br>MIN<br>TRS | All other |
| L4 | Groups | 7 | 4 | 5 | 4 | 4 | 4 | 6 | 6 | 6 | 6 | 2 |
| | + | TRS | MIN | EDU | EDU | EDU<br>TRS | COM<br>HOT<br>ELE<br>TRS | TRS | TRS | TRS | TRS | EDU |
| | – | AGR | AGR<br>FSH<br>MNF<br>TRD<br>CST | CST<br>RLE<br>AGR<br>MNF<br>MIN | AGR<br>FSH<br>ELE<br>MNF<br>CST<br>RLE<br>TRD<br>MIN | MIN<br>RLE<br>FSH | CST<br>FSH | CST | CST | AGR | FSH<br>MIN<br>RLE | AGR |
| L5 | Groups | **2** | 6 | 5 | 8 | 5 | 4 | 5 | 4 | 5 | 6 | |
| | + | EDU | TRD | ELE | TRD<br>HOT<br>HLT | TRD<br>AGR | TRD | HOT | TRD | TRS | HOT | |
| | – | All other | HLT | RLE | RLE | RLE<br>MIN | TRS | RLE | MIN | RLE | MNF | |
| L6 | Groups | 5 | 6 | 8 | 7 | 6 | 5 | 5 | 4 | 4 | 6 | 4 |
| | + | EDU<br>HLT | HLT | EDU | CST | FSH<br>CST | RLE | EDU<br>COM | CST | HLT<br>TRD | EDU | EDU |
| | – | ELE | MIN<br>MNF | ELE | ELE | ELE<br>MIN | MIN | ELE | MIN<br>ELE | ELE | ELE<br>MNF | ELE<br>TRS<br>MNF |
| L7 | Groups | 6 | 6 | 8 | 9 | 8 | 6 | 5 | 5 | 7 | 8 | 6 |
| | + | CST<br>TRD | HLT<br>CST | CST | CST | CST | TRD | CST<br>TRD | CST | CST<br>TRD | CST<br>TRD | TRD<br>CST |
| | – | ELE | ELE | MIN | ELE | ELE | ELE | ELE<br>HOT<br>TRS | TRS | ELE<br>TRS | ELE | HOT<br>RLE<br>TRS<br>ELE |
| L8 | Groups | 6 | 9 | 6 | 7 | 7 | 7 | 6 | **4** | 7 | 7 | 7 |
| | + | CST | HLT | CST | CST | CST | RLE | CST | TRD | HLT | EDU<br>TRD | CST |
| | – | ELE | ELE | MIN | ELE | ELE | ELE<br>MIN | ELE<br>HOT<br>TRS<br>AGR | RLE<br>TRS | ELE | ELE | HOT |
| L9 | Groups | 4 | 3 | 3 | 8 | 2 | 5 | 3 | 3 | | 4 | 3 |
| | + | TRD | TRD | TRD | TRD | TRD | TRD | TRD | TRD | | TRD<br>CST | TRD |
| | – | HOT | MIN<br>ELE | FSH<br>TRS<br>HOT | RLE | All other | TRS<br>COM | COM<br>EDU<br>HLT | TRS<br>MIN<br>ELE | | TRS<br>EDU<br>ELE | HOT |
| | | | | RLE<br>HLT<br>MIN | | | | | | | HLT<br>RLE | |
| L10 | Groups | 8 | 6 | 6 | 7 | 4 | 4 | 4 | 5 | 6 | 8 | 4 |
| | + | AGR | TRD | TRD<br>CST | AGR<br>FSH | TRD<br>AGR<br>FSH<br>MIN<br>MNF | FSH<br>CST<br>AGR | TRD | CST | AGR | FSH | TRD<br>MNF<br>FSH<br>AGR |
| | – | TRS | HLT | HLT | EDU | TRS<br>EDU<br>HLT<br>HOT | COM<br>TRS<br>ELE<br>HOT | TRS<br>RLE<br>ELE<br>HLT | TRS<br>ELE | TRS<br>HLT<br>ELE<br>EDU<br>HOT | EDU<br>TRS | EDU<br>TRS<br>HLT<br>RLE<br>HOT |
| L11 | Groups | 2 | | | 7 | **2** | | 2 | | | **2** | 2 |
| | + | TRD | | | HOT | TRD | | TRD<br>AGR<br>CST | | | HOT | HOT |
| | – | All other | | | RLE | All other | | COM | | | All other | All other |

Source: Calculations based on BACH database.

# Appendix 16. Selected Results of the Post-Hoc Analysis of Cross-Industry Variance for Debt Ratios (Disjoint Homogeneous Groups are Bolded)

J. Koralun-Bereźnicka, *Corporate Performance*, Contributions to Management Science,
DOI 10.1007/978-3-319-00345-0, 

| Ratio | Content | All | NL | B | FR | ES | I | A | D | P | FIN | PL |
|---|---|---|---|---|---|---|---|---|---|---|---|---|
| $D_1$ | groups | 4 | 3 | 8 | 6 | 4 | 4 | | **3** | 5 | **2** | |
| | + | HLT<br>MIN | MIN | ELE<br>HLT | MIN | TRD<br>COM | MIN | | MIN | MIN<br>MNF | COM<br>HLT<br>EDU | |
| | – | RLE | TRS<br>MNF<br>HOT<br>ELE<br>TRD<br>AGR<br>COM<br>RLE<br>FSH<br>EDU<br>CST | RLE | RLE | RLE | FSH<br>CST | | CST<br>RLE<br>TRS<br>TRD<br>MNF | RLE | All other | |
| $D_2$ | Groups | **2** | 6 | 9 | 8 | 5 | 5 | 4 | 6 | 6 | 7 | 5 |
| | + | EDU | HLT | TRD<br>CST | CST | CST | TRD<br>RLE | TRD<br>MIN | MIN | FSH | TRD | TRS |
| | – | All other | TRS | FSH | TRS | HLT | HOT | HOT | RLE | TRS<br>COM | ELE<br>RLE | AGR |
| $D_3$ | Groups | | 5 | 8 | 6 | 6 | 3 | | 5 | 4 | 6 | 3 |
| | + | | HLT | RLE<br>ELE<br>MIN | CST | TRD<br>FSH | MIN | | MIN | FSH<br>MNF | COM | TRS |
| | – | | TRS | FSH | TRS | HLT | CST<br>HOT | | RLE | COM | ELE<br>RLE<br>HOT | AGR |
| $D_4$ | Groups | 6 | | 8 | 6 | | | | **6** | | 7 | 6 |
| | + | MIN | | MIN<br>ELE | ELE<br>MIN<br>RLE | | | | MIN | | COM | AGR |
| | – | CST | | FSH | TRS | | | | CST | | HOT | TRD |
| $D_5$ | Groups | | | 2 | 5 | | | 2 | | | 2 | **2** |
| | + | | | COM | HOT | | | AGR<br>RLE | | | ELE | HOT |
| | – | | | FSH | CST<br>EDU<br>TRD<br>MNF<br>AGR<br>MIN | | | HLT | | | All other | All other |
| $D_6$ | Groups | 4 | 5 | 7 | 6 | 4 | 5 | | 5 | 4 | 6 | 4 |
| | + | RLE | MIN<br>CST<br>TRD | TRD | CST<br>TRD | TRD<br>MNF<br>CST<br>AGR<br>HLT<br>FSH<br>EDU<br>COM | TRD | | TRD | TRD | EDU<br>TRD | MIN<br>TRS |
| | – | TRD | TRS | RLE | RLE | RLE | TRS<br>ELE | | RLE | RLE | ELE | HLT<br>TRD |
| $D_7$ | Groups | 4 | 4 | 6 | 7 | 6 | 4 | | 5 | 5 | 3 | 2 |
| | + | MIN<br>TRS | MIN | CST | CST | CST<br>HLT | RLE | | CST | HLT | CST | MIN |
| | – | CST | TRS<br>HOT | MIN | RLE<br>TRS | TRS<br>RLE | ELE | | TRS | RLE<br>ELE | ELE | All other |
| $D_8$ | Groups | 5 | 7 | 7 | 6 | 5 | 7 | 4 | **4** | 5 | 6 | **2** |
| | + | MIN | MNF | RLE | AGR<br>HOT<br>RLE<br>TRD<br>FSH | AGR<br>FSH<br>CST<br>HOT | FSH | HOT<br>RLE | RLE | HOT | HLT<br>RLE<br>FSH<br>AGR<br>HOT<br>CST | MIN |
| | – | AGR<br>FSH | HLT | TRS | ELE | MIN | TRS | AGR | MIN | TRS<br>COM<br>FSH | ELE<br>MIN | All other |

Source: Calculations based on BACH database.

# Appendix 17. One-Way Analysis of Variance Across Countries: Values of F-Statistics and p; p = 0.05 (Deficiencies of Significance Were Highlighted)

J. Koralun-Bereźnicka, *Corporate Performance*, Contributions to Management Science, DOI 10.1007/978-3-319-00345-0, © Springer International Publishing Switzerland 2013

| Ratio | Content | AGR | FSH | MIN | MNF | ELE | CST | TRD | HOT | TRS | RLE | EDU | HLT | COM | All |
|---|---|---|---|---|---|---|---|---|---|---|---|---|---|---|---|
| $R_1$ | F | 23.35 | 5.553 | 4.841 | 42.37 | 8.624 | 9.680 | 34.05 | 19.78 | 16.80 | 30.58 | 6.770 | 34.14 | 14.39 | **1.899** |
| | p | (0.000) | (0.000) | (0.000) | (0.000) | (0.000) | (0.000) | (0.000) | (0.000) | (0.000) | (0.000) | (0.000) | (0.000) | (0.000) | **(0.049)** |
| $R_2$ | F | 26.67 | 9.494 | 1.943 | 37.96 | 4.603 | 23.96 | 31.77 | 14.01 | 6.300 | 32.72 | 10.24 | 30.14 | 18.29 | **10.40** |
| | p | (0.000) | (0.000) | (0.064) | (0.000) | (0.000) | (0.000) | (0.000) | (0.000) | (0.000) | (0.000) | (0.006) | (0.000) | (0.000) | **(0.000)** |
| $R_3$ | F | 31.12 | 8.637 | 3.728 | 19.49 | 3.716 | 7.613 | 5.181 | 5.493 | 1.010 | 1.932 | 3.069 | 34.62 | 16.58 | **4.445** |
| | p | (0.000) | (0.000) | (0.001) | (0.000) | (0.001) | (0.000) | (0.000) | (0.000) | (0.442) | (0.065) | (0.010) | (0.000) | (0.000) | **(0.000)** |
| $R_4$ | F | 4.008 | 1.110 | 2.415 | 1.352 | 0.784 | 25.80 | 6.587 | 7.159 | 1.164 | 3.129 | 1.499 | 0.542 | 7.344 | **1.241** |
| | p | (0.002) | (0.377) | (0.021) | (0.239) | (0.632) | (0.000) | (0.000) | (0.000) | (0.334) | (0.004) | (0.192) | (0.798) | (0.006) | **(0.267)** |
| $R_5$ | F | 21.70 | 4.665 | 8.932 | 6.024 | 9.368 | 12.58 | 3.611 | 10.90 | 1.071 | 2.893 | 3.220 | 50.45 | 66.31 | **4.266** |
| | p | (0.000) | (0.000) | (0.000) | (0.000) | (0.000) | (0.000) | (0.001) | (0.037) | (0.397) | (0.007) | (0.007) | (0.000) | (0.000) | **(0.000)** |
| $R_6$ | F | 19.55 | 1.296 | 4.829 | 5.232 | 1.224 | 4.393 | 16.34 | 1.764 | 0.915 | 0.518 | 5.505 | 1.199 | 2.832 | **1.439** |
| | p | (0.000) | (0.279) | (0.000) | (0.000) | (0.298) | (0.000) | (0.000) | (0.105) | (0.519) | (0.856) | (0.000) | (0.323) | (0.012) | **(0.167)** |
| $R_7$ | F | 18.70 | 11.61 | 11.19 | 8.243 | 14.41 | 7.284 | 44.79 | 28.55 | 11.32 | 15.93 | 12.52 | 21.68 | 44.00 | **43.45** |
| | p | (0.000) | (0.000) | (0.000) | (0.000) | (0.000) | (0.000) | (0.000) | (0.000) | (0.000) | (0.000) | (0.000) | (0.000) | (0.000) | **(0.000)** |
| $R_8$ | F | 53.30 | 5.554 | 35.70 | 170.0 | 27.54 | 81.51 | 79.11 | 124.5 | 20.00 | 585.1 | 6.755 | 96.74 | 48.29 | **7.738** |
| | p | (0.000) | (0.000) | (0.000) | (0.000) | (0.000) | (0.000) | (0.000) | (0.000) | (0.000) | (0.000) | (0.000) | (0.000) | (0.000) | **(0.000)** |
| $R_9$ | F | 53.29 | 9.971 | 31.20 | 175.5 | 29.84 | 51.00 | 70.39 | 134.5 | 24.80 | 29.46 | 15.68 | 45.04 | 55.83 | **7.655** |
| | p | (0.000) | (0.000) | (0.000) | (0.000) | (0.000) | (0.000) | (0.000) | (0.000) | (0.000) | (0.000) | (0.000) | (0.000) | (0.000) | **(0.000)** |
| $R_{10}$ | F | 29.37 | 6.160 | 6.560 | 22.99 | 10.05 | 195.6 | 22.35 | 99.32 | 10.67 | 24.36 | 12.18 | 44.78 | 28.70 | **4.060** |
| | p | (0.000) | (0.000) | (0.000) | (0.000) | (0.000) | (0.000) | (0.000) | (0.000) | (0.000) | (0.000) | (0.000) | (0.000) | (0.000) | **(0.000)** |
| $R_{11}$ | F | 44.99 | 60.01 | 72.84 | 42.53 | 47.85 | 131.5 | 27.52 | 119.7 | 2.359 | 68.64 | 27.71 | 31.92 | 35.31 | **7.762** |
| | p | (0.000) | (0.000) | (0.000) | (0.000) | (0.000) | (0.000) | (0.000) | (0.000) | (0.024) | (0.000) | (0.002) | (0.000) | (0.000) | **(0.000)** |
| $R_{12}$ | F | 150.9 | 11.55 | 71.44 | 323.8 | 47.65 | 76.04 | 321.0 | 347.6 | 64.98 | 571.2 | 23.52 | 105.1 | 30.36 | **96.16** |
| | p | (0.000) | (0.000) | (0.000) | (0.000) | (0.000) | (0.000) | (0.000) | (0.000) | (0.000) | (0.000) | (0.000) | (0.000) | (0.000) | **(0.000)** |
| $R_{13}$ | F | 3.438 | 2.217 | 5.611 | 19.82 | 2.410 | 3.347 | 4.774 | 4.150 | 3.653 | 82.92 | 13.57 | 10.77 | 3.471 | **2.176** |
| | p | (0.005) | (0.055) | (0.000) | (0.000) | (0.026) | (0.004) | (0.000) | (0.001) | (0.002) | (0.000) | (0.000) | (0.000) | (0.005) | **(0.027)** |
| $P_1$ | F | 28.64 | 7.836 | 7.994 | 30.37 | 27.18 | 6.050 | 31.85 | 45.18 | 12.39 | 14.72 | 4.567 | 152.5 | 2.830 | **12.05** |
| | p | (0.000) | (0.000) | (0.000) | (0.000) | (0.000) | (0.000) | (0.000) | (0.000) | (0.000) | (0.000) | (0.001) | (0.000) | (0.011) | **(0.000)** |
| $P_2$ | F | 39.58 | 1.374 | 9.073 | 49.12 | 17.82 | 52.55 | 37.25 | 42.78 | 13.23 | 17.98 | 40.71 | 151.5 | 2.290 | **11.03** |
| | p | (0.000) | (0.245) | (0.000) | (0.000) | (0.000) | (0.000) | (0.000) | (0.000) | (0.000) | (0.000) | (0.000) | (0.000) | (0.035) | **(0.000)** |
| $P_3$ | F | 24.78 | 8.793 | 10.66 | 9.457 | 13.76 | 26.10 | 45.77 | 33.21 | 7.762 | 24.97 | 37.29 | 71.49 | 3.804 | **24.85** |
| | p | (0.000) | (0.000) | (0.000) | (0.000) | (0.000) | (0.000) | (0.000) | (0.007) | (0.000) | (0.000) | (0.000) | (0.000) | (0.001) | **(0.000)** |
| $P_4$ | F | 29.82 | 2.578 | 38.07 | 8.131 | 28.38 | 2.202 | 9.167 | 21.32 | 10.88 | 66.49 | 4.718 | 8.372 | 29.30 | **10.39** |
| | p | (0.000) | (0.000) | (0.000) | (0.000) | (0.000) | (0.034) | (0.000) | (0.000) | (0.000) | (0.000) | (0.000) | (0.000) | (0.000) | **(0.000)** |
| $P_5$ | F | 15.80 | 5.904 | 4.831 | 182.6 | 21.44 | 160.0 | 73.13 | 28.58 | 0.085 | 155.4 | 11.88 | 181.8 | 13.17 | **2.618** |
| | p | (0.000) | (0.000) | (0.000) | (0.000) | (0.000) | (0.000) | (0.000) | (0.000) | (1.000) | (0.000) | (0.003) | (0.000) | (0.000) | **(0.006)** |
| $P_6$ | F | 20.52 | 22.45 | 19.99 | 20.64 | 39.01 | 39.17 | 21.42 | 75.79 | 19.62 | 80.24 | 18.70 | 38.75 | 43.00 | **39.41** |
| | p | (0.000) | (0.000) | (0.000) | (0.000) | (0.000) | (0.000) | (0.000) | (0.000) | (0.000) | (0.000) | (0.001) | (0.000) | (0.000) | **(0.000)** |
| $P_7$ | F | 73.97 | 44.68 | 21.69 | 183.6 | 23.70 | 10.71 | 53.24 | 61.80 | 19.48 | 187.1 | 24.04 | 214.3 | 47.94 | **9.580** |
| | p | (0.000) | (0.000) | (0.000) | (0.000) | (0.000) | (0.000) | (0.000) | (0.000) | (0.000) | (0.000) | (0.000) | (0.000) | (0.000) | **(0.000)** |
| $P_8$ | F | 60.67 | 11.13 | 16.62 | 123.7 | 23.26 | 48.43 | 60.63 | 66.50 | 18.94 | 191.6 | 36.61 | 177.7 | 45.19 | **15.83** |
| | p | (0.000) | (0.000) | (0.000) | (0.000) | (0.000) | (0.000) | (0.000) | (0.000) | (0.000) | (0.000) | (0.000) | (0.000) | (0.000) | **(0.000)** |
| $P_9$ | F | 30.49 | 1.428 | 0.162 | 9.221 | 1.073 | 42.88 | 14.66 | 1.646 | 1.035 | 0.051 | 4.032 | 1.321 | 3.262 | **1.822** |
| | p | (0.000) | (0.224) | (0.997) | (0.000) | (0.396) | (0.000) | (0.000) | (0.134) | (0.424) | (1.000) | (0.002) | (0.262) | (0.004) | **(0.061)** |
| $P_{10}$ | F | 62.22 | 23.54 | 51.77 | 86.63 | 38.58 | 36.11 | 37.24 | 27.78 | 29.88 | 67.93 | 4.800 | 13.61 | 12.76 | **6.356** |
| | p | (0.000) | (0.000) | (0.000) | (0.000) | (0.000) | (0.000) | (0.000) | (0.000) | (0.000) | (0.000) | (0.000) | (0.000) | (0.000) | **(0.000)** |
| $P_{11}$ | F | 33.85 | 1.616 | 0.335 | 6.134 | 1.240 | 12.10 | 16.27 | 1.981 | 0.895 | 0.156 | 7.033 | 1.369 | 3.260 | **1.677** |
| | p | (0.000) | (0.162) | (0.960) | (0.000) | (0.289) | (0.000) | (0.000) | (0.066) | (0.536) | (0.997) | (0.000) | (0.241) | (0.004) | **(0.091)** |
| $D_1$ | F | 0.878 | 1.734 | 5.553 | 19.67 | 9.345 | 43.56 | 32.42 | 21.49 | 6.255 | 37.84 | 1.697 | 4.533 | 39.01 | **8.634** |
| | p | (0.532) | (0.134) | (0.000) | (0.000) | (0.000) | (0.000) | (0.000) | (0.000) | (0.000) | (0.000) | (0.150) | (0.002) | (0.000) | **(0.000)** |
| $D_2$ | F | 47.26 | 66.95 | 1.848 | 59.83 | 27.94 | 20.96 | 25.71 | 59.26 | 8.336 | 172.4 | 5.745 | 41.76 | 24.30 | **1.882** |
| | p | (0.000) | (0.000) | (0.057) | (0.000) | (0.000) | (0.000) | (0.000) | (0.000) | (0.000) | (0.000) | (0.000) | (0.000) | (0.000) | **(0.060)** |
| $D_3$ | F | 35.31 | 49.87 | 0.460 | 47.22 | 23.63 | 14.74 | 17.83 | 0.084 | 8.570 | 105.8 | 0.006 | 12.21 | 20.35 | **10.75** |
| | p | (0.000) | (0.000) | (0.901) | (0.000) | (0.000) | (0.000) | (0.000) | (1.000) | (0.000) | (0.000) | (1.000) | (0.000) | (0.000) | **(0.000)** |
| $D_4$ | F | 104.5 | 12.39 | 17.96 | 72.69 | 27.77 | 15.11 | 25.38 | 81.69 | 9.854 | 158.4 | 13.40 | 64.14 | 26.51 | **15.49** |
| | p | (0.000) | (0.000) | (0.000) | (0.000) | (0.000) | (0.000) | (0.000) | (0.000) | (0.000) | (0.000) | (0.000) | (0.000) | (0.000) | **(0.000)** |
| $D_5$ | F | 30.22 | 1.699 | 1.798 | 2.971 | 1.169 | 2.015 | 15.64 | 2.055 | 1.139 | 0.099 | 6.755 | 1.275 | 1.934 | **1.476** |
| | p | (0.000) | (0.139) | (0.065) | (0.008) | (0.331) | (0.053) | (0.000) | (0.057) | (0.351) | (1.000) | (0.000) | (0.284) | (0.074) | **(0.162)** |
| $D_6$ | F | 5.958 | 11.95 | 47.79 | 47.32 | 28.08 | 20.44 | 9.832 | 25.41 | 6.582 | 44.73 | 9.754 | 39.48 | 31.90 | **2.657** |
| | p | (0.000) | (0.000) | (0.000) | (0.000) | (0.000) | (0.000) | (0.000) | (0.000) | (0.000) | (0.000) | (0.000) | (0.000) | (0.000) | **(0.007)** |
| $D_7$ | F | 3.020 | 4.309 | 2.562 | 16.52 | 12.30 | 21.24 | 16.17 | 16.66 | 11.54 | 13.22 | 21.79 | 14.46 | 5.699 | **8.451** |
| | p | (0.011) | (0.001) | (0.019) | (0.000) | (0.000) | (0.000) | (0.000) | (0.000) | (0.000) | (0.000) | (0.000) | (0.000) | (0.000) | **(0.000)** |
| $D_8$ | F | 233.6 | 24.71 | 84.59 | 917.8 | 212.5 | 343.2 | 502.6 | 279.1 | 59.35 | 67.75 | 76.48 | 970.4 | 18.23 | **72.07** |
| | p | (0.000) | (0.000) | (0.000) | (0.000) | (0.000) | (0.000) | (0.000) | (0.000) | (0.000) | (0.000) | (0.000) | (0.000) | (0.000) | **(0.000)** |

Source: Calculations based on BACH database.

# Appendix 18. Selected Results of the *Post-Hoc* Analysis of Cross-Country Variance for Profitability and Turnover Ratios (Disjoint Homogeneous Groups Are Bolded)

J. Koralun-Bereźnicka, *Corporate Performance*, Contributions to Management Science,
DOI 10.1007/978-3-319-00345-0, 

| Ratio | Content | All | AGR | FSH | MIN | MNF | ELE | CST | TRD | HOT | TRS | RLE | EDU | HLT | COM |
|---|---|---|---|---|---|---|---|---|---|---|---|---|---|---|---|
| $P_1$ | groups | **2** | 4 | 3 | 3 | 5 | 3 | 3 | 5 | 4 | 6 | 5 | 3 | 2 | 4 |
| | + | **FIN** | FIN | NL | I, PL, FR, NL | FIN | FR | P | P, ES | A | ES | D | PL, ES | All other | FIN |
| | – | **D, B** | ES | P | ES | D | B, D | D | D | FR, FIN, B | B | NL, I | NL | ES, PL, FR, P | A, P |
| $P_2$ | Groups | **4** | 3 | 4 | | 5 | 3 | 4 | 5 | 4 | 3 | 4 | **2** | 5 | 4 |
| | + | **FIN** | FIN | FIN | | FIN | ES | FIN | FIN, ES | ES | ES | ES | PL, FIN | NL, FIN | FIN |
| | – | **P** | ES | P | | D | PL, D, A | D | D | B | B | P | All other | ES | P |
| $P_3$ | Groups | **3** | 4 | 2 | 2 | **2** | 2 | 4 | 4 | 3 | | | 2 | 4 | 3 |
| | + | **FIN** | FIN | ES, FIN, NL | I, B | NL, FIN | ES | NL, FIN | FIN | NL | | | PL | NL, FIN | FIN |
| | – | **PL** | PL, I, B | PL, B, P | D, ES, PL | All other | PL, A, D | D | D | B | | | B | ES | P |
| $P_4$ | Groups | | 2 | | 2 | | | **3** | 3 | 4 | | 2 | | | **2** |
| | + | | All other | | NL | | | NL | NL | PL | | A | | | FIN |
| | – | | FIN | | FR, A | | | FIN | PL | FIN, ES | | B, FIN | | | All other |
| $P_5$ | Groups | **2** | 4 | 2 | 4 | 3 | 4 | 4 | 3 | 4 | | 2 | **2** | 5 | 4 |
| | + | **FIN** | FIN | FIN, ES, NL | NL | NL | B | FIN | FIN | FIN | | NL | FIN | FIN | FIN |
| | – | **All other** | PL, P, I | PL | ES | I | A, PL, FR | D | D, I | B | | PL, D | All other | ES | P |
| $P_6$ | Groups | | 4 | | 2 | 3 | | 3 | **3** | | | | 3 | | 2 |
| | + | | FIN | | NL | NL | | FIN, NL | ES | | | | PL, B, NL | | NL |
| | – | | PL | | All other | I | | P | D, FR, P, I, B, FIN, NL, A | | | | P | | A |
| $P_7$ | Groups | **4** | 5 | 3 | 4 | 3 | 4 | 4 | 5 | 5 | 4 | 5 | 3 | 6 | 4 |
| | + | **I** | I | I, ES | NL | ES, I, B | B, NL | I, P | B, I | B | B | B, I, ES | B, ES, NL | P | B, P, FR, I |
| | – | **PL, A, FIN** | PL | PL | PL | PL | A | PL | A | A | PL | FIN | A | FIN | A, PL |
| $P_8$ | Groups | **4** | **3** | 3 | 5 | **6** | 5 | 5 | 6 | **5** | 4 | **7** | 3 | **3** | 4 |
| | + | **D, PL** | ES | PL | NL, A | PL | PL | FIN | D | FIN | FIN | I | A | FIN, PL, FR | A, PL, FIN |
| | – | **P** | PL, P | P | ES | NL, FIN | A, FR, FIN, ES | I, P, ES | P, NL | P | P, I, ES | P, ES, B | ES, FIN | NL, B | P |
| $P_9$ | Groups | **3** | 4 | 4 | 5 | **5** | 4 | 6 | 5 | 7 | 5 | **3** | 4 | **3** | 5 |
| | + | **D** | I, ES, FR | I, FIN | A, NL | FR | D | FR | D | FIN | FIN | I | FR | FR, FIN, P | FIN |
| | – | **ES, P, B, NL** | PL | NL, P | B | NL, FIN | A, FIN, FR, ES | I | NL | P | P | P, ES, B, A, FR, D, FIN, PL | ES | B, A | P |
| $P_{10}$ | Groups | **2** | 3 | 2 | 3 | 4 | 3 | 6 | **3** | 6 | 4 | 3 | **2** | 4 | 5 |
| | + | **FIN** | FIN, FR, NL, PL | All other | PL | FIN | A, FR | A | A | ES | ES | NL, FR, FIN, ES | FIN | NL, ES, A, FIN | ES |
| | – | **I, B, D** | I | I | NL | ES | B | I | D, B, PL, I | B, FIN, I | B | I | All other | B | A |
| $P_{11}$ | Groups | **4** | 4 | 4 | **5** | 5 | **3** | 7 | 6 | 5 | 2 | 4 | 5 | 4 | 5 |
| | + | **A, FR** | FR | P | PL, ES | D | A | A | A | ES | FR | NL, FR | P | ES | ES |
| | – | **I** | I | I | NL | PL, ES | ES, P, B, NL, FIN, I, PL, D | P | PL | B | PL, NL | D | B | B | FIN, B |
| $P_{12}$ | Groups | **4** | **4** | 3 | 5 | 6 | 4 | 5 | 7 | 5 | 5 | 7 | **2** | 5 | 5 |
| | + | **FR** | ES, FR, PL | P, ES | ES | FR, B | FR, PL, B | FR | FR | FR | FR, B | FR | All other | ES | P |
| | – | **I, NL, D, A** | I, NL | NL, I | NL, I | NL, I | I | I | I | A, NL, I | I, D, A, NL | D | FIN, A, NL | NL, A | I |
| $P_{13}$ | Groups | **2** | 2 | | 2 | 3 | 2 | 2 | 2 | 2 | 2 | **4** | **2** | **2** | 2 |
| | + | **ES** | PL | | ES | NL | FIN | P | NL, PL | PL, ES | All other | P, B | FIN | NL | ES, PL, I, NL |
| | – | **NL** | I, ES | | All other | I, P, ES, PL, FR, B | NL | FIN, B | ES, D, I | FIN | NL | I, FIN, NL, D, PL | All other | All other | FIN |

Source: Calculations based on BACH database.

# Appendix 19. Selected Results of the Post-Hoc Analysis of Cross-Country Variance for Liquidity Ratios (Disjoint Homogeneous Groups Are Bolded)

J. Koralun-Bereźnicka, *Corporate Performance*, Contributions to Management Science,
DOI 10.1007/978-3-319-00345-0, © Springer International Publishing Switzerland 2013

| Ratio | Content | All | AGR | FSH | MIN | MNF | ELE | CST | TRD | HOT | TRS | RLE | EDU | HLT | COM |
|---|---|---|---|---|---|---|---|---|---|---|---|---|---|---|---|
| $L_1$ | groups | 6 | 6 | 3 | 4 | 5 | 6 | 3 | 5 | 6 | 4 | 4 | 3 | 4 | 2 |
| | + | FIN | PL | FIN | D | FIN | FR | NL | FIN | FIN | NL | FR, FIN | PL | NL | PL |
| | – | A | B | B, P | NL | B | A | ES, A, PL, D, B | ES, PL | A | P | D | FIN | PL, A | P |
| $L_2$ | Groups | 5 | 6 | | 2 | 5 | 4 | 6 | 7 | 5 | 4 | 5 | 5 | 4 | 2 |
| | + | FIN | PL | | D | FIN | D | NL | FIN | FIN, NL | NL | FR | FIN | NL | PL |
| | – | A | P | | All other | PL, B | A | D | PL, ES | A | P, PL | D | A | PL, A | P |
| $L_3$ | Groups | 5 | 4 | 4 | 3 | 2 | 5 | 6 | 5 | 4 | 3 | 5 | 3 | 4 | 2 |
| | + | FIN | FIN | FIN | B | D, FIN, NL, FR, P | B | NL | FIN | FIN | NL, FIN | FR, FIN | FIN | NL, FIN | PL |
| | – | I, P | I, P, ES | I | NL, P | I, ES | ES | I, P | D | I | I | I | A, P, FR | ES | All other |
| $L_4$ | Groups | 4 | 5 | 2 | 2 | 5 | 5 | 2 | 5 | 5 | 5 | 4 | 2 | 3 | 4 |
| | + | NL | ES | B | NL | NL | NL | NL | D | I | FIN, P | NL, I | B, ES | NL, B | I |
| | – | A | P, PL | All other | All other | PL | FR | D | A | A | PL | ES | A, FIN | A | P, ES, FIN, A, PL |
| $L_5$ | Groups | 2 | 2 | 3 | 2 | 5 | 4 | 7 | 4 | 3 | | 7 | 2 | 5 | 4 |
| | + | FIN | FIN | PL | PL | PL | B | FIN | PL, FIN, D | FIN, PL | | PL | FIN | FIN, PL | FIN |
| | – | All other | All other | P | All other | I, FIN, NL | ES, I FR, A, D | ES | I, P | I, P, ES, NL | | B | All other | NL, ES | I, ES |
| $L_6$ | Groups | 4 | 3 | 5 | 4 | 5 | 6 | 6 | 4 | 5 | 4 | 5 | 3 | 4 | 4 |
| | + | NL | NL, FIN | FIN | FR | PL, NL | NL | NL, PL, FIN | NL | FIN | NL | NL | NL, PL | NL | FIN, PL |
| | – | ES | P | I, P | ES, B, I | ES | ES | P | ES | ES | ES | ES | ES, FR, P | ES | ES |
| $L_7$ | Groups | 5 | 4 | 5 | 5 | 5 | 6 | 3 | 5 | 5 | 4 | 6 | 5 | 7 | 4 |
| | + | I | I, FR | I | A | I, FR | D | FR, D | D | I | FR | I | FR | NL | FIN, I |
| | – | PL | PL, FIN | B, NL | B | NL | A | PL | ES | A, PL | A, P, PL | PL | FIN | PL | A |
| $L_8$ | Groups | 6 | 4 | 3 | 6 | 5 | 6 | 5 | 5 | 5 | 4 | 6 | 5 | 7 | 5 |
| | + | I | I | I | D | I | D | FR | I | I | FR | I | FR | NL | I |
| | – | PL | PL, P, FIN | B, NL | B | B, NL, PL | A, FIN | D, FIN | ES, PL | A, PL | A, P, PL | PL | P, ES, PL | PL | P, A |
| $L_9$ | Groups | | 3 | | | 2 | | 5 | 2 | | | | 2 | | 2 |
| | + | | B, I | | | PL | | D, A | ES, PL | | | | B, FIN, PL, NL | | All other |
| | – | | PL, NL, FIN, FR, P | | | All other | | ES, P, NL | All other | | | | A | | A |
| $L_{10}$ | Groups | 4 | 5 | 5 | 6 | 5 | 4 | 3 | 5 | 6 | 5 | 5 | 2 | 3 | 4 |
| | + | D | P | FIN | A, ES | PL | FR | D | A | A | PL, A | D | A | A, PL | FIN |
| | – | NL | NL | B | NL | FIN, NL | NL, I | ES, FR, NL, PL | I, P | I | ES | B | FR, B, ES, NL, FIN | NL | I |
| $L_{11}$ | Groups | | 3 | | | 2 | | 4 | 2 | | | | 3 | | 2 |
| | + | | B | | | PL | | PL | ES, PL | | | | B, PL | | NL, B |
| | – | | PL, P, FR, FIN, NL | | | All other | | P | All other | | | | P | | A |

Source: Calculations based on BACH database.

# Appendix 20. Selected Results of the Post-Hoc Analysis of Cross-Country Variance for Debt Ratios (Disjoint Homogeneous Groups Are Bolded)

| Ratio | Content | All | AGR | FSH | MIN | MNF | ELE | CST | TRD | HOT | TRS | RLE | EDU | HLT | COM |
|---|---|---|---|---|---|---|---|---|---|---|---|---|---|---|---|
| $D_1$ | groups | **3** | | | 3 | **2** | 4 | 4 | 5 | 3 | 4 | 4 | | 2 | 3 |
| | + | **FIN** | | | NL | PL, ES, P, FR | PL, FR | FIN, FR | ES | FIN | FIN | I | | FIN | FIN |
| | – | **B, P** | | | ES, B | All other | FIN | I, D | B | B | FR | P, ES, B, FR | | ES, B, P, FR | P |
| $D_2$ | Groups | | 5 | **3** | | 5 | 3 | 5 | 5 | 6 | 4 | 4 | **2** | 4 | **5** |
| | + | | FIN | B, FR | | B | FIN | I, P | NL | A | FR, A | FIN, D, A FR, ES | FIN | ES | P |
| | – | | PL | PL, P, ES, I | | D | D, PL, B, I | D | I, D | PL | I | I | All other | NL, PL, P | I, FIN |
| $D_3$ | Groups | **5** | 5 | 5 | | 6 | 4 | 5 | 3 | | 3 | 6 | | 3 | 3 |
| | + | **FR** | B | B | | B | FIN, A | I | NL, FR, A, P | | FR | D | | ES | P |
| | – | **D, PL** | PL | PL, P | | D | D, PL, B | D | D, FIN, ES | | I, FIN, D, B | PL | | NL, PL, P, FIN | FIN, ES, I |
| $D_4$ | Groups | **5** | 6 | 4 | 6 | **4** | 3 | 5 | 5 | 6 | 3 | 7 | 4 | **4** | 4 |
| | + | **PL** | PL | PL, ES, P | PL | D, FIN, NL | PL, B, D | FIN, NL | FIN | PL | FIN, I | PL | ES | NL | FIN |
| | – | **FR** | B | B | A | I | A | I | I | A | FR | I | A | ES A | P |
| $D_5$ | Groups | | 4 | | | 2 | | | 3 | | | | 3 | | |
| | + | | B | | | B | | | ES | | | | B | | |
| | – | | PL | | | D, FR, P, I | | | D, FIN, FR, I, P, A, NL | | | | P | | |
| $D_6$ | Groups | **2** | 3 | 3 | 3 | 4 | **3** | **2** | 3 | **3** | 2 | 3 | **2** | 3 | 5 |
| | + | **B** | B | B | B, ES | NL | FIN | I, P | NL | NL, B, P, ES | NL, FR, D, P, ES | P, ES, B | FIN | B | P |
| | – | **PL** | ES, PL | PL, FIN, ES, P | D, NL, FR | ES, FR, D, P, PL | D, PL, B | All other | ES, FIN, D, FR | FIN | FIN, B | I, NL, PL, FIN | All other | FIN, PL, FR | FIN |
| $D_7$ | Groups | **4** | 2 | 2 | 2 | 4 | 4 | 4 | 5 | 3 | 5 | 4 | 3 | 3 | 2 |
| | + | **PL, NL** | NL | B | PL | FIN, NL | FIN | PL, P | NL, B | NL, B | D | FR | B, PL, P, NL | NL, B | PL |
| | – | **ES** | ES | ES, P, FIN | All other | ES | FR | ES, FR | ES | P, FIN, I | I | I | FIN | ES | All other |
| $D_8$ | Groups | **4** | 4 | 3 | 5 | **4** | 4 | 6 | 5 | 4 | 5 | 4 | 3 | **3** | 3 |
| | + | **D** | NL | NL, P | D | D | FR, D | D | D | NL, I | I | NL | NL | NL | I, NL |
| | – | **P, PL, B** | ES, P | PL, ES | P | P, PL | P, PL, B | P | P, PL | P | PL | B | PL, B | P, ES, PL, FIN, B | B |

Source: Calculations based on BACH database.

J. Koralun-Bereźnicka, *Corporate Performance*, Contributions to Management Science,
DOI 10.1007/978-3-319-00345-0, © Springer International Publishing Switzerland 2013

# Appendix 21. Two-Way Analysis of Ratios Variance – the Year Effect (Y), the Country Effect (C) and the Combined Effect (YC): Values of F-Statistic and p, p = 0.05 (Significant Effects Are Highlighted)

J. Koralun-Bereźnicka, *Corporate Performance*, Contributions to Management Science,
DOI 10.1007/978-3-319-00345-0, 

| Ratio | Effect | F | p | Ratio | Effect | F | p | Ratio | Effect | F | p |
|---|---|---|---|---|---|---|---|---|---|---|---|
| $P_1$ | Y | 0.393 | 0.758 | $L_1$ | Y | 0.248 | 0.960 | $D_1$ | Y | 2.767 | 0.041 |
| | C | 2.108 | 0.033 | | C | 11.26 | 0.000 | | C | 8.777 | 0.000 |
| | YC | 0.403 | 1.000 | | YC | 0.593 | 0.991 | | YC | 1.021 | 0.437 |
| $P_2$ | Y | 1.322 | 0.266 | $L_2$ | Y | 0.272 | 0.950 | $D_2$ | Y | 0.519 | 0.794 |
| | C | 11.78 | 0.000 | | C | 10.26 | 0.000 | | C | 1.682 | 0.090 |
| | YC | 0.830 | 0.795 | | YC | 0.606 | 0.989 | | YC | 0.680 | 0.962 |
| $P_3$ | Y | 5.815 | 0.000 | $L_3$ | Y | 0.717 | 0.636 | $D_3$ | Y | 1.235 | 0.286 |
| | C | 4.642 | 0.000 | | C | 24.04 | 0.000 | | C | 0.414 | 0.928 |
| | YC | 0.729 | 0.927 | | YC | 0.819 | 0.820 | | YC | 1.404 | 0.033 |
| $P_4$ | Y | 0.678 | 0.668 | $L_4$ | Y | 0.992 | 0.430 | $D_4$ | Y | 0.522 | 0.792 |
| | C | 1.293 | 0.237 | | C | 9.048 | 0.000 | | C | 16.41 | 0.000 |
| | YC | 0.963 | 0.552 | | YC | 0.496 | 0.999 | | YC | 0.331 | 1.000 |
| $P_5$ | Y | 0.812 | 0.561 | $L_5$ | Y | 0.437 | 0.854 | $D_5$ | Y | 0.264 | 0.953 |
| | C | 4.024 | 0.000 | | C | 2.354 | 0.013 | | C | 1.718 | 0.081 |
| | YC | 0.764 | 0.892 | | YC | 0.566 | 0.995 | | YC | 1.084 | 0.320 |
| $P_6$ | Y | 0.589 | 0.739 | $L_6$ | Y | 0.535 | 0.782 | $D_6$ | Y | 0.546 | 0.773 |
| | C | 1.146 | 0.328 | | C | 36.54 | 0.000 | | C | 2.530 | 0.010 |
| | YC | 0.999 | 0.479 | | YC | 0.518 | 0.998 | | YC | 0.462 | 0.999 |
| $P_7$ | Y | 3.627 | 0.001 | $L_7$ | Y | 0.063 | 0.999 | $D_7$ | Y | 1.344 | 0.235 |
| | C | 47.30 | 0.000 | | C | 8.468 | 0.000 | | C | 7.380 | 0.000 |
| | YC | 2.978 | 0.000 | | YC | 0.079 | 1.000 | | YC | 0.609 | 0.983 |
| $P_8$ | Y | 0.127 | 0.993 | $L_8$ | Y | 0.083 | 0.998 | $D_8$ | Y | 0.473 | 0.828 |
| | C | 6.971 | 0.000 | | C | 14.13 | 0.000 | | C | 67.45 | 0.000 |
| | YC | 0.083 | 1.000 | | YC | 0.152 | 1.000 | | YC | 0.253 | 1.000 |
| $P_9$ | Y | 0.092 | 0.997 | $L_9$ | Y | 0.713 | 0.639 | | | | |
| | C | 6.906 | 0.000 | | C | 1.756 | 0.073 | | | | |
| | YC | 0.068 | 1.000 | | YC | 0.740 | 0.917 | | | | |
| $P_{10}$ | Y | 0.363 | 0.779 | $L_{10}$ | Y | 0.434 | 0.857 | | | | |
| | C | 4.043 | 0.000 | | C | 5.804 | 0.000 | | | | |
| | YC | 0.520 | 0.998 | | YC | 0.156 | 1.000 | | | | |
| $P_{11}$ | Y | 0.183 | 0.908 | $L_{11}$ | Y | 0.118 | 0.994 | | | | |
| | C | 7.510 | 0.000 | | C | 1.484 | 0.150 | | | | |
| | YC | 0.391 | 1.000 | | YC | 1.023 | 0.433 | | | | |
| $P_{12}$ | Y | 0.468 | 0.705 | | | | | | | | |
| | C | 94.66 | 0.000 | | | | | | | | |
| | YC | 0.320 | 1.000 | | | | | | | | |
| $P_{13}$ | Y | 0.522 | 0.792 | | | | | | | | |
| | C | 2.089 | 0.035 | | | | | | | | |
| | YC | 0.443 | 1.000 | | | | | | | | |

Source: Calculations based on BACH database.

# Appendix 22. Two-Way Analysis of Ratios Variance – the Year Effect (Y), the Industry Effect (I) and the Combined Effect (YI): Values of F-Statistic and p, p = 0.05 (Significant Effects are Highlighted)

J. Koralun-Bereźnicka, *Corporate Performance*, Contributions to Management Science,
DOI 10.1007/978-3-319-00345-0, 

| Ratio | Effect | F | p | Ratio | Effect | F | p | Ratio | Effect | F | p |
|---|---|---|---|---|---|---|---|---|---|---|---|
| | Y | 0.863 | 0.521 | | Y | 0.377 | 0.894 | | Y | 1.431 | 0.200 |
| $P_1$ | I | 46.26 | 0.000 | $L_1$ | I | 7.684 | 0.000 | $D_1$ | I | 8.778 | 0.000 |
| | YI | 0.519 | 1.000 | | YI | 0.605 | 0.996 | | YI | 1.006 | 0.468 |
| | Y | 1.007 | 0.419 | | Y | 0.264 | 0.954 | | Y | 2.408 | 0.026 |
| $P_2$ | I | 19.95 | 0.000 | $L_2$ | I | 8.990 | 0.000 | $D_2$ | I | 4.043 | 0.000 |
| | YI | 0.630 | 0.992 | | YI | 0.532 | 0.999 | | YI | 1.683 | 0.001 |
| | Y | 5.170 | 0.000 | | Y | 0.634 | 0.703 | | Y | 1.571 | 0.153 |
| $P_3$ | I | 9.129 | 0.000 | $L_3$ | I | 13.39 | 0.000 | $D_3$ | I | 1.156 | 0.312 |
| | YI | 1.320 | 0.046 | | YI | 0.488 | 1.000 | | YI | 1.215 | 0.117 |
| | Y | 1.056 | 0.388 | | Y | 1.120 | 0.349 | | Y | 0.427 | 0.861 |
| $P_4$ | I | 1.122 | 0.339 | $L_4$ | I | 25.79 | 0.000 | $D_4$ | I | 19.69 | 0.000 |
| | YI | 1.264 | 0.077 | | YI | 0.314 | 1.000 | | YI | 0.419 | 1.000 |
| | Y | 2.750 | 0.012 | | Y | 1.874 | 0.083 | | Y | 0.419 | 0.867 |
| $P_5$ | I | 4.400 | 0.000 | $L_5$ | I | 5.295 | 0.000 | $D_5$ | I | 1.474 | 0.129 |
| | YI | 1.618 | 0.001 | | YI | 1.358 | 0.031 | | YI | 0.903 | 0.700 |
| | Y | 0.798 | 0.572 | | Y | 0.130 | 0.993 | | Y | 1.439 | 0.197 |
| $P_6$ | I | 1.241 | 0.250 | $L_6$ | I | 33.68 | 0.000 | $D_6$ | I | 11.66 | 0.000 |
| | YI | 0.788 | 0.898 | | YI | 0.310 | 1.000 | | YI | 0.948 | 0.600 |
| | Y | 4.086 | 0.000 | | Y | 0.255 | 0.957 | | Y | 1.527 | 0.167 |
| $P_7$ | I | 39.80 | 0.000 | $L_7$ | I | 117.3 | 0.000 | $D_7$ | I | 6.650 | 0.000 |
| | YI | 0.191 | 1.000 | | YI | 0.268 | 1.000 | | YI | 0.662 | 0.985 |
| | Y | 0.883 | 0.507 | | Y | 0.282 | 0.945 | | Y | 0.411 | 0.872 |
| $P_8$ | I | 106.5 | 0.000 | $L_8$ | I | 53.84 | 0.000 | $D_8$ | I | 12.63 | 0.000 |
| | YI | 0.287 | 1.000 | | YI | 0.224 | 1.000 | | YI | 0.067 | 1.000 |
| | Y | 0.361 | 0.904 | | Y | 0.696 | 0.653 | | | | |
| $P_9$ | I | 125.4 | 0.000 | $L_9$ | I | 17.23 | 0.000 | | | | |
| | YI | 0.138 | 1.000 | | YI | 0.728 | 0.954 | | | | |
| | Y | 1.237 | 0.285 | | Y | 0.540 | 0.778 | | | | |
| $P_{10}$ | I | 36.31 | 0.000 | $L_{10}$ | I | 106.2 | 0.000 | | | | |
| | YI | 1.058 | 0.356 | | YI | 0.247 | 1.000 | | | | |
| | Y | 0.597 | 0.732 | | Y | 0.245 | 0.961 | | | | |
| $P_{11}$ | I | 107.8 | 0.000 | $L_{11}$ | I | 2.040 | 0.019 | | | | |
| | YI | 0.371 | 1.000 | | YI | 0.708 | 0.966 | | | | |
| | Y | 0.284 | 0.944 | | | | | | | | |
| $P_{12}$ | I | 18.08 | 0.000 | | | | | | | | |
| | YI | 0.219 | 1.000 | | | | | | | | |
| | Y | 1.417 | 0.206 | | | | | | | | |
| $P_{13}$ | I | 13.96 | 0.000 | | | | | | | | |
| | YI | 0.726 | 0.955 | | | | | | | | |

Source: Calculations based on BACH database.

# Appendix 23. Tree Diagrams in Countries Based on Average Ratios for 1999–2005; Ward Method, Square Euclidean Distance

J. Koralun-Bereźnicka, *Corporate Performance*, Contributions to Management Science,
DOI 10.1007/978-3-319-00345-0, 

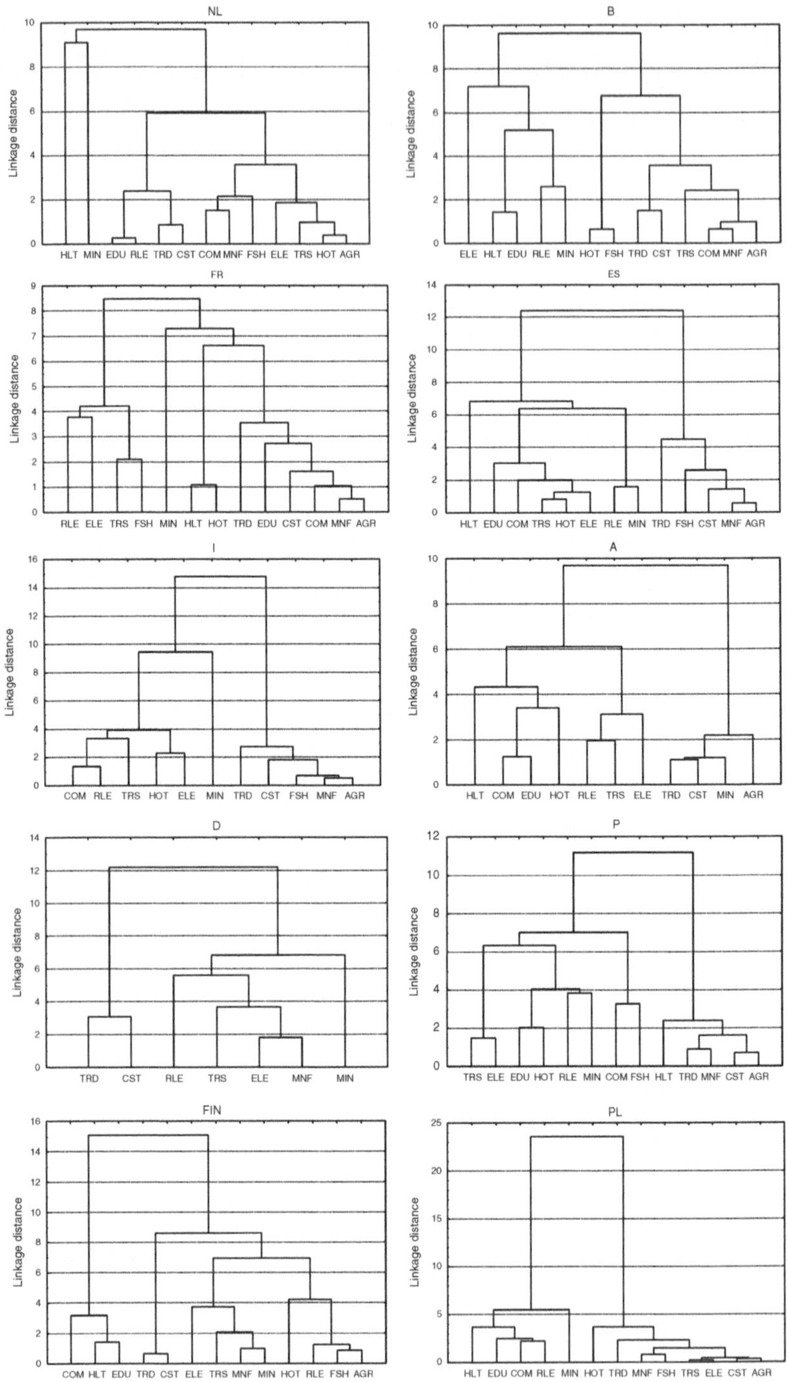


Source: Calculations based on BACH database.

# Appendix 24. Tree Diagrams in Industries Based on Average Ratios for 1999–2005; Ward Method, Square Euclidean Distance

J. Koralun-Bereźnicka, *Corporate Performance*, Contributions to Management Science, DOI 10.1007/978-3-319-00345-0, © Springer International Publishing Switzerland 2013

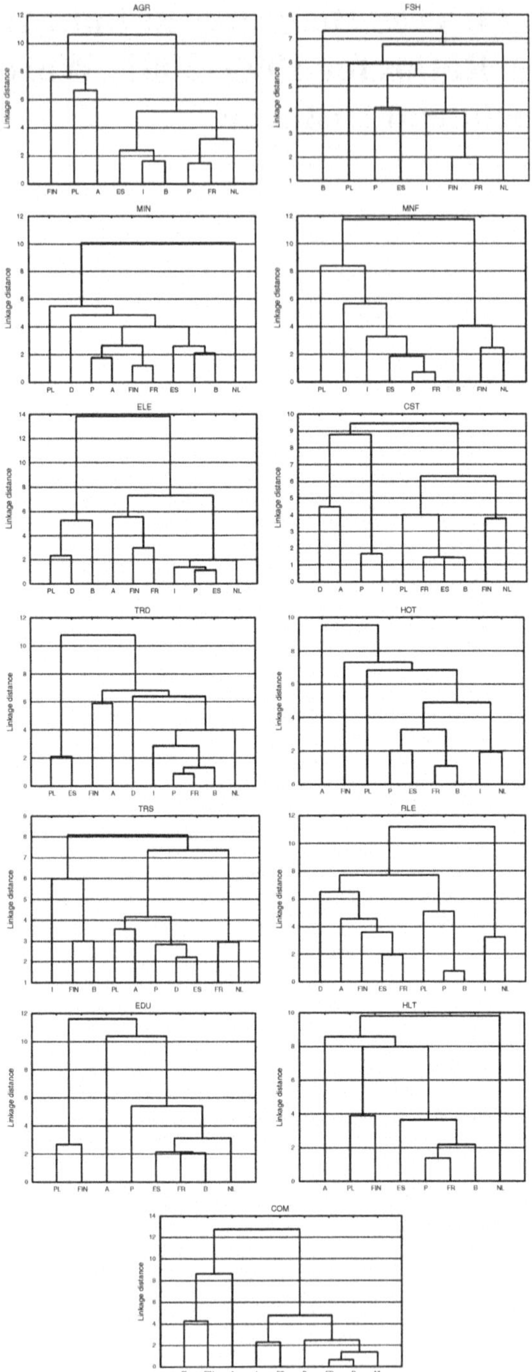


Source: Calculations based on BACH database.

# Appendix 25. Tree Diagram of Industries in Countries Based on Average Ratios for 1999–2005; Ward Method, Square Euclidean Distance

J. Koralun-Bereźnicka, *Corporate Performance*, Contributions to Management Science,
DOI 10.1007/978-3-319-00345-0, 

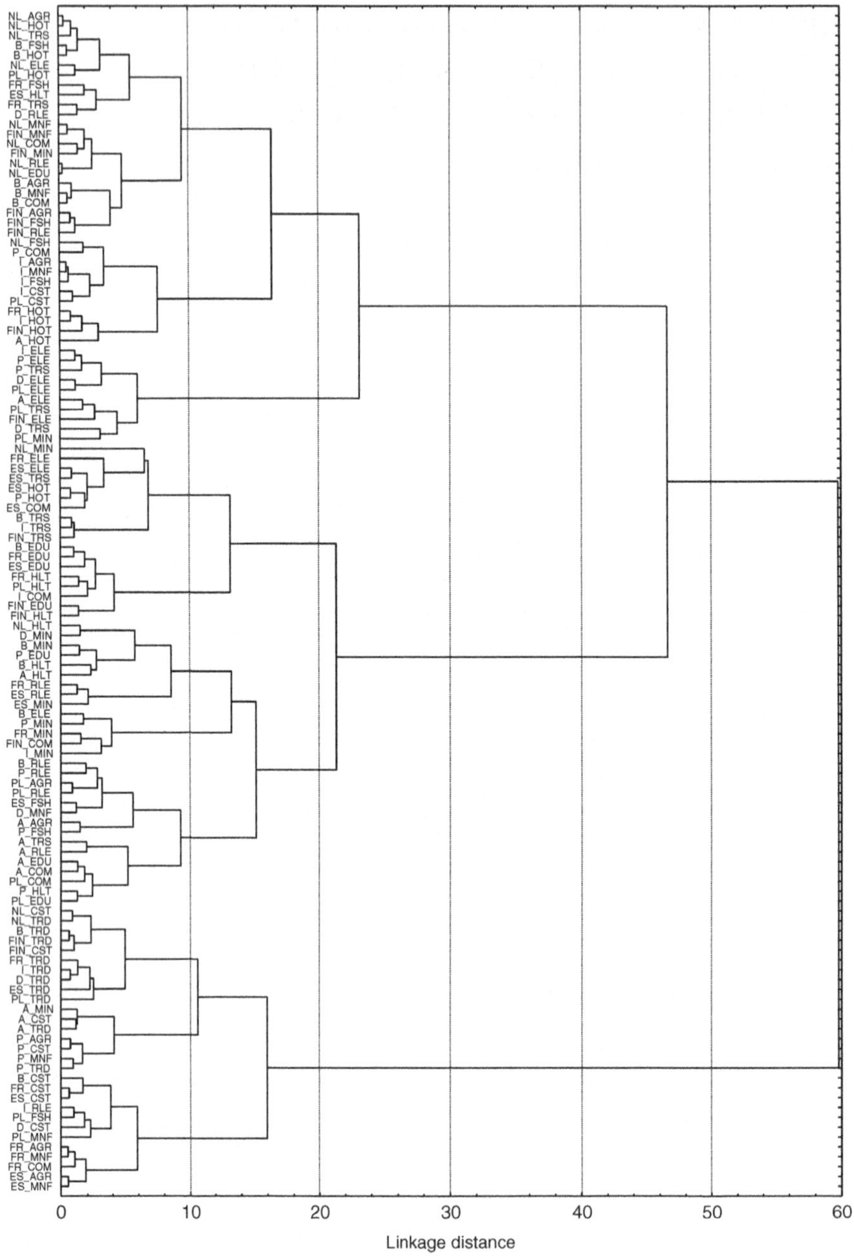


Source: Calculations based on BACH database.

The manufacturer's authorised representative in the EU is Springer
Nature Customer Service Centre GmbH, Europaplatz 3, 69115 Heidelberg,
Germany. If you have any concerns regarding our products, please
contact ProductSafety@springernature.com

Printed and bound by CPI Group (UK) Ltd, Croydon, CR0 4YY
25/09/2026
02222857-0006